FREUDIAN PASSIONS

FREUDIAN PASSIONS
Psychoanalysis, form, and literature

Jan Campbell

KARNAC

First published in 2013 by
Karnac Books Ltd
118 Finchley Road
London NW3 5HT

British Library Cataloguing in Publication Data

A C.I.P. for this book is available from the British Library

ISBN-13: 978-1-85575-616-8

Typeset by V Publishing Solutions Pvt Ltd., Chennai, India

Printed in Great Britain

www.karnacbooks.com

CONTENTS

PREFACE

The Freudian Passions of Jan Campbell's title—the passion for psychoanalysis that is everywhere in the remarkable readings and writing of this book: and the question of what psychoanalysis has done to, and with, our more traditional ideas about the passions—are both a reminder and a puzzle. Campbell wants to remind us that there is no passion without forms of representation, which are essentially mobile and vagrant, in search of hospitality but prone to sabotage; and that there would be nothing that we call passion without what Freud called—in a phrase that weaves together for psychoanalysts, the biological and the fictive—"our mythology, the drives". The passions that conventionally define us are at once conventional and innovative and on the loose. Psychoanalysis is an always elusive essentialism, telling us who we are, and showing us that we never quite, or nearly, know. And where we might like there to be a knowing there is only a sensing.

What is puzzling, for both the theorist and the clinician—the theorist mostly stuck with an obsessionally limited and reiterated set of preoccupations and vocabulary, the clinician forced to focus on the patient's suffering (and pleasure) in a similarly limited set of prized and painful symptoms—is how and why the individual's extraordinary capacity for improvisation, for vision and revision, is so readily stultified. How it is that what Winnicott called "the imaginative elaboration of physical function" is so often radically constrained? Why is the ego so tempted to fix itself in an image that it then needs so violently to defend? Or, to put it slightly differently why, in the account of Freud and so many of his followers, does the ego prefer mastery to movement, security to vitality, intelligibility to enigma, paranoia to personal and impersonal intimacy? How is it that, in psychoanalysis, the arts have been reduced to forms of sublimation and reparation; and sado-masochism, by the same token, has become the modern self-cure for intimate exchange? And of a piece with these questions, that Campbell so adroitly addresses, is the fact that psychoanalysis has so little to say about new styles of relating ("symptoms", she writes in one of her many illuminating formulations, "run backward but they are also affects that move forward. As an escape from the ego's boundaries they are in search of new forms beyond the self"). Much psychoanalytic theory and clinical practice, she intimates, may be somehow complicit with the closed symptoms it claims to open up, fostering too small a repertoire of all too recognisable forms of exchange.

Campbell starts from the principle, spelled out in her riveting account of telepathy as somehow at the heart of the matter for psychoanalysis, that our attunement to others has always already happened. Not that we are in some sort of harmonious accord with others, which the Freudian passions—the passions redescribed by Freud and Campbell—preclude; but that the passions on their quest for form are a seeking out, an eking out, of others. And by the same token psychoanalysis becomes, among other things, an after-education in a primary and informing receptive intelligence. So Campbell assumes, rightly, that what she calls "maternal form", which requires considerable tact and subtlety to both evoke and explicate—"we might think of the mother", Campbell writes, "as more of a genre mix"—is essential to development; which is always, whatever else it is, the development of imagination, the ongoing and always obscured and provisional formulating of, the finding of forms for, unconscious desire. And by attending to what she calls the rhythms of the unconscious as integral but not opposed to the so-called content of the unconscious she manages to do that most intriguing and difficult thing—she manages to think differently, to write differently about the unconscious. Campbell can make us feel that the genial and the elemental may not be incompatible.

In *Freudian Passions*, a genuinely original piece of contemporary psychoanalytic writing, Campbell, as a clinician and writer herself, gives us, in William James words, "something to be going on from", something that is all too rare in psychoanalytic writing. No-one has been able to mix personal reminiscence, psychoanalytic theory and practice, and readings of literary texts, in quite this way. "Something in other words, must be added to desire to make it work", Campbell writes in her reading of Woolf's *To the Lighthouse*. In *Freudian Passions* she is showing us, through her other words, how psychoanalysis might work; and in doing this, she is showing us how a lot of other things work as well.

Adam Phillips

We cannot know the unconscious in any straightforward way because it is repressed and thus unknowable. As Freud often acknowledged, the unconscious never "is"; it is not something waiting deep down in our psyche, ready to be uncovered by the right analytic interpretation or dream. Rather, it waits, and lurks as a potential for different forms of expression, dangerously residing behind—and in quest for—the forms that will give a shape to our desires and allow them to travel and communicate. To experience our passions we must have forms through which they can be carried, borne, and represented, and our first forms are arguably the most incestuous or familiar, but also the most unknowable; uncanny because they are so intense. Our passionate affects come dressed and undressed in familiar and unfamiliar clothes; those comfortable Oedipal slippers, uncannily styled, as the forms into which we need to step in order to express and fit what we feel.

In *Freudian Passions* I argue that something has to be added to Freud's model of repression to make sense of how our passions move in the transference and communicate. Our repressed unconscious passions are unbearable, and so unavailable to life and experience, and it is through the unconscious communication with another that these passions can find forms in an answering and telepathic response. Unconscious telepathy, in other words, which begins with the mother, happens as our first non-human interaction with objects in the world; non-human, because for the baby and the mother, this early telepathic forming and informing of the passionate attunement between them is before the baby has any sense of a psychological ego or self. Telepathy and the unconscious forms to which it gives rise are what we return to, in therapy and in life, as a way to sublimate the ferocity of our most intense and unbearable affects that have been repressed.

Telepathy was in a sense Freud's dream, one he was determined to keep secret. When Sándor Ferenczi, Freud's much loved colleague wants to offer his experiments in telepathy as public proof of psychoanalysis, Freud tells him authoritatively "Don't do it". Freud advises Ferenczi that the only new thing that he could add to the existing literature would be the "personal influence that must radiate from it. By it you would be throwing a bomb into the psychoanalytical house which would be certain to explode. Surely we agree in not wanting to hasten this perhaps unavoidable disturbance in or development".[1] Freud had misgivings about making public his beliefs in telepathy. These reservations were fuelled by entreaties from Ernest Jones that psychoanalysis must eschew any relation with telepathy if it is to be accepted without prejudice. "In your private political opinions you might be a Bolshevist," he tells Freud, but that is no reason to halt the spread of psychoanalysis by telling people. Freud replies, that in regards to telepathy he is convinced it has been the great experiment of his life, but if anyone asks, Jones can tell them that his conversion is "my private affair like my Jewishness, my passion for smoking and many other things, and that the theme of telepathy is in essence alien to psychoanalysis."

But if Freud publicly disavowed his private belief in telepathy, it was through his friendship and work with Ferenczi that telepathy worked its influence on psychoanalysis. Freud and Ferenczi loved each other. If Ferenczi's love was more openly transmitted, Freud's was arguably more secretive and repressed. Their telepathic transferences, the thoughts and feelings, hidden at times and then shared and transported between them, mirrored the inescapable links between psychoanalysis and telepathy, and between a repressed and unrepressed unconscious. And yet the telepathic and non-psychological objects of Freud's desires; his smelly cigars, his beloved dogs or his Jewish ancestry are his most personal and non-personal forms that arguably take him back not just to his mother but to the wider world of cultural forms in which Freud and his early Oedipal loves were situated. If telepathy sublimates our early repressed passions it can only do this through the wider cultural objects and forms carried by the mother (but not just the mother) that begin and continue to surround us.

The telepathic forms that give a dress sense or style to our passions are the unconscious rhythms that move our passions and sublimate them in relation to the corresponding or non-corresponding forms that exist within us and outside us as objects in the world. Besides the neurotic desires we repress and the perverse ones we express, are the circuitous and proliferating desires and spaces of the ego, that can come into being provided they have a dress design and shape through which they can travel and communicate.

In Virginia Woolf's *To the Lighthouse*, Lily Briscoe strives to uncover what lies beneath the painter Mr. Pauncefort's view, the green and grey pictures "with lemon coloured sailing boats and pink women on the beach".[2] The fashion of Mr. Pauncefort, not unlike Mrs. Ramsay, is for "pale, elegant and semi-transparent" art. If Mrs. Ramsay's rose flowered beauty is there for all to see and admire, it only goes so deep. She only "appears" beautiful. Mrs. Ramsay captures the rosy appearance of love, but not the dark and double side that is part of its essence. Mrs. Ramsay is wilfully unaware of love's ambivalence. As Lily realises, in order to really make art and life sublime you have to look beneath the fashion for pastel, or rose tinted colours. For "beneath the colour there was a shape".[3]

Sharon Kivland's work is sublime in Lily Briscoe's aesthetic sense, showing the uncanny hiding of the ferocity of our desire, along with the evocative dress designs, through which our ego makes its unconscious into art and shapes. In an alluring but discomposing photograph from *Du cou au genou*, 2011, Kivland gives us the anonymous female form, the maternal form. A torso cut off at the head with enough of the protruding neck muscle and suggestion of hair to know this woman has her head turned to what? She is in movement, and the dress that both corsets and waves around her body provides the movement to the body and its desires. The white curves of this dress, the way it fits close but reveals the female form through the pleats and folds of the material puts in play both the rhythm and the unconscious desires of this woman's body: together they make up her body/ego. Is this, then, her passion? On the one hand, art as the ideal and impersonal female form, and on the other, unmodified passion. Always threatening to dissolve into the non-personal "itness" of the id-like torso perhaps, until it ripples into, and is carried by the dress shapes of her ego that form and inform that ever moving but always enigmatic response.

In Kivland's non-personal image of the female form we see beneath the colour to the unconscious artistry of her shapes. The dress design of Kivland's image is a maternal, telepathic form unconsciously communicating, carrying (and hiding) the Freudian Passions, to which we respond by giving them life.

Notes

1. Sigmund Freud and Sándor Ferenczi, Letters Vol. 3, letter 1007 20 March, 1925 in *The Correspondence of Sigmund Freud and Sándor Ferenczi. Vol. 3 1920–1933*, edited by Ernst Falzeder and Eva Brabant, trans. by Peter T. Hoffer, intro. by Judith Dupont, Cambridge, MA: The Belknap Press of Harvard University Press.
2. Virginia Woolf, [1927]. *To the Lighthouse*, Introduction by Hermione Lee, London: Penguin Books, 1992, p. 17.
3. Woolf, V. (1992). *To the Lighthouse*, London, Penguin Books. [1927]. p. 23.

ACKNOWLEDGEMENTS

This book brings together my clinical and literary interests in psychoanalysis, not just because I think these two worlds have so much to say to each other, but because the arts of unconscious reading at work in these two encounters are ones that bring our experience to life. I am grateful to my editor Rod Tweedy at Karnac, for his patience. I want to thank Adam Phillips, for his return of forms. I am ongoingly grateful to Steve Pile for his inspiring intellect, companionship, kindness and for joint adventures in telepathic thinking and space travel in relation to psychoanalysis. I am lucky to have found in Roger Lippin his friendship when I needed it the most, and for finding a co-therapist who is so passionate about literature. I also want to express gratitude to Russell Rose for friendship, conversation, care and for his quite exceptional healing powers with my body. Many thanks to my friends Pam Howard, Mark Varhmeyer, Sam Jahara, Tanya Smart, and Trisha Hynes for being my companions in the world of therapy. Thanks also go to friends in London for making me feel at home, to Erica Carter (for everything!), and to Emma Francis for the *Psychoanalysis, Literature and Practice* Seminar at Senate House. Gratitude also goes to my friends in Lewes, Geraldine Pass, Peter Hadyn-Smith, Susanne Hoebbels, Prue Green, Liz Bang-Jones and in loving memory of Helmut Frielinghaus.

I want to specifically thank Danielle Fuller for all her kindness and for being so brave in the face of injustice; a special thank you to Steve Ellis, for his support and kindness. Thanks also to all my other friends in academia for their integrity and solidarity, Julie Rak, Jim Mussell, Claire Barker, Dave Gunning, Hera Cook, Sarah Kember, Anita Rupprecht, Mark Erickson, Sara Wood. For those of you at Birmingham, I will miss our reading group! My gratitude also goes to Lisa Brown and Heather Harris for their friendship and their humour that has lasted since our midwifery days until now. I also want to thank Dr. Patrick Gordon at Kings College Hospital for all his excellent care and his open minded-ness to chinese herbs, during my recent illness. This book would have been the poorer without the amazing cover image from Sharon Kivland; I wish to thank her for her generosity. Thanks also go to all my students (undergraduate and postgraduate) who have always been an inspiration, especially my PhD students and my students from *Literature, Sexuality, and the Body*. My biggest gratitude goes to my therapy clients and patients, past and present, who have given and who continue to give and teach me so much. All clinical material in this book is entirely fictional.

Finally I wish to thank Mike Van Duuren for his love and support, and for being him and being there when things have been bleak. This book is dedicated with much love to my daughter Esmé—for the joy she gives me in being her.

CHAPTER ONE

Passions in search of form

W hat questions do our passions raise for psychoanalysis? For Freud, passions are our life, and death drives, that unhappy marriage between our affects and representations; the love we can bind and the sexuality we cannot bear or formulate. Our unmanageable passions have a history that predates psychoanalysis. In one sense the very word passion belongs to an older vocabulary that psychoanalysis came along to deconstruct or explain. In Freudian language we have affects which can lean towards biological instincts or rest on their representative qualification in relation to feelings, emotions, moods, and drives. And yet passion evokes that vital capacity which makes us feel alive; makes life worth living. Moreover, passion is always directed towards something. We could call that something an object, but before the object exists, or after it is destroyed or lost, passion is in search of a form in which it can be dressed and carried. Are passions, then, our desires? In some ways, yes, but passion suggests a more passive relation. We suffer our passions, they are something that seems to visit or invade our very being, whereas desire suggests a more active relationship to our wants. Desire, perhaps, involves the ego's participation; we might need to loosen or lose our egos to find our desire, but the ego has not disappeared. Whereas in a blind passion, whether that is in terms of love, lust or hate, we are literally beside ourselves. Passion, here, has driven us to a place beyond the ego and all reason, to the madness that resides at the heart of love. So we could say that passionate affects are the part of our desires that are on the move in search of form. And our desires are the travel of those passionate forms seeking further elaboration.

Psychoanalysis as literature and a means of reading, translates, carries, and performs our passions. It can explain, along with literature, not just how we read and translate the world around us, but also how we read each other in relation to our personal history, and how we read in order to move towards our future, to something new. Reading is not necessarily seeing, nor is it confined to language. We can read a person like a book, so the saying goes, suggesting it's easy. But reading books, as any reader knows, can be done in an infinite variety of ways. Roland Barthes is probably the most famous literary critic to suggest that readers are also writers, that texts don't belong to authors. Texts and writing can't be confined to the author's life, and are indeed born after their death, in relation to the wider public circulation of their translation. In a similar way we can say that within the genre we call the family, there are sub-genres of mothers, fathers, and siblings. For the child, pleasure and the sense of a personal self entails the repression and translation of desire into the genres we call mothers and fathers. Too much sameness, or too much difference, results in a dead genre, or mother, and so the ingredients for pleasure in the family are the translation of secrets into genres: the recognisable forms that mediate desire and yet keep it circulating. Passions without forms to translate and communicate them to another, remain incestuously prohibited and blocked off. Without this transfiguration of affect and passion into genre, genres become repetitive and stuck; the same old pattern or script. We can see this repetition of sameness in the transference; and the analyst's task is not simply as Freud realised in his classic essay *Remembering, Repeating, and Working-Through*, to get the client to remember repressed drives or to "abreact" the emotions attached to them. "Working through the resistances" is what distinguishes psychoanalysis from hypnosis in Freud's opinion because it effects more lasting change.

And this is, I suggest, because in hypnosis, symptoms are washed away, only to return once our defences are erected, more forcibly than before. Symptoms, here, are not respected as they are in analysis, as the bodily forms and spaces through which we seek to speak and relate our passions. Symptoms are inherently relational, they are our forbidden desires on the move, seeking conversation, demanding to be read in similar and yet different ways. Reading in psychoanalysis, and in the analytic session, translates secrets and our symptoms into genres that can give living form to our desires. The Oedipal complex explains how we identify with and desire both parents, and it is this sameness and difference that makes our mothers and fathers into 'alive' genres, where we can re-find our first loves and yet fashion them differently, again, and again. The daughter needs to find her unique mother and yet also locate her as a mother within a succession of mothers, referring the girl on to her future, symbolic identity. In psychoanalysis we are used to the idea of a phallic genre and the need for the child to desire beyond the mother to what is called the father's language or law. But the mother also needs to belong to a genre, although I will suggest, as other feminists have done historically, that the mother's language is poetic and gestural, rather than linguistic.

We might think of the mother as more of a genre mix, as it is the lived form of our love for our mothers that carries us forward to participation in the cultural symbolic. And by this, I mean maternal form as an allegiance to the real of the mother's body, but its other side links up with what psychoanalysis has called the phallic desire that travels beyond the mother to the cultural world. So maternal form will be in rhythm with the body, but is also a continuing presence in relation to Oedipal conflicts allowing us to bear the ongoing frustration of those different desires.

Maternal form would then be a means of mediating our opposing desires, translating the sameness and difference of the Oedipal stage, enabling the primary passionate forms in relation to the mother to be broken up in a generative manner and translated into more active desires within the cultural and social field. Where the phallus opposes the mother's body, you will always choose between being a victim and perpetrator, one or the other—in a condition of divorce. It's the difference between your parents arguing (sometimes terribly), and "father" beating "mother" up. In families, between couples, arguments can be won and lost: understandings, guile, comings and goings are all involved. Bodily gesture and language join up as different languages that on some basic level still recognise and relate to each other. But what kind of conversation, we might ask, are we in when we are simply being kicked or punched? Maternal form adds something to the stand-off between the phallus and the maternal body; it translates that sadomasochism in its creation of ego routes and shapes, moving us from the original attachment drives in relation to the mother, towards more erotic fashioning of the self within a wider cultural world.

Maternal form

Lived form in relation to the mother is how our passionate affects become rhythmically and unconsciously distributed and intimately engaged with other personal and non-personal objects. Lived form, as Susan Langer understands it, is a "significant form", in that it gives shape and expression to what we feel, through non-verbal and aesthetic symbols that are pre-verbal and occur before the advent of language and what we would now call the Lacanian Symbolic. If living form is the bodily and artistic symbols that express the pre-Oedipal and imaginary relationship with the mother, then it is this form that replicates itself within the shared Oedipal genres that agree and organise conventions and exchange within our culture. In this book I want to explore how affects are in search of the living forms associated with the early mother. In other words lived form expresses and helps to sublimate the bodily drives in the realm of the imaginary before the advent of language and the Symbolic.

My argument for maternal lived form is indebted to the different understandings of the unconscious forms or idioms that are communicated between mother and child in the work of Christopher Bollas and Kenneth Wright. Both Bollas and Wright develop ideas of a maternal aesthetic that follow Winnicott in understanding how the child's early self, and being, is elaborated through a generative maternal object, that can accurately reflect her babies moods, but also allow those affectual drives to use and alter her. Developing Langer's notion of significant form to an understanding of the reciprocal attunement between mother and baby, Wright suggests that the mother's ability to identify and respond to her infant's changing affects and rhythms is an unconscious mirroring that transforms and returns the child's patterns with her own particular form, expressing the child's experiences in similar but different ways. But this is not simply mimicry:

> She does not copy the baby's behaviour, but grasps its *experience*, which she then replays it in a way that bears her own stamp. (Wright, 2009: p. 146)

For Wright, the resonant forms that become elaborated in the holding relationship between mother and child (in all their vocal, visual, and kinetic diversity) are integral to the developing life of the self or ego. It is Wright's use of aesthetic form in relation to Langer's thinking that interests me, the idea that inherent to the imaginary is an ongoing sublimation of affects in relation to the mother that is carried through the non-verbal presentational symbols that directly express lived feeling and experience. Langer writes, "everything actual must be transformed by imagination into something experiential" (Langer, 1953: p. 258). It is the virtual powers of art, poetry, and music that make them able to express what we feel, because it is only through this symbolic illusion that we can really experience them. The first passionate forms of the child are related to his mother and his immediate environment, and the mother is a virtual form for the child in an uncanny and a poetic sense. By this I mean she must be enigmatically alien, and yet a similar semblance and form that the child can use symbolically and analogically to bring his feelings to life, constructing the multiple changing shapes of his ego. The child's passionate drives imitates the form of the mother, just in the way she returns her child's affects with her particular form attached. But this mimesis between the two is never simply mimicry, there is always a vital improvisation at work, through the rhythms of the senses, that makes these forms analogous: similar but not the same.

And it is through these analogous forms the designs of the ego begin to grow and travel. And yet there is more to this story than just these ideals, what Bersani would call, inaccurate replications of the mother's and the child's forms. For the child's affects are always in excess of the available forms to frame it. Our passions always overspill into a world that is alien and to some degree un-digestible to the self. In his essay *On Narcissism* Freud asks,

> what makes it necessary at all for our mental life to pass beyond the limits of narcissism and to attach the libido to objects? The answer which would follow from our line of thought would once more be that this necessity arises when the cathexis of the ego with libido exceeds a certain amount. (Freud, 1914b: p. 85)

When passions become too much for the ego they overflow to the objects that exist around them. A strong ego says Freud, protects us from becoming ill, but, "in the last instance we must love in order not to fall ill" (Freud, 1914b: p. 85). We might say that repression bolsters the ego in the boundaries it erects between the self and the world, but this mastery does little to elaborate our excessive passions.

Repression of our desires is always in relation to the ideal ego or self, who forbids and fixes what we feel for our first love objects. What we can't have we will forever want, and repression ensures that we will always be running back home in pursuit of these ideal desires. Freud makes clear in *On Narcissism* that repression and sublimation are different things, if the construction of the ego ideal,

> heightens the demands of the ego and is the most powerful factor favouring repressions; sublimation is a way out, a way by which those demands can be met *without* involving repression. (Freud, 1914b: p. 95)

Some alternative must be found to repression, if our passions are to travel and become shaped into liveable experience. In psychoanalysis, the transference follows the familiar ego lines and boundaries that take us back to the scene of what is repressed, and yet the transference is not to wean someone from what they feel, but to provide new shapes in which the ego can elaborate its loves. Symptoms run back to the excessive fixed passions of our past, but they are also in search of new forms of conversation, and the transference is how we allow our affects and passions this elaboration in terms of a search for more relational forms.

We might think of this early expression of maternal form and feeling in relation to Kristeva's notion of the semiotic; a poetic chora that precedes the symbolic but is also heterogeneous, playing alongside the Law, and helping to mediate the bodily drives with language and the stand-off between the maternal body and phallic prohibition. Lived form, what I call maternal form, has a more intimate relationship with the bodily drives than language. Whereas language represses the drives, maternal form mixes with them and unconsciously translates and communicates with them telepathically. Without maternal form, we have a repression of the body through language with no sublimation! Consequently, maternal form predates the Symbolic but is at work mediating and translating the passions associated with the mother's body. Julia Kristeva makes clear in her book *Black Sun* that the unconscious is not structured through language, but;

like all imprints of the Other, including and most particularly those that are most archaic, 'semiotic', it is constituted by preverbal self-sensualities that the narcissistic or amorous experience restores to me. (Kristeva, 1987: p. 204)

In Lacanian thinking the body is only available as a repressed entity, and Kristeva's understanding of the semiotic is different, in that it brings the material body back as something that has to work at the level of the imaginary and the symbolic. This brings Kristeva's work much closer to what Freud saw as a necessary sublimation or mediation of the drives, a sublimation that I contend is not just achieved through repression, a fixed ego ideal or castration through language. Of course Kristeva's work moves from an emphasis on the semiotic aspects of the maternal body to the nature and necessity of its abjection.

As Kelly Oliver's brilliant reading of Kristeva makes clear, rejection and negation of the maternal body occurs in the pre-symbolic, a gestural expulsion which Kristeva locates in Freud's Fort Da game. Negativity moves through the symbolic, Kelly informs us, "because it moves through the corporeal" and this pre-symbolic negation of the mother's body shows how this body, "acts not only as a lack but also as an excess" (Kelly, 1998: p. 56). It is this excess of the maternal body characterised as both semiotic and abject that makes up some of the most interesting aspects of Kristeva's thinking. And yet these excesses, the poetic, and the thing repulsed, are always structured for Kristeva in relation to a repressive Oedipal Symbolic. In this book I want to concentrate on an excess to the maternal body, the Freudian passions, that are carried by a telepathic maternal form that is non-discursive and anterior to the Symbolic. This maternal telepathy can be in touch with reality without necessarily being conscious. The imaginary, in other words, is not simply fantasmatic, but has a relation to reality and the material body, carrying living forms and primary symbols that shape our affects and move them into a more friendly less punitive relationship between the ego and its ideal. So, here, maternal form is not repressed under the Symbolic but partakes of a different kind of sublimation of sexuality, one which is non-repressive, reduplicating the primary identification with the mother in ways that form and de-form, shape and re-shape the ego.

Paul Federn's understanding of the way that the ego has many different boundaries is instructive. He argues that the ego has many boundaries that are flexible and moveable, and that the bodily ego feeling associated with the ego is "compound" being made up of motor and sensory memories but also with the somatic organisation. Bodily ego feeling "is not identical with the somatic organisation, with the unity of correctly ordered perceptions of one's own body" (Federn, 1952: p. 27). Ego feelings can coincide with our perception of our body, but there are plenty of ego states where we transcend or dissociate from the experience of our bodily boundaries. Federn talks of the bodily ego feeling as a mental one, and when we are awake these things feel synonymous, but there are times, in Federn's view, for example in dreaming or falling asleep, or in particular hypnotic states, where it is easy to see how distinct our mental and bodily ego's are.

Didier Anzieu develops Federn's understanding of the ego's moveable boundaries to conceptualise "a skin ego" (Anzieu, 1989). For Anzieu, the ego is a skin ego covering the psychic organism and beginning as part of an envelope with the mother. Thus it acts as,

> a containing, unifying envelop for the Self, as a protective barrier for the psyche; and as a filter of exchanges and a surface of inscription for the first traces, a function which makes representation possible. (Anzieu, 1989; p. 98)

Although the first skin ego is established by touch, there is also an early sensory sound envelop with the mother, and these skins give way to visual envelopes supporting the psyche as it develops. Thinking about our different skins is a rather wonderful way to encapsulate the embodiment of different selves that are initially enveloped in relation to the mother's body. The skin ego returns us to the early sensorium that is the bedrock of Freud's thinking. Steve Connor is disconcerted with the therapeutic emphasis in Anzieu's work on the suffering and repair of the ego's skin. The "model of the skin as a case or container is just not extensive or various enough to account for the psycho-social life, or lives of the skin", Connor writes. Being happy in one's skin is the ability to live "the skin's multiplicity, its many foldedness" (Connor, 2004: p. 92).

One way of thinking about Anzieu's skins and Federn's ego boundaries that does not return them simply to a model of suffering or repair is to understand them as different descriptions of living maternal forms associated with an early unconscious communication between mother and child. Federn suggests that ego feelings (be they memories, affects, or perceptions of somatic or external reality) are not predicated on consciousness, and when ego feelings are absent we become aware of them as estranged sensations. Something is affectually lacking in the ego's experience. "Whenever there is a change in ego feeling cathexis", Federn writes, we sense the "boundaries" of our ego.

> Whenever an impression impinges, be it somatic or psychic, it strikes a boundary of the ego normally invested with ego-feeling. *If no ego feeling sets in at this boundary, we sense the impression in question as alien.* So long as no impression impinges on upon the boundaries of ego feeling, we remain unaware of the confines of the ego. (Federn, 1952: p. 64)

Or another explanation would be that without the ego's boundaries and forms, our feelings, affects, memories and perceptions can't be experienced as something lived. We feel strange and dissociated when ego feelings have shrunk away, or moved beyond the available boundaries and forms which can carry and express them. Anzieu ends his book on *The Skin Ego* with an example of the hysteric, who lacking an adequately protective and holding skin, is subject to one that is overly excitable and stimulating. Like Masud Khan's famous grudge, this hysterical personality is caught up in an endless sadomasochistic seduction which is actually a demand for more ego capacity in relation to holding maternal care. This argument, that the hysteric is in search of protective maternal care and not desire, is part of a long oscillation in psychoanalytic thinking that makes the hysteric too full of desire, or too empty; too much of a child stuck auto-erotically to the mother, or too frustrated in relation to a paternal naming or symbolic place she desperately wants and rejects.

Unconscious reading

Passion in relation to the early mother is something that is excessive, traumatic and unbearable, and yet without it we are left inhibited; an ego forever at odds with its punishing ideal. Freud is most well known for his theorisation of the psychic repression of our passions, but as I shall argue it is the unconscious reading and communication in the analytic session, the telepathic transfer of our desires and needs, providing forms for what we feel, that is also at stake. Telepathy, as myself and Steve Pile have argued, constitutes the other side of Freud's theory of repression and is a necessary part of understanding how the unconscious moves and communicates (Campbell and Pile, 2010). Moreover the importance of telepathy for psychoanalysis is not just how it explains a non-repressed unconscious constantly at work transferring the repressed. For a telepathic and a receptive unconscious is also the medium through which the passions in relation to the maternal body are shaped and translated into new forms of the ego as an alternative sublimation to repression.

Learning to read together, for the mother and baby, is a storying of love and hate; the weaving and fashioning of new egos, internal and external worlds that can carry and shape our affects. The baby reads the mother long before she is able to understand language. She reads and construes the mother's body and the maternal response using this reading to shape and illustrate her own love. The mother reads too, identifying with her baby and returning and regulating its affects, with her own particular form of idiom attached. Reading, as Barthes says, is always a form of translation or writing; it produces our identifications differently. So reading is a continuation of love. It is how we render our passions and other people into something more durable and real. Without reading there is no exchange, no reality principle, and love simply becomes a narcissistic extension of the same.

If on one level desire is not sociable based on fantasies and wishes that have little to do with the object at hand, it is also true to say, as Lacan reminds us, that because desire is based on an impossible demand to the other, it leads us beyond the certainty of our fantasy wants and wishes to a world beyond the ego. And this supposes that we can't know what we want, because what we desire will always exceed our current wardrobe. Finding the right clothes that fit what we feel means inevitably following old patterns, but because it is in the nature of desire to move beyond the available object, or kit, then we have to submit to the unknowable objects; those shapes or forms that exist outside the self. This is one way we can think of objects and things that live in us but also surround us as having a virtual life of their own. Responding to these living virtual living (maternal) forms occurs through telepathy and unconscious reading, but this is not a matter of second sight. As Freud realised, telepathy as the other side to repression can never be an act of foreseeing the future; it is the elaboration of the uncanny.

The uncanny, Freud tells us, resides in the unfamiliar objects we bump into that cover over the repressed familiar scene of our relation to the maternal body. But because this passionate scene was always beyond our ability to experience it then what is new is always located in relation to the familiar but beyond it, in the non-human objects that exist in our repressed psychic existence, but also outside in the world in which we live. It is with the mother as the first familiar and non-human object that we learn to unconsciously read our desires and because reading is also writing, this maternal telepathy inscribes and elaborates our affects beyond the fixity and certainty of familial objects and wants. And yet it is important to stress that there will always be the passions that exceed the shapes or objects that are at hand to pattern them. Telepathy or maternal form can never fully translate or sublimate the excessive passions of our relation to the mother's body, what Kristeva calls the maternal thing. Any telepathy that purports to know with certainty what is unconscious, is a foreclosure to accept what lies beyond our understanding. Psychotic disturbance is a good example of this, because psychotic patients are often very sensitive and receptive to unconscious communications, but it is their certainty on the face of these messages that is problematic, their refusal to accept the contingent status of reality.

If we fall so madly in love that we can't distinguish where we end and the other begins, then unconscious reading is a continuation of this passionate love, but one that begins to translate that love, to produce and write it, in more plural ways. One of the things that psychoanalysis has always been concerned with is the inability and the ability to bear the intensity of what we feel. When someone can't carry or bear their feelings, we call them mad. But what does this mean? More succinctly, what does it entail? Babies arrive in the world with the most unbearable needs; we can't ignore her scream, for good reason. The scream makes us act and do something to change those agonised cries, into some more bearable form of feeling. Whether we feed the baby, hold, or rock her, the human interaction, the rhythm that occurs between the baby and the other is a beginning of finding the forms that will fashion and shape the self. For without forms to carry and translate our affects, we would have no idea what they were.

Rhythm is on the way to form and form is on the way to language. And so maternal form is harboured within the rhythms of body and yet moves towards language and the social genres of our genders, our sexualities and our families. Affects move through these different forms, the rhythm of bodily sounds, tactile holding, painterly images and finally language to emerge in a more qualified or stylised fashion. For Wilfred Bion, thoughts exist before we have the apparatus to think them. These thoughts are the beta elements or undigested sensations or experiences that have to be transformed into alpha elements (processed or digestible experience) so they can be thought and stored in the unconscious (Bion, 1962). But we can equally say the same thing about affects or passions because "unthought" thoughts and "unfelt" feelings are in fact, indistinguishable. In order to feel our passions, we need forms through which we can bear, carry and communicate them. These forms are initially the ones borrowed from the mother, the sounds, touch, facial response and bodily gestures through which she receives the child's early affects and returns them in similar, and yet crucially different ways. Eventually the child shifts and elaborates these non-discursive forms to more representational meanings within language.

Mad love and the dress sense of the ego

In his discussion of unconscious emotions, Freud points out that, "to suppress the development of affect is the true aim of repression and that its work is incomplete if this aim is not achieved" (Freud, 1915: p. 178). We repress our unconscious affects and feeling because they are too much for us to experience or bear. Indeed, it was Freud who argued that love was a state of being akin to psychosis; that when we are in love we are in fact quite mad. Our loving passions are of course, inextricable from the feelings of hate, jealousy and paranoia that accompany them. And this is especially so when the love we feel can't travel or find a form, an ideal form in which it can be borne and elaborated as part of our ego. So we can say that our passions are always in search of forms, and these forms initially originate from the outside world. But what exactly are these forms? In Freud's thinking they are the various patterning and structures of our unconscious experience; the representations, ideations, images, rhythms, dreams, spaces and objects that carry and house our passionate affects, most visible in our night dreams.

Although certain forms might be seen to exist innately within the baby as a kind of pre-historical and pre-geographical pattern or prototype, most forms come initially to the baby from the outside world in the shape and rhythm of the mother's body and voice, in the mirroring of her responsive face and gestures. The baby is also in touch with other forms of nature and culture that come from everyday life, which stretch from the immediate family and its environment to the wider life that takes place on streets, countryside, of a particular culture and community. Initially the baby does not differentiate between itself and the surrounding world. And it is through telepathically reading that non-personal world that the young ego borrows the forms through which to sublimate his affects and shape the ego. Repression is the defence through which the young ego wards off the affects and passions it cannot bear or translate, but it is my contention that repression and telepathy are always in concert and without the initial, telepathic sublimation of our affects, the ego would not make an appearance.

Freud made several maps or topographies of the ego and the unconscious. We can see these maps in terms of Anzieu's various skins, and the metaphor of skin is useful in thinking about the early embodiment of the psyche. We don't have to return the skin ego solely to images of destruction and repair. Freud saw the unconscious beginning in the biological instinct of the Id, developing into an ego whose repressions and ideals are always in harsh dialogue with the cultural and moral imperatives of the super ego. He also saw the mind not so much divided from the body, but as a kind of form, a form of dress or garment we could say, that grows around it and shapes the material body in various styles. The mind is an immanent form that grows and changes, and changes shape in accordance with the affectual passions of our body. So neither our minds, nor our affects are simply an individual concern. They are always in unconscious traffic and communication with the forms, minds and affects that emanate from another. I want to suggest that we can see the ego as a series of styles and designs that can give new shapes and dress sense to the self. The ego is not so much a smooth skin, but one that changes shape to become decorated and elaborated in various ways. In the same way we would design a dress or a house, the architect of our ego is concerned with the various shapes and rooms that light up aspects of our self experience, in contrast to other aspects that are hidden, or in shade. Some of these rooms have connecting doors, whilst others remain firmly shut, and like the Reading Room in Virginia Woolf's famous essay, the ego's unconscious reading room is one that looks out onto a wealth of typological forms and flowers that exist outside its walls in the virtual landscapes beyond the self.

The infant has to learn how to read and reach the forms to which he can match his passions. At first with the mother, but then over time he has to move beyond the mother to arrive at the varying cultural forms that make up a human world. When our passions can't find adequate patterns and forms to fit them, then they become repressed and we become ill, our desire becomes trapped in our body rather than being able to travel beyond us in relation to another. One of the things that Lacan explained in relation to the Oedipal complex was how the child has to be able to formulate a place beyond the mother, a space of her desire and absence, so that the child can move in the world and culture, what Lacan calls the symbolic order signified by the phallus. If this space of the mother's desire is not a question or a subject of interest and enquiry for the child, then the child can't place their desire beyond the mother, and they become locked up, not just with the too powerful mother, but also within themselves. Desire and meaning become located and trapped within the child's body, rather than being allowed to travel beyond the child and establish meaning in relation to a symbolic and cultural world.

The key to this crucial movement of desire beyond the maternal dyad to the phallic third term is language according to Lacan, and yet Freud saw language somewhat differently as a medium for connecting the unconscious to word presentations and consciousness. So the unconscious, for Freud, remains a thing like presentation, thick with affect. Thus we have unconscious forms and these as he has shown us are multiple in their design, their shape and their ability to elaborate or defensively fix our passions. Psychoanalysis is all about how we repress, elaborate and translate our unconscious passions; how we develop these into a succession of forms so that our experience of life can be widened. And this experience as Freud keeps telling us is largely unconscious.

One of the problems of the opposition in psychoanalysis between the body of the mother and the sign of the father is that it trumps the intelligence of the unconscious maternal dream world with the superior insignia of conscious and repressive mental representation in the "Name of the Father". As I have argued before, this has made psychoanalysis problematic for women, for feminism, and for queer theory because it makes the so-called pre-Oedipal sexualities, the mother daughter relationship and homosexuality into something more neurotic, closer to unconscious conflicts. At worst, it makes the pre-Oedipal, as in Julia

Kristeva's damning critique of the mother-daughter bond, closer to psychosis. I want to suggest, in relation to this dilemma at least two things. First, what if it is true that certain sexualities associated with say femininity, are closer to the unconscious, closer in other words to the dream worlds of our imaginary existence? If we read psychoanalysis in terms of a purely developmental and linear timeline, then the paternal Oedipal signifier is the transcendental ideal and the dream body of the mother, merely where we start from, a carnal imaginary from which we must escape. And yet, Freud was always emphasising how we return to our first forms, the fixations of pre-Oedipal desires.

Return to form, in other words, is also a return to first forms and the imaginary affects of the maternal body. And without this circuitous retreat, without the formulations of our unconscious world, nothing new can be experienced or achieved. The unconscious draws us back home, to our bodies and to our mothers, but this return to the familiar, it seems, is necessary if we want to move to anything different or new. Pure difference is impossible, because we need sameness—the mimesis to the mother—to mould and fashion those primary similar forms, in different ways. Psychosis, whether we see it through a Lacanian or object relations lens is a position of too much sameness, a retreat into the body of the mother and a refusal or foreclosure of the category of the meaningful insignia of the father. For the Lacanians, this difference is categorical, there is no half way house between a neurotic and a psychotic structure. In other words, your psychic world is structured by the symbolic difference of the phallus, or it is not. Object relation analysts believe that there are graduations between psychotic and neurotic, the borderland country where the bodily real and the mental imaginary fight it out. The Lacanians disagree; you cannot be, according to them, just a bit mad. You are mad, or you are neurotic and if you are mad, the question for the analysis is how to stop you going mad, or triggering a psychosis.

Although I think the Lacanian school is vital in thinking through the importance of meaning in the therapy situation, along with the idea that shared meaning for the psychotic is always problematic. I also wonder if their structural approach to questions of madness and language, is too absolute. Language is not the only means, or indeed the only form, which carries unconscious affects and makes those affects communicable within, and in relation to, a symbolic and cultural world, neither is madness simply a question of psychosis. Neurotic people also go mad, but in a more related way, as Freud's *Studies on Hysteria* so eloquently showed. For Freud, hysterics go mad in their longing and their need for love, but they are still able to read and translate the other in creatively unconscious communications.

The hysteric's excess and maternal form

And yet hysteria is saying something very interesting about the way the unconscious works, because the hysteric can't just submit to the phallic principle. The hysteric is full of melodramatic affects, repressed and dissociated, that exceed mental representation. But hysteria is also always a refusal of leaving the mother's body and entering into the phallic domain of language, the law of the father. A refusal of that crucial third symbolic presence, which for Lacanian's acts as a metaphorical substitution and deferral of the love mother and child feel for each other, thus redirecting the child's desire into the world. The phallus, we might say, has become fetishised within psychoanalytic theory as the sole means which springs the child free from its passionate embrace with the mother. As hysterics we keep are fantasy and reality apart; we are always racing back to our past loves in a refusal of present reality, and yet if our primary passions are always going to be the most real thing, then we must find ingenious routes and ways of being able to both satisfy those primary loves, by staying in touch with them, and finding the secondary forms that will bear and carry those passions somewhere new. And yet it is not a question of choosing between the mother and the father, and weighing up which is better. If the dangers of an object relations approach to psychoanalysis and to the hysteric in particular, is that it keeps the patient mired in a maternal order with not enough establishment, or mobilisation, of meaning or desire; then Lacanian approaches often find themselves at a loss when it comes to the hysterical patient whose passionate flesh simply won't accept the paternal law of the signifier.

Masud Khan writes about how the hysteric manifests a sort of false sexualised self, over sexualising and objectifying herself in relation to men when really she is looking for the maternal care and ego support that was missing in her early years. Seduction with men is a cover for seeking maternal holding that was too absent earlier on. Contemporary psychoanalysis categorises the hysteric in both Oedipal and pre-Oedipal terms. Freud understood hysteria, illustrated by his most famous patient Dora, as a neurotic failure to accept her love and desire for the father, so retreating into a twilight world of fantasy and affectual memories. Whereas, more contemporary object relations analysts understand the hysteric as a pre-Oedipal refusal, the child's insistence in staying with the mother is an asexual and autoerotic reverie. This narcissistic retreat with the mother, the need to stay a child, is a defence against maturing. The hysteric's grudge, here, is in simple terms a refusal to grow up, to reach a stage where sexuality, reality, and object exchange allow a re-creation of our Oedipal loves. But more importantly this is also the hysteric's inability to elaborate her characters in plural ways, to move within the world and use its cultural objects dynamically, or as Bollas would say evocatively.

And so the hysteric is someone, like the character of Mrs. Ramsay in *To the Lighthouse*, who is unable to dress up and design her body-ego. She remains shabby when it comes to having a good ego dress sense. Unable to choose, the hysteric is always trying everyone's clothes, selves, and desires on for size. So, just in the way close female friends and daughters and sisters copy each other's appearance, the hysteric mimes other people's ego fashions, their differing characters. Hysteria is interesting in that like melodrama it is both a character and a genre that is mobile. Distinguished by its ability to mime and dress up in the other's clothes, the ability to impersonate another person's ego and their desires defines hysteria. And yet this mobility of identification, this inability to select what, or who she can become is another refusal on the part of the hysteric, to acknowledge the benefits of reality over fantasy. Hysteria, is as clinicians will testify, a dressing up in potential future forms, which are then discarded in favour of the first or most "authentic" passions associated with the mother.

So, the hysteric refuses her own status as an artist, her own ability to be a fashion designer of her ego, rather than just a slavish follower of fashions. Being a designer of your ego, so to speak, means the end of identification, and the beginning of something unknowable and new. As Freud tells us, the hysteric's mobility; her flight into a transferential identification with the other, is a regression on a temporal and struc-tural level:

> The flight from unsatisfactory reality into what, on accounts of the biological damage involved, we call illness (though it is never with-out an immediate of yield of pleasure to the patient) takes place along the path of involution, of regression, of a return to earlier phases of sexual life, phases from which at one time satisfaction

was withheld. This regression appears to be a twofold one; a temporal one in so far as the libido, the erotic needs, hark back to stages of development that are earlier in time, and a formal one, in that the original and primitive methods of psychical expression are employed in manifesting those needs. Both these kinds of regression, however, lead back to childhood and unite in bringing about an infantile condition of sexual life. (Freud, 1910: p. 49)

Hysteria in its very basic meaning for Freud was simply repression of sexuality, which existed in moderate quantities in the normal person, but reached excess proportions in full blown neurosis. So hysteria in this simple sense means a difficulty in love, a struggle in finding the way through to what we want, or love. Because for hysterics, the most loved object is an old one, fantasised and stored in the body erotically and narcissistically. As Freud keeps telling us, reality is disappointing, and if this disillusion becomes excessive, or the patient's ability to adapt to it is weak, then regression into wishes and illness is the result. The hysteric flies back home to her past loves, because her present ones are so inadequate; these present desires are un-fulfilling, precisely because they are not the first. And yet we all do this; it is not just the so-called full blown hysteric who runs back to a familiar past as an escape from facing current realities.

So, we have to take seriously Freud's statement that the reality of the world lets us down, and that where we love in the present, there is always the pull between disappointment and an original ideal that on some level we can't give up, because it harbours our most intense affectual passions. At the end of his *Five Lectures On Psycho-analysis* Freud warns the audience against too much adherence to the civilised ways of life. "We ought not", he writes "to exalt ourselves so high as completely to neglect what was originally animal in our nature" (Freud, 1909b: p. 54). Freud then gives the example, a story from German literature of a town, where the citizens owned a gifted and strong horse that ate too many expensive oats. They trained the horse to live and work on less and less, until one day they found it had died. The moral of the tale, says Freud is that we all need a "certain modicum of oats" (Freud, 1910: p. 55). Our sexuality like the oats is a precious commodity and there is only a certain amount of harnessing, sublimation, or work that can be achieved. Some pleasure, Freud seems to say, is essential; some amount of un-sublimated, unrestricted and unrepressed pleasure is a modicum for a happy existence.

The hysteric is like the greedy horse, whose hunger is out of balance with the economies of love, life, and work. In other words, she is excessive when it comes to what she wants. But of course we are all versions of the hungry horse; we all have dreams, needs, and wants. We are not simply workhorses. There is in all of us a discrepancy between our dream selves and our real selves, the parts of us that dream and wish, and the parts of us that have to negotiate that dream, libidinal self in terms of the world. Our reality selves can sublimate wishes, but more commonly according to Freud, we replace repression by the "condemning judgements" of a mental rationality trying to wipe our desires away. These rationalisations can be "along the best lines" says Freud in mastering the impulses that were initially unusable by us. Qualifying this, he adds:

> the extirpation of infantile wishes is by no mean the ideal aim of development. Owing to their repressions, neurotics have sacrificed many sources of mental energy whose contributions would of been of great value in the formation of their character and in their activity in life. (Freud, 1910: p. 53)

Sublimation is a halfway house between our dream and reality selves, because it depends on the partial lifting of repression. And this makes hysteria interesting, because symptoms are the stuff of our sexual desire that have escaped or refused the ego's admonishments. Symptoms are the stories and the art materials of the ego, on the move in a different guise. Symptoms are relational, they are always in search of a conversation, which is why in therapy we need to really listen to them, be interested in what symptoms are telling us, rather than just trying to boss them out of the way with drugs or positive thinking techniques. "If a person who is at loggerheads with reality possesses an artistic technique" says Freud, then, "he can transform his phantasies into artistic creations instead of symptoms" (Freud. p. 50). But by the same token, the hysteric and her symptoms are a pre-requisite to the artist she can become. No symptoms, no excessive wants, implies no art-work by the ego. The hysteric is fixated within old ego forms that keep her stuck, and yet at the same time her bodily symptoms are the passions that have escaped the boundaries of a familiar ego and are in search of new forms and encounters.

Symptoms are on one level seen culturally to be pathological, but on another they are a reserve power, an unconscious power that refuses silence. Whether we think of the power of the phobic symptom or the hysterical one, these symptoms are all distinguished by their ability to move beyond the confines of the ego. Thus symptoms are always in a creative process of becoming something else. Hysterics are people whose symptoms express their psychological conflicts through the body. They are the men and the women who repress and dissociate their sexuality and then have an unconscious relationship with it. But as I have said that makes us all hysterics. Sexuality is always the too much or the not enough of our libidinal relationships with our first loves. And it is because sexuality is so excessive that the hysteric figures as both the emptiness of desire, and as a personification of passionate madness. We all desire on our own, in the sense that our desires are always in excess of the object available and it is the hysteric who enacts this furious wanting which is simply the other side of desire's impossibility. And so it's not true that the hysteric or the woman can't access desire; if anything her desire is too much, it is the extremeness of the passion that renders it obscure. The problem is not that the hysteric can't desire, but a question of how she desires. What fashion and forms will allow her to elaborate her innermost wishes in relation to the world in which she lives?

Freud tells us in a paper on hysterical attacks, that these fits are made up of condensed material, just like dreams, combining recent wishes with infantile phantasies (Freud, 1909: p. 232). However much we see the hysteric as locked into a world of autoerotic fantasy, melodramatically enacted through the body, hysteria is never just a private theatre, it demands an audience and it is always simultaneously a refusal and an appeal to the other in terms of the shaping and formation of desire. Hysteria is a return to childhood sexuality, says Freud, mimicking the stages of repression, failure of repression and the return of the repressed. When it comes to women, Freud continues, hysteria is a re-awakening, "of a piece of sexual activity in women which existed during their childhood and at that time revealed an essentially masculine character" (Freud, 1909: p. 234). What Freud means here is the woman's active desire for her mother. Hysteria, in women, leads to homosexuality and this is just the normal repression and return of sexuality that they experience. Primary sexuality for the woman is for their mothers and without this revival of love women don't get symptoms, but equally, they don't experience their most intense sexuality either. So a lot must depend on the nature and the love between mother and daughter from a psychoanalytic point of view. In a companion piece composed in the same year, Freud also points that hysterical symptoms are always bisexual, they are, "the expression on the one hand of a masculine unconscious sexual phantasy, and on the other hand of a feminine one" (Freud, 1908: p. 165). Freud is saying quite clearly here, that women desire both parents excessively and accordingly they express symptoms in relation to both sexes.

Christopher Bollas argues that it is the mother's inability to celebrate or acknowledge their child's genital sexuality that leads to the hysteric's typical refusal of the paternal order which issues in all the complex exchanges with reality.

> As the mother relates to the infant's genital with a dead hand, she declines both to celebrate it and to word it, thus leaving the genital excitation untransformed. It is of interest that the hysteric suffers an excess of non-genital erotic transformations, often verging on exhibitionist theatre, but when it comes to the genital moment the self is suddenly and dramatically an infantile creature with no sense of erotic destiny. (Bollas, 2000: p. 51)

I think this delineation of an asexual maternal order needs some consideration. Surely the kind of early non-sexual relationship to the mother is a fantasy projected backwards of a world before all the trouble began. Infantile sexuality is around from the beginning, but in its primitive states it remains untranslatable. Bollas's description of a mother unable to celebrate her child's genital sexuality is actually a refusal to read and translate that sexuality into forms that can carry it forward. This would imply that the mother is required to read her child's sexuality in all its myriad and perverse designs. For the infant's sexuality erupts, as Freud keeps telling us, in polymorphous ways, not as adult genital sexuality, but through fantasy and through the body.

Neither is the so-called paternal order the only route out to reality. According to Bollas, the father needs to be experienced as an obstacle in order for the child to move forward to his future. Thus, the father doubles as "the impingement of the real upon any self's unconditional relation the mother" (Bollas, 2000: p. 75). However, I suggest that the father's role can be helpful or unhelpful in mediating castration anxiety for the child. The infant might need the father as an obstacle but she also needs him to be a loving frustration. Castration happens, reality happens, separation from the imaginary maternal circle happens, without fathers necessarily being present emotionally or physically. In fact we can say that castration is an ongoing and necessary separation from the mother that begins with birth. The mother mitigates her leavings of the child with milk and love and then the forms or response that enable the child to elaborate and design the inner envelope of its sensory perceptual and affectual ties with the maternal bond. Thus, it is the nature, or the kind of reality that the so-called third term brings that is really the issue. If castration is our wake up call to reality, then it's destruction of the maternal imaginary must go hand in hand with enabling the child to elaborate its maternal world of forms.

In other words castration is the painful acknowledgement of the mother as a sexual and desiring, leaving being. Although we run into the prohibitive and repressive "No" of this reality, it is the ability to recreate the original sexual tie with the mother in differing unconscious ego shapes and forms that will allow us to mould and translate this sexuality into something we can actually experience. Psychosis arises when the child remains locked inside the maternal imaginary, but this is often just as much a reaction against the brutality of reality; a violent separation say, can cause psychosis just as much as a mother who refuses to let her child to experience anything outside of her maternal embrace. Complete madness is very frightening, but total sanity equally so. For, if psychosis is simply a refusal of unbearable reality and the subsequent retreat to the fairy world of our imagination, where fancy rules; then we all need to be a little mad. For without this fanciful and imaginary capacity we occupy a sane, but ultimately dead world of reality bereft of its illusory capacity. It as if the hysteric knows in all of her delays journeying towards reality, taking in many imaginary detours and circuitous routes, that she needs her sexuality (not just her baby needs), holding and shaping.

Freud was very open about what constituted sexuality: femininity, masculinity, perversion, part-objects, arbitrary objects and narcissistic desires were the polymorphous mix that made up the life of every child. Neurosis arrives for Freud, when a return and fixation to earlier forms of loving takes place. But if as Freud also thought infantile pleasures are the only real ones, then how do we distinguish between a return to past loves that makes us ill and a return that makes us happy? And this makes hysteria interesting because the hysteric is the character in psychoanalysis which is most fluid and labile, and also the most stuck.

On the move but forever fixated in her ideals, being flung backwards and forwards over loving the mother or her father, the hysteric expresses what Gregorio Kohon calls her "divalence". This lability is I suggest not just the hysteric's refusal to choose between her mother and father, but her need for the translation of these passions through forms that are telepathically read and responded to by another.

Dora's search for maternal form

This search for a maternal telepathic form is played out in Freud's analysis of Dora. Christopher Bollas interprets Dora's case as an autoerotic retreat into the embrace of a virginal mother; "a primary denial of sexuality" and the conflicts associated with the place of the father that such rebuttal brings (Bollas, 2000: p. 28). Freud's more Oedipal interpretations centred on Dora's repressed heterosexual desires and he is famous for missing Dora's maternal and homosexual transference onto Frau K. Separating the meanings of hysteria into maternal or paternal orders is to forget that the hysterical symptom is the failure, and return of the repressed, that is asking for a telepathic response from another. Something for the hysteric needs to be added to her love of the mother, in order to mitigate the savage prohibition of the father's law.

Leo Bersani argues persuasively that it is the very incompletion of our pre-Oedipal and Oedipal narratives; their escape from repression or closure that enables our perverse sexualities their continuation and sublimation through art. Thus, with Freud's essay on Leonardo da Vinci, it is precisely the failure of the paternal phallus to end the "radically mobile sexuality" between mother and son that leaves Leonardo with so many shifting positions in relation to an excessive maternal sexuality (Bersani, 1986: pp. 45–46). Leonardo's painting of the Mona Lisa sublimates traumatic excess with the mother not as a repressive substitute of his Oedipal desires but as a continuation of those fantasies, illustrated in that legendary smile as desire and menace. Bersani suggests that this de-oedipalising of the father gives him a "function as a duplicating generalisation of that love and not as its repudiation" (Bersani, 1986: p. 47). I would add to this that the inaccurate replications of desire that Bersani attributes to a generative paternal function in the Leonardo essay, could equally be seen as a maternal living form that mimetically reproduces are familiar identifications whilst telepathically translating them. The Oedipal complex is an arena where identification and desire, ego and object love are inseparably intertwined and mimetically replayed in melodramatic style, and yet it is precisely the ability of this melodrama to change its style or genre that makes a difference.

Evidence of Dora's autoerotic and idealistic identification with the mother is found, as Bollas suggests, in Dora's dream association of standing rapt in front of Raphael's Sistine Madonna. And yet this identification with a spiritual mother, is not, as I have argued, simply a return to asexual narcissism, or a regression to babyhood, that so many psychoanalysts have ascribed to the hysterical condition. Dora's rapt associations to the Madonna were her attempt to symbolise her homosexual relation with the maternal order; to find a living painterly form with which to paint and shape her passions for Frau K, whom she adored. Both these ideal women, the real and the painterly, have to be read as Dora's repressed excess in terms of her own mother whose "housewife's psychosis" (hysterical lack of desire) had posed the initial problem for Dora. Dora's passions, as Freud eventually realised, were bisexual. For Dora's talk of the "delightful whiteness" of Frau K's body was not solely born out of rivalry. It is in addition to her jealous love over her father, that Dora's "masculine" desire for the woman emerges: "The jealous emotions of a woman were linked in the unconscious with a jealousy such as might have been felt by a man" (Freud, 1905: p. 7). In other words Dora wants something in relation to her mother as well as her father, and these wants can't be seen as alternatives, both desires needed to be elaborated in relation to each other.

Perhaps the two most lasting perversions in psychoanalysis are that the pre-Oedipal is simply a place of asexual maternal holding, and that Oedipal sexuality is heterosexual, i.e, that the daughter does not actively desire her mother, or the son his father. We are always in the process of returning to the caring and holding of a maternal envelope, and the conflicts of the Oedipal stage. Affectionate love and sexuality are the two currents that reside in both of these descriptions or stages, although it is in the Oedipal phase that the frustration between these two currents really gets going. In his essay *Concerning the Most Universal Debasement in the Erotic Life*, Freud argues that neurotic tendencies and impotence are a result of the failure of the affectionate and sensual currents to coincide. "Of these currents" Freud says, "the affectionate is the older. It derives from the earliest years of childhood, was formed on the basis of the interests of the drive to self-preservation and is aimed at the members of the family and those with the responsibility of caring for the child" (Freud, 1912: p. 251). He goes on to say that from the very outset the affectionate current "has admitted contributions from the sexual drives, components of erotic interest that are more or less clearly apparent in childhood" (Freud, 1912: p. 251).

The older affectionate drives are our loving identification and idealisation of parental figures which are all powerful. And it is these loving identifications that are incestuous and create obstacles to more sensual loving. So that is why, according to Freud, men have to debase women in order to desire them (remove them from their idealised and incestuous position), and women tend to forget and obscure from themselves what they desire. Women spend "a long time away from sexuality" in fantasy, or their sexuality can thrive once a prohibition has been placed upon it. Prohibitions on their sexuality do for women what debasement of their sexual object do for men: protect both from the impotence that arises when there is a "non-confluence of the affectionate and sensual impulses" (Freud, 1912: p. 257).

Dora's flight from her desires is a protection against the conflict and non-confluence of her romantic and sexual longings. This young woman wanted romance and yet she was saddled with parents that made the joining of her ideals and her sexuality difficult. There was nothing whatsoever romantic about Herr K's sexual advances or Freud's literal key turning interpretations of the case, designed to unlock her mysteries within. Frau K was the obvious person for Dora to love because she was both an ideal mother, and sexually desirable, she was iconic of what Dora wanted to be, and also figured as a homosexual erotic object. For Dora's passionate search was arguably about working out a relation between her ideals and her sexual desires. We all begin with loving and identifying both parents, Freud's affectionate currents. Sexuality is around from the start but gets going in relation to the incestuous ideal authority figures, complicating the picture. How we bring together our ideal and sexual loves is never easy; we both identify with, and idealise both parents in the affectionate so-called "pre-Oedipal phase" and our sexual drives and fantasies in relation to these figures is both polymorphous and repressed. Bollas says the mother's desire is necessary to lift the child out of narcissistic relating, and with this I agree, but only partially. For the daughter, particularly, the forms her sexuality can take will have to be both the same (ideal) as a mother, and different. Or to put it differently, the daughter has an affectionate attachment to her mother and her repressed sexual drives don't preserve this bond but perversely shatter it into multiform parts and fashions. And this means that the difficulty for the daughter is as much how she achieves her autoeroticism, as it is how she leaves it behind.

Qualifying his great paper *On Narcissism* Freud controversially suggests that women have more problems than men in moving past the narcissistic stage. But we could argue that narcissism for the girl is never so assured, because it is always complicated by her simultaneous desire and identification with the mother. As Freud says, "real happy love corresponds to the primal condition in which object-libido and ego-libido cannot be distinguished" (Freud, 1914b: p. 100); and yet in adulthood this is not so easy to achieve. Ego ideals get solidified into punishing super-egos, the movement between our sexuality and our romantic (incestuous longings) inevitably hits recurrent obstacles. Although I am framing this as a particular dilemma for the female hysteric, I think this is also problematic for men. It might be easier for men to regulate their desires for the mother because these desires are not such a direct threat to their egos. Nevertheless, there is a loss for men it seems to me, in that the marriage of their narcissism and desire is so often at the expense of maternal identifications. Projection of this loss and envy is institutionalised in the historical sexism of our cultures.

And so how does the hysteric, or Dora, elaborate her sexual desires in relation to her loving identifications with the mother? How does she move from mother love to sexual love, if accession to the paternal order is not the magic cure? To love someone is not simply a matter of caring for them because passion is involved. When we love someone we want to merge with them, they embody our ideal selves or egos. The deeper the intimacy, the more boundaries between self and other disappear and yet psychoanalysis seems bent on only heralding the destructive nature of this so-called symbiosis, as if merging is only violent, and a separate sense of the relation between subject and object is the most mature and therefore the most ethical way to love. I am not so sure. If love is attributing our ideal ego or self to someone else and loving ourselves in them, then this ideal love is of course bound to fail once reality and the difference or separation from the other begins to manifest itself.

And yet this story presupposes that we lose our egos in love, only to re-find them in someone else, our love object, who has to then be protected and guarded from anything that might seem alien to the project of the self. Thus, love is premised on keeping our ideals as safe and maybe as secret as possible, and this is of course more practically done in fantasy, rather than reality. But if love is to last, then surely it must not be dependent on the resurrection, or the projection of the familiar ego into the other. For when this happens, the fury invoked when the other does not match this ideal, or becomes separated from it, kills love, because that love can't be reconciled with the other's difference. In this sense masochism becomes the only lasting way to love, because in masochism, passion is borne along and through the ongoing pain and loss of the ego's boundaries.

Leo Bersani and Adam Phillips have recently suggested impersonal narcissism as a way of envisaging a non-violent love, premised on the dissolution of the ego, where recognition by the lover, of his ideal ego in another, leads him to narcissistically love the other in the way he loves himself. Rendering the Platonic dialogues, "In Freudian terms", Bersani describes how,

> the boy sees and loves his ideal ego in his lover-except that this ego is not something he has lost and that he projects onto someone else, the over-valued object of love. On the contrary it is what the lover loves in him. In a sense, the lover recognises *his* ideal ego in the boy; desiring the boy in a way that is both the boy's and the lover's. The lover's desire waters the smaller, less well developed wings of a soul very much like his. And as the wings of the beloved's ideal nature grow, the lover is transported—driven divinely mad—by his vision of the boy becoming more and more like himself (the boy), like him (the lover) and like the god they both serve, the type of being to which they both belong. (Bersani, 2008: p. 84)

The ego ideal here is no longer unattainable, no longer in the service of making an injunction against our desire. Because this ego ideal has found its counterpart in the reality; albeit the virtual reality of another, then it can spread its wings as an agent of actual desire and becoming. For Bersani, with impersonal narcissism, the other person's difference is an "envelope" which is also "our sameness", and yet this envelope is not part of the knowable personal ego of either person, it is a potential of what they both can become. (Bersani, 2008: p. 108)

As Phillips says this Platonic account of relational and impersonal narcissism can be directly related to the primal bond where mother and child are attuned, narcissistically, impersonally, to "what each is becoming in the presence of the other" (Phillips, 2008: p. 113). We can see how this impersonal narcissism is also the medium of telepathic maternal forms, unconsciously on the move, reading and translating the passionate affinities between the mother and child, so they evolve into the different ego shapes that are produced between them. Such unconscious reading would then be a way of translating the hysteric's excessive passions into forms that did not just fly back to old and familiar fixations. Mimetic identification in the pre-Oedipal dyad is, as Borch-Jacobsen describes, the dissolution of ego and object love. Such mimesis is not just the replication of sameness, that is often implied in this identificatory love, but a movement of similarity; the relational and impersonal narcissism of Bersani's platonic lovers, where mother and child unconsciously read each other in relation to a virtual type of being they are becoming together. The divine reference in Bersani's account of a universal type is arguably a genre: the rhetorical forms that make up our being in relation to a wider cultural world.

If this is so, then how the daughter reads the mother, and the mother reads the daughter, unconsciously, telepathically, narcissistically, is how the genre of this female desire becomes pleasurably mobilised through both sameness and difference. Dora's rapture in front of the Sistine Madonna is a retreat into an autoerotic reverie with the mother which is also the daughter's passionate search for rhetorical forms of similarity which can elaborate her sexuality. Dora reads the Sistine Madonna as a virtual form of the female divine, not as another version of a transcendental female symbolic, or an over-weaning maternal super-ego, but as a living genre; a repository of actual love and virtual forms through which Dora can fashion her becoming ego, in relation to her mother and other women. Dora's passions are in search of a maternal form through which she can read and articulate both the identity and difference of her desire; a search in other words for a love that can both marry and move her ideals towards a real exchange with another.

The Sistine Madonna, for Dora, is her ego ideal found in another and in this case it is the virtual form of what she can be, abstracted in a painting. Furthermore, it is the actual bodily passion in Dora that meets and is reconfigured in relation to the painterly image, as a lived form of something she both finds and yet recreates. This is no different from the play between passion and forms in the mother-child relation, or the analytic session where there is a kind of dream-work in operation. The analyst thus features as a non-personal envelope, a virtual skin-ego reflecting the patient's passion and her sameness; and yet this passion is returned and unconsciously read by both parties into a new reality and exchange. Arguably, the analyst is a similar and yet better carrier of dream forms, than Dora's Madonna painting, because the analyst is also real. Like in a dream, he is a painting/an object that feels and responds and talks back. If Freud had recognised Dora's need for a virtual and actual mother in her passion for the Madonna painting, then perhaps together they could have translated that dream mother, into future possibilities of what Dora could love and become. And that would have meant Freud being open, to being loved as a woman, and as a man in the transference. Rather than providing unreadable keyhole interpretations of Dora's repressed affects, he would have realised psychoanalytic technique as his ability to be a poem in the crafting of Dora's desires.

In his paper *On Narcissism* Freud spells out the difference between idealisation and sublimation of the instincts. He writes, "the formation of the ego-ideal is often confused with the sublimation of the instinct, to the detriment of our understanding of the facts" (Freud, 1914b: p. 94). Continuing, Freud explains that when someone exchanges his narcissism for an elevated ego ideal, this does not mean that sublimation of the instinct has taken place. Quite the reverse, for the higher the ego's ideals, the more hard work and therefore the more repression is expected from the ego. And yet, if we read Dora's ideal love of the Sistine Madonna, as a relational and impersonal narcissism, and let us not forget this Madonna is a painting, then the ego ideal does not substitute for the narcissistic identification, as some kind of strict super-ego. Rather it puts this ego identification into movement: the daughter's unconscious reading and replication of maternal similarity and forms; a rhythm where the figure of Dora and the lines of the painting ripple and blend into the virtual and possible outlines of a future self she can become.

Conclusion

Sexuality, in Freud's thinking is a much more complex entity than has often been acknowledged. It is much more wild and anarchic, menacing, and buried, than contemporary ideas of fantasy and sexuality seem to suggest. And so telepathic reading of our sexuality and the transference is always at stake in communicating and translating the uncanny repression of our passionate ties. As I will argue in this book, a Freudian sense of telepathy is always partial in its ability to translate the traumatic otherness of our sexuality. For the daughter, a telepathic reading of her passions in relation to her mother is arguably a primary sublimation. Homosexuality, for Dora, becomes the necessary creative work, a relational narcissism that signifies the flowering of passion into exchange and love. In *Mourning and Melancholia* Freud distinguishes between a narcissism that eschews object choice, as in melancholia, and a hysterical identification where narcissism is on the lookout for something in common with the other:

> The difference, however, between narcissistic and hysterical iden- tification may be seen in this: that whereas in the former object cathexis has been abandoned, in the latter it persists and mani- fests its influence, though this usually confined to certain isolated attacks and innervations. In any case, in the transference neurosis, too, identification is the expression of there being something in common, which may signify love. (Freud, 1917: p. 250)

Love is the unconscious work and reading of the hysteric's relational symptoms in the analytic session; a telepathy which perhaps Freud missed out on with Dora because he failed to see how she needed his return of maternal forms within the transference. That Dora needed to love Freud first as a mother and secondly as a man, that she needed her homosexuality more, and before she could access heterosexual love, is perhaps well known. And yet Dora's case shows us easily the hys- teric can be misread by psychoanalysis, just as Dora was misread by Freud, because the opposition that the hysteric is caught in between fantasy and reality, the mother and father, repressed bodily desire and the authority of the superego, can't be resolved by a phallic law or a language of desire that suppresses sameness under the privileged het- erosexual signifier of difference. Hysteria, and Dora insist, that we take homosexual desire as the relational narcissistic matrix upon which all future forms of desire for the daughter depend. Not because heterosex- uality is foreclosed in this account, but because a happy love depends on the ego ideal attaining same sex affiliation, the lived form of our potential self in another, who is the same.

If as Judith Butler says, the melancholia of gender is the ungrievable loss of same sex desire, then bringing this same sex desire back to life is through the telepathic way we unconsciously perform, read and trans- late those repressed desires as living forms and genres (Butler, 1997).

The dead mother, for the daughter is a dead genre. This frightening mother is the emptiness and excess of passions the daughter cannot translate; a mother in other words who cannot reflect back the necessary living forms through which her daughter can access pleasures. And so making this mother into a living genre, whether she is an actual mother or a male analyst, entails an unconscious reading of the excessive passions associated with this early bond. This lived unconscious form is something we read telepathically everyday as therapists in our consulting rooms. But it is also arguably alive in the reading and making of literature, film and poetry. For the telepathic reading of our passions, through analysis, art and literature is their sublimation; an unconscious reading that does not substitute for our symptoms, but moves them into new configurations and possibilities. In the next chapter I will explore the unconscious reading of the mother as both a meeting and elaboration of both passions and form.

CHAPTER TWO

Unconscious reading of mothers and flowers

To read what was never written. Such reading is the most ancient; reading
before all languages, from the entrails, the stars, or dances.

—Benjamin, 1978: p. 336

What does the understanding of a telepathic, unconscious maternal form add to the debates within psychoanalysis? I shall argue in this book that telepathy, intrinsic to the travels of a repressed unconscious within Freud's thinking, is part of an unconscious and receptive unconscious that is located in relation to the earliest relationship with the mother. Grasping the unconscious work of a telepathic receptive unconscious enables us to understand, not just how the dynamic Freudian unconscious works, but also how such a receptive unconscious can be linked to the creation of unconscious lived forms that both create the "self" and shape and give expression to our affects. Unconscious perception goes on all the time in waking life, and is associated with what Freud calls the dream day. We are constantly collecting our unconscious perceptions as we go through life and these join up with unconscious memory and affects. At night, in our dreams, this transference between our unconscious wishes and our

33

perceptions is more intense because the barrier between conscious and unconscious is less rigid.

And so telepathy which collects our unconscious perceptions through the day continues through the night, connecting with our more repressed unconscious passions and translating them into dream wishes. "The preconscious dream-wish", is formed, Freud tells us through, "giving expression to the unconscious impulse in the material of the preconscious days residues". (Freud, 1917: p. 226) In other words, our dream desires are created through a telepathic translation of forms that begin with the day dream collector, and then carries on this dream work through the night. Telepathy is the transference and the route to the unconscious; through its dream-work or translation our wishes are brought to life. It is this dream-work, an unconscious reading by day and by night, that sublimates our deepest desires. Unconscious memory points backwards towards our earliest sensations and is a mimesis, an imaginary repetition of their sentient form, but it is only through the transference, and a more telepathic perception of these earliest memories, that they can be brought to a vivid light.

In Lacan's view, the memories and stories—the reminiscences that lead back to our primary desires—are always imaginary, they are the deceitful and narcissistic defenders of the ego, and it is these memories that have to be re-written symbolically in analysis. So, in this Lacanian reading there is no pre-Oedipal experience that is not imaginary, and true memory is a rewriting of history from the perspectives of the present and the future. This is then Nachträglichkeit or deferred action, the time of psychoanalysis where the present and future control the past. We can only know of the past what we remake of it in relation to the future, and so the reality of pre-Oedipal experience is, from Lacan's point of view, simply the fairy-stories in the land of the ego that have to be replaced by Symbolic memory and desire.

Rewriting or translating primary passions, symbolically, is how we can access our desire and replace imaginary reminiscences with true history. Post-Lacanian feminists have struggled with trying to redefine the phallic nature of this Oedipal Symbolic in more positive feminine terms, of re-defining the female symbolic at the level of language, and I think the most successful attempts at doing this have been through the notion of maternal poetics. You cannot replace or substitute the maternal body by the Symbolic in feminine terms because quite simply women have more trouble finding a perverse route to working through their desire and loss of the mother. Women objectify their mothers with more difficulty because, as Luce Irigaray tells us, there is a relationship of sameness, a mimesis with their mothers partaking of the body that needs to be acknowledged and expressed. So I think we need to add to a deferred notion of time, the idea of lived time. Lived time is the time of the affectual body that exists prior to the representational subject.

We can think of this time as "Women's Time" in the sense of Julia Kristeva's famous essay; a time cyclical and eternal, linked specifically to the idea of a maternal and unconscious space and place. For Kristeva this time is linked to a female subjectivity that gives itself up to intuition and thus,

> becomes a problem with respect to a certain conception of time: time as project, teleology, linear and prospective unfolding; time as departure, progression, and arrival-in other words, the time of history. (Kristeva, 1981: p. 17)

And yet Kristeva also sees this maternal recurring time as a problem for women and feminism, in that like the hysteric's reminiscences, it refuses the puncturing and mastery of a more masculine language and symbolic. I want to suggest that there is a lived maternal time and form, associated with a poetics of the maternal body, that is not oppositional to the repressive linear history of the subject, and the symbolic that Kristeva describes. Lived maternal form is an early telepathic reading between the ego and its other which can elaborate our more repressed and hysterical passions through a more receptive unconscious. This receptive and telepathic unconscious transfers the repressed unconscious and gives living form to our imaginary reminiscences so they can be moved and shaped in new ways by the ego.

Undoing the ego's masterful repressions and imaginary stories of a Personal self is not simply a confrontation with a more impersonal Symbolic or Law that would seek to translate those stories of plenitude in relation to lack or castration. Lacan sees ego psychology as a cover-up for the radical splitting of the subject through his or her desires. Although we could say he fails to see that the ego, in its more unconscious forms, is also our friendly negotiator. The ego, in other words, is not just imaginary but has an early pre-Oedipal relationship with reality. In a repressive unconscious, the realms of the imaginary maternal body and the Symbolic are in opposition. But in a more receptive unconscious, associated with a telepathic reading of lived maternal form and space, reality and fantasy communicate. And it is this lived maternal form that moves memory as a repetitive and unheard reminiscence into a more embodied experience.

Some contemporary psychoanalysts have focused on the importance of elaborating a maternal idiom or poetics associated with the early mother and child bond. Luce Irigaray's understanding of maternal gesture, Julia Kristeva's work on the semiotic chora and Christopher Bollas's conceptualisation of maternal idiom, are all in different ways trying to formulate a theory in terms of the lived practice of maternal form. The figure of the hysteric has been emblematic in psychoanalysis in showing the repression of sexuality and its accompanying symptoms. However, the hysteric is also a key to understanding how the unconscious communicates. The hysterical character shows us the nature of passion and its repression; but she also makes us the audience for her performance of affects in search of lived form. This lived form is not conscious; it cannot be placed within language and conscious meaning, although if language is going to live and move in time, then its signifiers need a connection to the lived form of affects that underpin them. Desire, in other words, might find its representation through language, but its force and subterranean vitality, the push we feel when we want something, or are excited by somebody, that comes from our passions. But in order for passions to travel, in order for them to communicate and be borne and carried along, they need a form, a dress or design to be elaborated, read, and hopefully translated.

Untranslatable passions are literally unbearable, they are repetition of the same, the same need; the same loneliness, the same death in life that is the fate of passions if they become stuck and non-negotiable. We begin, as babies with extreme passions and affects. The baby's needs, its cry, is not ignorable. Demand is met initially by the mother, and her return of the baby's passions is not simply the same. The mother's responsive passion is a mimesis with difference attached, as she returns her baby's affects along with gestures, smiles, facial mirroring or her playful response. So affects are passed backwards and forwards between mother and child, but if the mother is attuned to her baby, this mimesis is never just simply the same, a perfect match, because the mother returns the baby's passions slightly differently, with form attached and with some delay. There is a difference between an unconscious symbiosis where the mother and child are one and yet open to the unconscious similarities and differences between them, and an idealized symbiosis where fantasies of harmony, Narcissus and Echo, enacted between adults, or projected onto a child, are a defence, or restoration of loss. In the former case we have an unconscious conversation but in the latter both the ego and the object substitute for each other but can't melt or move in any way. They remain mute and fixated.

Christopher Bollas and Kenneth Wright are two contemporary psychoanalysts in the Winnicottian tradition who have understood a pre-verbal, unconscious language, or communication between the mother and baby in terms of a maternal aesthetics. For Bollas this aesthetic, as the "unthought known" defines an unconscious self which arises from what Freud called the Id, and yet instead of being repressed this unconscious is receptive and generative. The receptive unconscious is the part of our libidinal drives that express operational structures of being and character which are developed in relation to our first objects. The mother as the first transformational object is something we use evocatively, along with other objects in the world to structure and develop our personal being and idiom. Bollas writes:

> Our private idiom and its operational matriculation into processes of care that are theories of being leave each of us as adults with a substantial part of our self somehow deeply known (profoundly us) yet unthought. The theory of id was a crucial first step in conceptualising an important "itness" to us, something at our core, something that drives consciousness: a figuration of personality that conjures specific objects to unravel its code by such objectifications. Above all, our itness, or our idiom, is our mystery. (Bollas, 1993: p. 51)

Bollas thinks of this unconscious elaboration of the self mostly in terms of objects, both external and internal, that can release our idiom into being. He also thinks that the process of this generative creation of the self is a kind of dream work, where we use objects unconsciously releasing them into self-expression within reality. For Bollas, all generative processing of the "unthought known" begins with the mother's idiom of care and the infant's reception of this unconscious form. Informed by the earliest aesthetic we are held and transformed; "The uncanny pleasure of being held by a poem, a composition, a painting", according to Bollas, lies in "those moments when the infant's internal world is partly given form by the mother" (Bollas, 1989: p. 32). This experience of the unthought known is, for Bollas, a kind of "deja vu" or existential memory that is non-representational because it is carried in experiences of being, that correspondence with the other, before mind and the wording of the self is established.

In *A Sketch of the Past* Virginia Woolf writes of some of her earliest memories associated with the family holiday home at St Ives. At least these memories are the ones that open the way for her to what must be the first and foundational moment of being:

> If life has a base that it stands upon, it is a bowl that fills and fills and fills—then my bowl without a doubt stands on this memory. It is of lying half asleep, half awake, in bed in the nursery of St Ives. It is of hearing the waves breaking, one, two, one two, and sending a splash of water over the beach; and then breaking, one, two, one two, behind a yellow blind. It is of hearing the blind draw its little acorn across the floor as the wind blew the blind out. It is of lying and hearing this splash and seeing this light, and feeling, it is almost impossible that I should be here; of feeling the purest ecstasy I can conceive. (Woolf, 1990:p. 73)

But of course this is not just a memory, it is a work of art; an act of the imagination. Woolf is using language here, to bring her earliest memories to life, but what is interesting is not that these images and impressions in her memory are just lying in wait to be given expression through words. Rather, the images themselves only become vivid images or pictures once they have been painted through Woolf's poetic language. So, language here is used to paint rather than just represent. Woolf speaks of the balcony wall of the nursery that connected with the balcony of her parent's dressing room. Her mother comes into view in a white dressing gown and then we see purple passionflowers growing on the wall, "with great starry blossoms, with purple streaks, and large green buds" (Woolf, 1990: p. 74). As Woolf paints these early impressions for us, of the pale lemon blind, the sea's green splash and the shimmering passionflowers, she talks about sight and sound becoming indistinguishable; shapes that coalesce with light making them move and reconfigure. Rather than language being a reflective representation of a bodily image, it works here poetically, condensing colour, sound, and sense, as a kind of dream-work on the page. A dream-work that we participate with as readers, producing the image vividly: our aesthetic response inseparable from the feelings conveyed.

Woolf's poetic impressions can't simply be ascribed to discursive meaning. The one two, one two of the sea green waves, and the acorn running along the floor attached to the billowing sunny blind, will evoke different forms, for Woolf as a writer and for us as readers. The words are the materials, for what Susan Langer calls, the non-discursive art forms that makes up poetry. Woolf's moments of being are an expression of what Langer calls virtual reality, an illusion of life that is more significant than the real world or thing. "To be imaginatively coherent", Langer writes,

> the "world" of a poem must be made out of events that are in the imaginative mode—the mode of naive experience, in which action and feeling, sensory value and moral value, causal connection and symbolic connection, are still undivorced. For the primary illusion of literature, the semblance of life is abstracted from immediate, personal life, as the primary illusion of the other arts-virtual space, time, and power—are images of perceived space, vital time, felt power. (Langer, 1953: p. 217)

Of course the most interesting thing about Woolf's first impressions is that they have to be moulded and sculpted into being. She writes, "those moments—in the nursery, on the road to the beach—can still be more real than the present moment" (Woolf, 1990: p. 75). So what is happening in those moments where we imagine so strongly, it is like we are actually there? Woolf supposes that her memory supplies what has been forgotten, "so that it seems as if it were happening independently, though I am really making it happen" (Woolf, 1990: p. 75). What do we do then, to make these memories happen? What needs to be added to memory to make it, as it were, come into such lucid perception and view?

Imagining is not simply fantasy. "I am hardly aware of myself, but only of the sensation" says Woolf of her first nursery impressions, "I am only the container of the feeling of ecstasy, of the feeling of rapture" (Woolf, 1990: p. 76). What Woolf describes through her wordy materials are memories that become imaginatively vivid through the act of unconscious perception. Elaine Scarry describes our imagination, whether it occurs in our daydreams, or under the instruction of literary authors, as being a perceptual mimesis. Our daydreams, according to Scarry, are a poor substitute for sensory perception. Imagining, in Scarry's opinion, is weak whilst it remains in our imaginary, but once brought to life through the act of reading and subject to authorial instruction, our imagining and images, "acquire the vivacity of perceptual objects" (Scarry, 2001: p. 5).

> How does it come about that this perceptual mimesis, which when undertaken on one's own is ordinarily feeble and impoverished, when under authorial instruction sometimes closely approximates actual perception? (Scarry, 2001: p. 6)

The vividness of imagination is due to the way it reproduces perception. In other words, according to Scarry, the strength of the imagination is due to the acuity of the mimesis of perception that gives rise to it. Although Scarry uses a cognitive psychological explanation to ground her understanding of perceptual mimesis, and the imaginative power of reading, I want to explore the difference she points to between fantasy and imagination, in rather different psychoanalytical terms. But first I want to distinguish what I mean by perceptual mimesis, which I will argue has both a conscious and unconscious side. Scarry uses the term mimesis in its classical sense, as an artistic representation of reality or nature, and so for her there is a distinction between immediate sensory perception and its mimetic representation in literature. What literature gives us, according to her, is a set of instructions for imagining something. So, for Scarry, Emily Bronte gives us instructions for imagining Catherine's face in *Wuthering Heights*, and yet we don't really see it.

> In imagining Catherine's face we perform a mimesis of actually seeing a face; in imagining the sweep of the wind across the moors, we perform a mimesis of actually hearing the wind. Imagining is an act of perceptual mimesis, whether undertaken in our own daydreams or under the instruction of great writers. (Scarry, 2001: p. 6)

But if imagining in this account, is weaker in daydreaming becoming stronger through reading, then what might be the unconscious stakes for imagination? A common way of thinking about daydreams is to see them as conscious sentimental abstractions. I don't personally think all daydreams are this fixed, but if we compare the idea of a weak but conscious daydream with the art of reading, then does the more vivid imagination, brought about by reading, mean that it is more or less conscious than a daydream? And if reading is more unconscious, then how is it? Is the strength of perceptual mimesis in reading a book always dependent on the skill of authorial instruction? What about the reader's unconscious sense perceptions, which always leak back into memory? I want to explore the idea that reading moves unconsciously and telepathically between equivalent objects, as a kind of dream-work, before it can be illuminated through a more subjective, conscious light. The idea, then, that there might be an unconscious dream work operating between the reader and the text that dissolves the reader's subjectivity in a mimetic becoming with the images offered up through the film, or the literary work. Thus authorial instruction plays its part through crafting the virtual world that the reader enters into, but elaboration of that artistic object is also dependent on the reader's ability to lose their conscious ego and enter into an unconscious mimesis of deeper sensory perception.

Walter Benjamin would only partly agree with Scarry's distinction between immediate sensory perception and its mimetic representation through art. For him, the mimetic capacity works immanently between the sensuous and non-sensuous. And like Freud's unconscious, this mimesis has both a phlyogenetic and ontogenetic meaning. Phylogenetically, mimesis can be linked back historically in ancient times to a magical sense of a compulsion "to become and behave like someone else" and it can also be connected ontogenetically with children's mimetic play. Children's play, Benjamin tells us, is shot through with mimetic modes of behaviour and this is not just limited to impersonating people. "The child plays at not only being a shopkeeper or teacher, but also a windmill and a train", Benjamin remarks and then asks, "Of what use to him is this schooling of his mimetic faculty?" (Benjamin, 1978: p. 333).

The ancient mimetic faculty of magic and astrology is for Benjamin evidence of a kind of unconscious reading where sensuous similarities are perceived "in a flash", and cannot be held onto. These flashes of unconscious perception are momentary, offering themselves up to our view as fleetingly "as a constellation of stars". If magic, telepathy and the identification of sameness in the other (or the object) is the earlier form of mimesis, then language for Benjamin is a more developed manifestation:

> Language is the highest application of the mimetic faculty: a medium
> into which the earlier perceptive capabilities for recognizing the

similar had entered without residue, so that it is now language
which represents the medium in which objects meet and enter into
relationship with each other, no longer directly, as once in the mind
of the augur or priest, but in their essences, in their most volatile
and delicate substances, even in their aromata. In other words: it is
to writing and language that clairvoyance has, over the course of
history, yielded its old powers. (Benjamin, 1933: p. 68)

Telepathy, according to Benjamin is at the heart of mimesis, the
forgotten and magical side to language and communication with the
other; thus it is a form of mimesis where identification with the other
(in terms of similarity) meets reality. Telepathic mimesis is where sensuous similarity connects self and other. This telepathic mimesis is also
sentient, filled with affect, and thus undoes the distinction that Scarry
makes between immediate perception and a more representative copy.
A mimesis that as Benjamin remarks characterises children's play. Play
in childhood is a way of repeating earlier, strong impressions, and play
is more adept than say a hallucination in being able to re-work an earlier experience because it has more multiple forms, and is more under
the sway of the ego. Reminiscences, like the ones that pour out of the
hysteric's mouth and body are an imaginary repetition and mimesis of
early sense perceptions, and yet what distinguishes the compulsion to
repeat in children, from the repetition in neurotic adults, is that with
children the mimesis seems more open and receptive to new objects
and new experiences.

In children, unconscious perceptions of the dream day are not so at
odds with their desires: new forms and old make friends more readily. Dominated by repression the hysteric's mimesis is different. She
repeats past desires onto the analyst, but she can't, as it were, get to
anything new. We can also see this hysterical mimesis as making up
what Borch-Jacobsen calls the indissoluble and hypnotic emotional
tie, between the ego and its first object, the mother (Borch-Jacobsen,
1992). But mimesis in Benjamin's sense of being an unconscious reading or telepathy is not simply locked into the imaginary; or distinct
from reality. On the contrary, what Benjamin calls the "profane illumination" is the shock, explosive meeting of memory, together with
our unconscious perceptions of the everyday object. Here, the object
is made both uncanny and surreal, through our unconscious reading. Explosion of the object and the subject occurs, as the fusion and

unconscious translation of what has hitherto been distinct produces the profane illumination.

Like children playing at being shopkeepers and windmills, we become the objects we read, and their new-found vividness goes together with the experienced intensity of our desire. Present and past are also dissolved together; a forgetting and a remembering as we remake our pasts into new imaginative experiences. For Benjamin, it is the Proustian involuntary memories clustering around the everyday objects we encounter, that enables us to deeply illuminate the world around us. In Benjamin's view it is the telepathy of reading that is at stake in making this happen:

> The most passionate investigation of telepathic phenomenon, for example, will not teach us half as much about reading (which is an eminently telepathic process), as the profane illumination of reading about telepathic phenomenon. And the most passionate investigation of the hashish trance will not teach us half as much about thinking (which is essentially narcotic) as the profane illumination of thinking about the hashish trance. (Benjamin, 1978: p. 190)

But how, exactly, can we profanely illuminate a hysterical or hypnotic state? Or how can the hysteric produce a profane illumination out of her desired object? In the analytic transference the hysteric communicates all the time, but there is no correspondence, because the analyst and patient are speaking different languages. Conversation cannot happen as long as the analyst simply keeps interpreting the hysteric's desires through his conscious mental representations.

As Sándor Ferenczi noted, the only way to really illuminate the repressed material, in the transference, is through a loving telepathy, where the unconscious minds of analyst and patient can meet, think, and talk together. Thinking unconsciously is not the same as thinking in a conscious way. For one thing, the kind of knowledge we store and acquire consciously is absolutely no help in being able to intuitively grasp the client's unconscious. The unconscious reading or telepathy in an analytic session means, as Freud said, that the analyst has to open his receptive and perceptive unconscious, like a telephone receiver, to communicate telepathically with her patient. Unconscious telepathy is also involved in the way the analyst listens to her client's free associations and in the way she listens to her own. But telepathy, in analysis, can't be just understood through the notion of free association; it is also involved in all forms of conversation and reading between analyst and client. It is speaking through gestures that are exchanged, and read, and that are present in the way the body talks. And telepathy is right there, at the heart of the transference, in the way the analyst and patient love and read each other.

If we liken this reading to Bersani's notion of impersonal narcissism, then analyst and patient are in a process of a loving mimesis with each other, where unconscious similarity becomes the ground for each person's becoming and their profane illuminations in relation to each other. As Adam Phillips says the analytic dyad is like the mother child tie; drenched in an impersonal narcissism where both parties are attuned, we could say telepathically tuned in, "to what each is becoming in the presence of the other" (Phillips, 2008: p. 113). Repressed unconscious desire gives way in analysis to the loving telepathy of the transference where analyst and patient read, and get to know each other through unconscious desire. If this sounds idealistic, then it must be added that there is plenty of conflict, frustration, and hate that also circulates in therapy and must accompany any intimate relationship. And yet it is through love and loss, not hatred, that we construct identifications. Telepathic sublimation of our passions is always incomplete and so unconscious reading can never fully translate the ferocity of our repressions. Psychoanalysis always wants to water down the love that takes place between analyst and client, as though it's only through inhibiting our love, that we can help our clients. And I simply don't think this is true. However, because unconscious desire takes time to be assimilated, because it is so strong, then the unconscious conversations taking place in analysis go on over time, before they suddenly surprise us, flashing up to illuminate their sensuous and similar correspondence.

So much psychoanalysis unconsciously adheres to a distinction between reality and the imaginary, in its separation of pre-Oedipal from Oedipal, whereas as Freud noted so succinctly in *The Interpretation of Dreams*, the unconscious and conscious are always on a continuum. And it is in the active and receptive notion of telepathic mimesis— the unconscious perception and reception of the child in relation to the mother, but also to other sensuous objects in the world, that reading and imagination begins. Unconscious telepathy and reading joins up our senses with our memory and through connecting the real and the imaginary versions, the mother is brought to life. Thus, we are reminded of Winnicott's famous transitional object where the child has to both find the object in the world and make it up. Telepathic reading, the early sensuous reading of our mother is both a real and virtual event, the particular way that we remember, and forget, notice, and half notice her sounds and smells; the patterns of light on her face and hair, or the flower patterns on her dress. In a similar way, we unconsciously read our patients in the analytic session. Like experiences with the mother, such unconscious perceptions of the client build over time. The way a person comes into a room, the awkwardness or exaggeration of movement that accompanies speech, the flushing of skin we begin to associate with a particular emotion or idea, the rhythm of someone's breathing and body as she or he opens up, or closes down in the episodic motion of the analytic hour. Telepathy—our unconscious reading of the other is the sublimation and the communication of our repressed desires. Without this unconscious communication there is arguably no real rhythm to analysis and no movement; everything just becomes a stuck repetition of the same.

Telepathy and unconscious reading is arguably at play in Christopher Bollas' notion of a maternal aesthetic "the unthought known" which describes the particular style of the mother's care of the infant's needs. It is memory, regression, the falling into this "maternal idiom" or mimesis that gives rise to aesthetic experience. Kenneth Wright follows many of Bollas' ideas and acknowledges their mutual debt to Winnicott's idea of primary creativity and the child's transitional ability in finding early internal forms through first objects. Yet Wright is unhappy with the emphasis Bollas puts on the transformational maternal aesthetic, as being a nostalgic memory or history. As he says:

> for Bollas, the revival of early memory—the sense of being *in the presence of* a transformational object—seems more important than the value of the forms themselves as integrating agents in the contemporary life of the subject. (Wright, 2009: pp. 150–151)

Wright thinks that Bollas makes the artwork nostalgic because he is privileging the memories that the artwork evokes, rather than seeing the art object as a container of evocative forms in the present, which would of course make the elaboration of aesthetic form in the clinical situation something current and new, rather than just a evocation and re-working of the past. I think Wright's observations are important, for of course this maternal aesthetic experience is both current and nostalgic, but Wright is also pointing to the role of unconscious perception in the clinical session. And yet our perception and unconscious generative use of objects will always summon up and leak back into memory and our repressed passions. Wright is interesting when he suggests that the analyst, like the mother, might be an art object in his or her own right; that there is a generation of forms by the object, in the here and now, that can elaborate emotional expression within the self. Maybe, though, we don't have to choose between Bollas' ideas of maternal idiom as an aesthetic memory, and Wrights ideas of the mother as a current perceptual object that generates art forms and emotional expression in the subject. Indeed, I think the idea of the mother as a currently perceived generator of artistic forms, is embedded in Bollas notion of her as a transformational object. In fact, we could characterise this transformational mix of memory and current perception as Walter Benjamin's surreal, profane illumination.

If we think of Virginia Woolf's beautiful evocation of her first moments of being, we can see that the aesthetic moment she is describing is both a memory of the past and her ability to shape that memory imaginatively through her writing. The one, two, one, two, of the waves as they splash on the beach or break behind the yellow blind, arise from her memory, but they are brought into life and form by her creative and mimetic identification with these images. This mimesis is a sensuous perception of similarity, but one that yields at the same time a non-discursive form, in Langer's meaning of the term. "I am only the container of the feeling of ecstasy" writes Woolf of her sensuous early memories (Woolf, 1990: p. 80). For the self here is reduced to its most simplest form, like a dream, this unconscious perceptive memory is a sentient pattern of sight, sound, and smell, which belongs, or seems to belong to another.

When we identify strongly with something, we become it and behave like it. The object suggests itself to us and we identify and surrender ourselves to its significant form and structure. Kenneth Wright describes maternal mirroring, particularly the mother's face, as an art form that in turn, creates the forms of feeling and emotion for the infant. However, I suggest that this maternal mirroring or mimesis combines the mother's response through song, sound, smell, and bodily gesture as much as it figures visual perception. The mother's telepathic response to her infant yields forms for his feelings, just as our dreams are initially given form by the residues of everyday events and objects we have encountered. In these simple forms of sentient life, Freud's primary processes, we are always elsewhere, just as we are in our dreams. And when our early passions exceed the forms we are given, when the mother stops being attuned to her child's needs, or when what the child simply feels is too much for the suggestive forms on offer, then these passions become unavailable for our experience.

In *A Sketch of the Past* Virginia Woolf describes three shocking examples of childhood memory to illustrate this point. The first memory is of her fighting with her brother on the lawn, when suddenly the young Virginia becomes paralysed and can't hit her sibling back. She remembers hopeless sadness and a feeling of "something terrible; and of, my own powerlessness" (Woolf, 1990: p. 80). The third memory is again a trauma, the suicide of a man who had been staying at the family holiday home in St Ives, and Woolf remembers being in the garden at night and the moonlit embrace of grey-green bark of the apple tree reflecting back the horror she feels. The middle memory or shock is, however, pleasurable, and it is simply of happening upon a flower in the garden:

> That is the whole", I said, I was looking at a plant with a spread of leaves; and it seemed plain that the flower itself was part of the earth; that a ring enclosed what was the flower; and that was the real flower; part earth; part flower. (Woolf, 1990: p. 80)

Flowers are particularly suggestive to our perceptual mimesis, in Scarry's view, because they inhabit a place that is halfway between the material and the immaterial world. As Aristotle describes, flowers exemplify the ability of humans to love something without eating it. We smell out our mothers, I suggest, for the whole of our lives, and that smell is either enticing or repelling. To begin with we love our mother and want to both eat her and spit her out, as Freud says of our early cannibalistic drives. But the fact that we learn to smell our mother without wanting either to eat her, or expel her, is evidence of how we can learn to love her continuously, regardless of her ability to feed us. To put it another way, the reason why we can eventually smell our mother without eating her, is because when we initially digested her, the experience was good enough for it to last. Scarry cites Aristotle's example of smelling flowers to explain how the flower exemplifies the relationship between imagination and perceptual mimesis. "What is imagining like?" she asks,

> Like being a plant. What is imagining? It is not-perception; it is
> instead the quasi-percipient, semi-percipient, almost percipient,
> not yet percipient, after-percipient of perceptual mimesis. (Scarry,
> 2001: p. 66)

We imagine the reality or solidity of things, according to Scarry,
through authorial instruction. She gives the example of how Proust
gets us to imagine the solidity of Marcel's nursery room in Combray,
by juxtaposing the light and images from a magic lantern playing on
the walls. The translucent quality of the light filled images works to
foreground the authenticity and density of the domestic objects. It is
"The glide of the transparent over the surface of something" says Scarry
that makes the walls seem real (Scarry, 2001: p. 6). And this movement
of a transparent surface over a solid one is how authors bring the vividness and solidity of their literary worlds to life. Scarry's explanation for
authorial instruction is that the reader is coaxed or pushed into a reliance on deep perceptual habits. In other words, it is not the imaginary,
in Scarry's view that is central to either the imagination or aesthetics:

> only by decoupling "vividness" from "the imaginary" (where
> we unreflectingly and inaccurately place it in many everyday
> conversations about aesthetics) and attaching it to its proper
> moorings in perception, can we then even recognize, first, that the
> imagined object is not ordinarily vivid, and second, that its not
> being vivid is tautologically bound up with its being imaginary.
> (Scarry, 2001: p. 4)

But of course psychoanalytically we would say that the unconscious
imaginary always gives way to a deeper sensual perception, once the
boundary of the more conscious ego is cracked or broken. Conscious
perception is always shadowed by both an unconscious sensory perception and our virtual and affectual memory, thus giving our desires
their shape in the present moment. Whereas Scarry wants to privilege
perception and make it a distinct structure, I suggest that perception
and memory are always twinned in the act of imagination at an unconscious level. Indeed, the mimesis of perception that Proust engages the
reader with in relation to Marcel's nursery is a translation satisfying
the reader's passionate wish by recreating earlier scenes of satisfactory
illusion.

Imagination depends on keeping both imaginary and real on the move in relation to each other, and perhaps the most important concern lies in accepting that we can't decide what is our memory and perception: they bleed into each other. The illusion of Marcel's nursery walls through the lights and images of the lantern are what make the reality of objects come into view. It is the transparent movement over objects, which gives them the right form and fit, thus bringing them into solidity. And so it is with flowers whose thin and transparent petals are nearer to the imaginary mental image; as they bloom out of and reflect the more earthy stalks and ground. In Freud's work we are often given the disparity, through repression and conflict, between the primary and secondary processes. As Winnicott says in his essay "Primitive Emotional Development", the baby will only come to love reality if her experience of hallucinating and wishing for the breast, happily coincides with the real thing coming along (Winnicott, 1984: p. 152).

Perhaps, it is no accident that Woolf gives us her flower memory as an example of a transformational and evocative object that provides a form and shape to her early experiences, thus bringing them to life. In the first memory or shock of the punch fight with her brother there is no description of a form to fit the feeling, just the terrible powerlessness at not being able to translate her rage into anything else. The flower comes next, and this is the pleasurable shock, which she can symbolise and make into an imaginative pattern and whole. The third memory of the suicidal man, is of course, a return to trauma, but the difference with this third memory, is that it is accompanied by an ability to symbolise her horror through the silvery green bark of the moonlit apple tree. Woolf learns later as an artist to receive these shock and surprises, and to pattern them through her writing. She learns that what was once in childhood experienced as the enemy blows of reality behind the cotton wool of daily life, can be recaptured through the imagination and made "real" in a more bearable way. She says, "I make it real by putting it into words" (Woolf, 1990: p. 81).

Flowers are easy to imagine, as Scarry notes, not just because of their outward appearance, their size and shape, but because they act as elementary forms, as internal rhythms and patterns that can marry our perception and memory. Forms, then, that can gather our disparate and unbearable passions, and make them into something expressive and communicable. Flowers are like a version of the virtual mother we all need, the one we can continuously smell and not eat, until she can be made real again in the mimetic identifications we make with objects in our current life, the here and now.

But there is something more about the virtual status of flower mothers, in that they are transient, they bloom and die, and so have to be re-invented as it were, again, and again, between the real and the imaginary and through the imagination. And this is what makes flowers and our imagination, and hopefully a version of our mother, different, and distinct from an imaginary fantasy. Because a fantasy, as Winnicott says, is a fixed thought and idea that can never be transformed, it just keeps on repeating in an unchanged way, whereas a mother that is a flower rather than simply a fantasy moves all the time like our dreams between the inside and the outside. There is a beginning to Woolf's first memory, we could call it her first passionate form, before the moment in the nursery at St Ives, where she sees the,

> red and purple flowers on a black background—my mother's dress; and she was sitting either in a train or in an omnibus, and I was on her lap. I therefore saw the flowers she was wearing very close; and can still see purple and red and blue, I think, against the black; they must have been anemones, I suppose. (Woolf, 1990: p. 72)

This flower memory of the mother is the preliminary mimesis which leads on to what feels the most important part of the memory, the moment in the nursery, the waves breaking one, two, one, two, the splash of the water on the beach, breaking behind the yellow blind. This is the memory that fills and fills, the dream memory that Woolf bases her imaginative self on, but it begins, we notice with the flowers on her mother's dress, the designs and forms from the mother that will shape her feelings and give the right dress designs to her ego. Imagination is not fantasy, neither is it simply memory, or simply perception. Rather it is the ability to move between memory and perception, between our fantasies and reality, through an unconscious mimesis with the other; a telepathy that connects our virtual and real lives. Imagination, then, is an early structure of the ego that participates with the imaginary, but is also distinct in that it is based on real, as well as imagined experiences with the mother. Flowers in this psychoanalytical sense are the version of our mother that can be smelled rather than eaten, although they can only bloom because there has been some earlier plant-like mother, call her a vegetable, that has been eaten in a nourishing way.

Charles Rycroft has insisted the pleasure principle, and the reality principle, or the ego, and the id, must be seen as a much more co-operative pairing. Whether we regress to our libidinal selves as Ernst Kris says in the service of the ego, or whether as Rycroft seems to think, the pleasure principle has always been a companion rather than a pre-cursor to our real selves, happiness depends on finding forms for our affects. And this procuring of forms, even in the privacy of dreams, is much more dependent on our mimetic and sentient identifications with, and responses to, everyday objects in the world. We don't just move from passions to discursive language and representation in the traditional pre-Oedipal to Oedipal story, of merger to independence. We are always at the mercy of our passions, as the so-called obsessive and hysteric show us in different ways. And yet if the obsessive keeps his affects secretly encased in dead forms, the compulsion of repeating this form or symptom is precisely because it kills off any desire, any-thing new. The dilemma for the hysteric is different because her affects are not constantly punished, just over-dramatic, in search of the right form or bowl to fill. Affects are repressed and hidden in the obsessive because they are forbidden enliveners of reality, and yet for the hysteric, affects are repressed and hidden because the reality that brings those vital forms is rejected.

The obsessive hates his pleasure, although he knows sure enough what it is. Whereas, the hysteric is always characterised by having affects that are in search of form, which can't be found because it is real-ity that is the obstacle. So the obsessive heterosexual man thinks and thinks, and hates pleasure associated with the woman, albeit a known intimacy which he avoids. Whereas, for the hysterical straight woman it is real men who are rejected—in favour of a fantasy man; intimacy is longed for by the passionate hysteric, but the reality that will usher it in, is often rejected because it is felt to be too frustrating. Another way of putting this is to say that we all have to learn to eat and read our mothers and that these two things are connected but not the same. Reading adds something to the cannibal passions of our early loves, making frustration and arguably intimacy more bearable. And reading, although it is often equated with words, has arguably got as much to do with a question of lived maternal form, which is pre-discursive. Read-ing adds living form to our affects because it mimetically brings them into reality through an unconscious perception and telepathy, which is also tuned in to our memories. Woolf describes how she turns up the past, like a plugged in radio, to listen into her childhood. In-between eating our mother and being able to lovingly imagine her, we have to learn to read her.

In Mary Jacobus's wonderful book *Psychoanalysis and the Scene of Reading* she puts together Woolf's famous essay, "Reading" with an argument for the melancholic incorporation of the object which she gathers from Freud and Karl Abraham. Using Woolf's essay, by way of illustration, Jacobus explores the introjective, projective, and incorporative mechanisms that are in play when we read a book. Woolf's description in this essay moves between her experience of reading a book in a country house and looking out onto a garden landscape, dreaming, and reading between the two. As Jacobus notes, this is the same glide of the transparent against solid surfaces that Scarry talks about, with the book and the garden dissolving and reappearing, first as a dream and then coming more vividly into view.

At the heart of Woolf's essay is the early memory, the famous escapade of the Stephen children as they go hunting for moths in the woods. Jacobus calls this hunt "the dream time of the essay"; the imaginary flight of the filmy, transparent grey moths against the dark stolid woods, which is also a play between perception and memory: the "irregular beam of light" from the lantern, leading the children with their butterfly nets and poison jar, deeper and deeper in the unconscious (Jacobus, 1999: p. 43). Jacobus emphasises the oral ingestion of the moths, drunkenly sucking rum, and sugar off pre-placed scraps of flannel, pinned to the trees. For her, this summons up our greedy absorption as readers. There in the densest part of the forest the children perceive through the moving search light, insects, blades of grass that are lit up as if through a magnifying glass, "every blade of grass looked larger than by day, and the crevices of the bark much more sharply cut" (Woolf, 1988: p. 140). The crackling sound of the insects in the wavy grass, as there emerges,

> here a grasshopper, there a beetle. And here again a daddy longlegs, awkwardly making his way from blade to blade. Their movements were all so awkward that they made one think of sea creatures crawling on the floor of the sea. (Woolf, 1988: pp. 150–151)

The insects, by "common consent" slither up the glass panes of the lantern conducted towards the light. Sounds are acute and the fascination of the dying moths quivering with stuck wings in the treacle is matched by the sight of a brilliant scarlet underwing on the most remote tree.

The flight of the grey moth, whose drinking pleasure seals his fate, is caught by the poison jar, illuminated as "a flash of scarlet within the glass". The reader experiences the motionless dead moth as a "glorious moment" which is accompanied by the shocking volly of shot, a "rattle of sound" signalling the fall of a tree, the fall perhaps of something unconscious (Woolf, 1988: p. 151).

For me, this scene is an orgy of the senses, and one where psychic memory illustrated by the flying grey moths is both caught and profanely illuminated by an unconscious perception. The death of the moth is a "glorious moment" because it is only when memory is caught like this in a flash of intuitive reading and perception, that the death means new life of the creative imagination. Woolf likens these moments to shocks of experience, a "loosening of the fabric? Breaking something away?" and yet for her, this is not so much a destruction of the moth, as it is the birth or creativity of the image (Woolf, 1988: p. 152). The birth, we could say, of new imaginative forms, where our first perceptions and memories meet within the body ego. I love the idea, promoted by Strachey and more recently by Jacobus that the literary reader is gustatory, one that is more than amply expressed in a variety of Woolf's writings. If eating our mother is satisfying enough, we can move from eating to smelling her scent like a flower, to sensing her gestures, sounds and colour. And like the insects in Woolf's wood of memory, these sensory perceptions are on the move towards more conscious illumination; and yet they remain as in a dream, equivalent and non-separate; an unconscious seeing.

What Woolf describes in her dream sequence in the forest is a description of very early and unconscious sense perceptions where seeing, hearing and feeling are more mixed up. Shocks are what the baby experiences in its perceptual awakening to the world. As Freud tells us, these shocks work two-ways, they come from inside and outside. But for the baby there is no such distinction, the baby apprehends everything outside as identification with its sensory and bodily experience. And so the body ego is formed as a mimesis with the mother, where her gestures, voice, smile—are us. We are in this primitive dream world, elsewhere, outside of ourselves as it were. We don't just perceive our mother's, or the garden she might be sitting in, we embody the leaves, the smell of hair and scents of sweat or summer air as parts of ourselves.

This mimesis and melody between child and mother is enabled for Daniel Stern by attunement, the ongoing tracking of the baby's feeling states, by the mother, who identifies with the baby's passionate affects and responds in a finely tuned, communicative way. Kenneth Wright adds to this by describing how the tuned in mother, holding the baby in her mind, responds through returning the baby's affects in symbolic and pre-symbolic ways. Wright does not mean Symbolic language, but uses Susan Langer's ideas of non-verbal, artistic form to explain how the mother tunes in to the child's affects and returns them symbolically. This music making between mother and child, where sense perceptions and affects come together to create in the child living forms, is the communication that is both telepathic and pre-discursive. Such telepathy is not extra-sensory, but intensely sensory, a reading between mother and child where a language of gesture, sound, colour, and shape, is qualitatively so much more vivid. Only as we grow older as people and as a society, do we forget our unconscious languages. And yet this telepathy comes back in the way we read objects, even if it is not always immediately clear what we are reading. As readers, or writers, we perceive and communicate telepathically with the virtual worlds we create. In analysis, the therapist and client read each other telepathically too. If Woolf talks about tuning into the past and turning it up like a radio, then Freud also uses the metaphor of a radio transmitter to describe the analyst's receptive unconscious, telepathically picking up the unconscious communications of her patient.

Freud speculates at the end of his essay *Negation* on how thinking and judgement come about through the same processes of ingestion and expulsion that originally created the ego. Thinking is how we free ourselves from the object, through expelling or losing it, and subsequently reproducing our perception of it. The test of reality is for Freud dependent on an object being "lost which once brought real satisfaction" (Freud, 1925: p. 238). A lot of psychoanalysis has historically read this to mean mental representation means the successful repression, the leaving behind of the primary processes. But I don't think this is what Freud meant at all. For this seems to make the act of thinking and mental activity dependent on the banishing of our primary sensory processes. And we can see in this essay on *Negation* how Freud tells us that the prelude to thinking is a sort of palpating of the ego which was learnt before:

> It happened at the sensory end of the apparatus, in connection with sense perceptions. For, on our hypothesis, perception is not a purely

passive process. The ego periodically sends out small amounts of cathexis into the perceptual system, by means of which it samples the external stimuli, and then after every such tentative advance, it draws back again. (Freud, 1925: p. 238)

But in his paper *A Note Upon the "Mystic Writing Pad"* written a few months before, Freud writes that it is the unconscious that stretches out these feelers:

It is as if the unconscious stretches out feelers, through the medium of the system Pcpt-Cs., towards the external world and hastily withdraws them as soon as they have sampled the excitations coming from it. (Freud, 1925b: p. 231)

These two quotes are only contradictory if we assume that in the first one, written in his paper on thinking, Freud is referring to conscious perception. It seems to me that Freud is talking in both cases of an unconscious perception and mimesis which is active, not just passive, like the insects in Woolf's forest, moving unsteadily, their feelers extended towards the light. In Freud's view the primary processes such as dreams, where images and things are condensed and displaced in a symbolic equivalence feed into, and feel, their way into reality. If reality is premised on the loss and introjection of the pleasurable object, then this primary pleasure must still be on hand through early perceptual memories in order to provide the living forms that connect love with thinking.

In order to think we have to spit out, or get rid of our mothers. And yet lived reality and the virtual reproduction of the mother is also dependent on her initially being something good and pleasurable to eat. Thinking is how we recreate the lost maternal object; or how we reproduce it, "as a presentation, without the external object still having to be there" (Freud, 1925: p. 237). For this virtual make-believing of the object to happen, the binaries of presence and absence, love and hate, self and other (what Freud called the fundamental ambivalence of psychic life), has to be captured by the oblique nature of the imagination. If in repression it is either our ego, or the other that is acting, then in "negation", both are on stage, so to speak. And it is in the unconscious reading and re-making of the mother (or the object), the virtual, and the real, our memories, and our perceptions, uncannily correspond. In negation, our mother is present and absent, loved and hated, perceived in reality, and made up through fantasy. When she is repressed, none of this ambivalence is available to feed the virtual forms that will re-present her. Telepathy as the imaginative prerequisite to thinking is the uncanny poetry of our minds, the living form of our mother, which moves and exists between full presence and total absence. It is through the virtual reading of a like object, a mother who is here, and there, ours, and an alien, that living expressions of what we think and feel can be found.

In reading our mothers, there is a plasticity of the ego at stake; we must be both able to taste the mother and yet communicate with her unconsciously and reciprocally in ways that allow the imagination to flower. If the mother is a plant she must be both edible vegetable that is satisfying and a flower that we can ongoingly imagine and love. The senses and the imagination need to work together, and for this to happen the mental imaginary cannot be too cut off from the real. Primary and secondary processes have to work together, not so much in harmony, as in what I would call a friendly ambivalence. Telepathy is crucial in grasping the edifice of the Freudian unconscious because it is also central to understanding how the pleasure principle moves towards a non-discursive form in relation to another. Unconscious reading between the ego and other creates the living forms of the ego that are part of reality: they are not simply imaginary. Without this telepathy, we have the mutually exclusive poles of passion, or thinking (hysteria, or obsession), one repressed out of sight under the other. Reading the mother as both an edible object we can digest and as a flower that has more reflective and translucent qualities of what we can become, allows us to combine passion and thinking, and to connect ourselves intimately to the world.

I want to give some examples of this telepathic communication in relation to the analytic session to underline not just how primary and secondary processes work together in the clinical setting, but also to show how telepathy is an unconscious perceptual reading, that is not really magical, although it is often perceived that way. Perhaps this is the main reason that Freud always disavowed telepathy whilst always secretly believing in it. Once we place telepathy in the realm of magic we abandon its very real work in crafting the ego, we perceive it as an instrument of the imaginary rather than the motor of the imagination. Perhaps the easiest way to describe telepathy operating in an analytic session is to talk about how the analyst is always unconsciously listening, perceiving, and being aware of the client's gestures. Reading the client is not just about listening to what he says but the way he says it, the tone and rhythm of his voice, the way he smiles and frowns, those little imperceptible signs, that gradually with time and repetition, become a language all of their own. And our patients read us too; they get to know us unconsciously and telepathically. In this sense, it is intuition, not conscious knowledge that becomes the attuned two-way instrument of analysis. Conscious thinking of analytic interpretations cannot access the uncanny negations, the imaginative and ambivalent poetry of the analytic session. It is only through a telepathic sense, the unconscious reading of each other as real and virtual editions of each other that the analyst and patient can truly communicate.

By way of illustration I want to give a simple, fictional, clinical example. A woman who is good, too good at managing everything in her life, strides into every session with me in a very purposeful way; she sits down and clears her throat, and I wait for her to start. She tells me numerous stories about how she competes, as a mother, in her career and with her husband, a competition she seemingly never loses. She describes her ideal family and about how they are on "happy street" what she talks about is a string of achievements and a needy husband who can't match up. I listen and drift with my own unconscious impressions and again this is something that happens over time, it is a repeated sense that at some point flashes up into awareness. Her muscular body, the management techniques she utilises with other people, to get through life are of apiece with how strong this woman seems, and how capable. But the way she suddenly just stops with the sound of the frog in her throat and her eyes are suddenly those of a child; opened wide and wet with tears, and we are encountering the helplessness she cannot really bear or experience.

When I speak, it is not from any rational reflection of what she is saying, but from a sharp intuition that I am both someone who is a longed for, and a refused resource, and this is linked to her childhood with a mother who similarly denied her own needs. I tell her that her husband's helplessness is her refused dependency and desire; it's all the need and wants she can't have. Unconscious reading like this happens all the time in therapy. The analyst, more often than not, is working with unconscious messages and perceptions that she senses but may not initially really understand. And why would it be otherwise? Repressed affects and ideas are transmitted telepathically to another, but won't necessarily be received in any comprehensible way, whether it is the repression of therapist or the client that is getting in the way. Therapy is a place where the half said, the not yet known, and the frankly incomprehensible become simply the familiar signs that we are working with unconscious material.

And so it is the secrets of our repressed desire, our traumatic and unmodified passions, what Woolf calls the "sudden shocks" that constitute her as a writer. These shocking affects are a mimesis that is always telepathically in search of form. Woolf moves from the beaten hurt from her brother's fist to the form for her feelings in a flower; her realisation that the flower was real, a growing plant attached to the ground, "part earth, part flower". Thus the flower is the lived and becoming expression of Woolf's being. In this way we can see the mother and our mimesis with her, as a flower—as something both virtual and real; a non-personal composition that is always driven by a more underground furnace, of our more earthy and primitive affects. Unconscious reading of our mother and of objects is always this mix, this inter-relationship between affects and form, between the secrets of our desire and the identification of our mother as an alive genre, a growing flower that we can version again and again as both the same and yet different. We all need mothers and fathers to belong to living rather than dead genres; we need to be able to version them again, and again; inside, and outside, as both personal, and non-personal; as uniquely ours, and as characters who are socially reproducible. Unconscious reading with our mothers, gives our repressed affects the right psychic garden in which they can grow into lived, maternal forms. And it is the unconscious telepathy of desire, a movement of loving similarity between child and mother, between lovers and between analyst and patient (for they are also similar lovers), that shapes and re-shapes our private desires in relation to another. Telepathy, in short, is a reading of the mother as a lived form that transports our repressed desires into the becoming or blossoming (ever renewable) genres of our families, our sexualities and our cultural identities.

Telepathy as a reading of maternal lived form constitutes a time and space of the early ego that is receptively attuned to external cultural forms and reality. It is this lived time of the unconscious, we could call it "Women's Time" (albeit a time which men can partake of), that allows us to see how we can learn to house the world and paint it inside of us. And through the ego's radical yielding and unconscious reading of the living forms beyond its familiar shell, we are able to sublimate our repressed desires, not as a substitution of what has been lost, but as a movement towards our futures.

CHAPTER THREE

Rhythms of the unconscious

W e all have rhythm. Memories have a rhythm and so has the unconscious. Character is built through rhythm. A rhythm to begin with, is like the dream. Far away, on the horizon of what seems our distant past we perceive this indistinct and shadowy ghost and then, as it suggests itself to us, the memory begins to grow and move closer. We can imagine it and colour it in. As gradually our sensations begin to give this memory body and materiality; a character, a scene, or an event come into view. The rhythm of memory therefore suggests, and we answer mimetically with, an affectual bodily rhythm that brings ourselves to life. The past is always beating in relation to the present, but as a dream other, this history is only sensible, can only become composed as character, when we can carry and remake these dreams in relation to the world.

Dreaming pleasure

We are all aware of those memories, often summoned by evocative objects in everyday life sending us into a kind of reverie and dreaming; bringing to life, like Proust's Madeleine cake, the memories of child-hood. Time, here, returns through the image, but it is an image that is brought into being by what we sense and feel, as if our senses can put us back there: into a landscape of what we have forgotten. For me, it is the smell of sandalwood and I am back sitting in what my grandmother used to call her summerhouse, but was in effect just a wooden hut with big windows at the back of her garden. I follow my daydream, dissociate and float in my mind, until the image comes, faint at first and then stronger. There it is: an octagonal shaped white house with a thatched roof, my bedroom with the grey sea-light streaming through slanted windows. Free association and images pan out, cinema-like, to reveal the hill on which my Granny lived, the beautiful curve of Lyme Bay below. And then, another image of me and my brother, swinging legs side by side in the sandalwood shed, or sitting together on the top of a flight of crustacean studded, stone steps that lead down to the beach. Although this is a memory, it is inseparable from the objects that materialise and embody it. Sandalwood reminds me of summer as a child and being with my brother, when we were like twins, exploring the rock pools for sea anemones and crabs. The beach at Lyme also reminds me of my father in a photo holding my hands and laughing as I scowl furiously into the camera. Sea-light is also the grey-blue of my mother's eyes, as she puts up her hand to shield herself from cross children or perhaps the sun's glare.

Lyme Regis conjures up some of the more intense pleasures of my childhood, but it is more than that, it is also a memory that goes back historically through my mother's genealogy to her ancestor Jane Austen. I teach *Persuasion* now to my students and when we come to the bit in the novel where Louisa falls senseless down those very same stone steps that me and brother used to sit on, I realise they are called "granny's teeth". An apt name, perhaps, for my actual granny and her stern middle class ways that my mother did everything to escape from. And yet, as I read this novel with my students, my lifelong rebellion against Jane Austen starts to melt as I begin to lose myself in the book that rhymes with both childhood memory and historical legacy. Lyme Regis and my granny's thatch are part of the rhythm of my memory. As such they are part of my character, or at least a dreamy bit which summons some of the more ideal aspects of my childhood. We all have our own particular rhythms, our preferred ones. Culturally, physically, and emotionally we inherit our personal rhythms and create them, in relation to the wider unconscious rhythms that surround us. It is not just pleasure or the unconscious rhythms of our past that come to us with the beat of repetition and memory. Think of the wave like pain of birth contractions or the rocking of an autistic child, warding off the world. Trauma is also rhythmic, images that can repeat as dissociated and dreamy, or the literal repeats that are sensational, putting you back into the full physical and emotional horror of the event.

Uncanny rhythms of the true self

Rhythm, or what Michael Eigen calls "psyche-music" is perhaps the first form of psychic life. Following Winnicott and Bion, Eigen emphasises the unconscious primary processing of feelings as a rhythm that moves between injury and recovery, death and life. Developing Bion's understanding of the primary processing of raw, un-digestible experience through what he calls Alpha function, Eigen enlivens the term calling it Alpha work. Thus he describes how a brilliant dancer will have "alpha feet" or a musician "alpha hands", or a psychoanalyst might have "alpha intuitions" (Eigen, 2004b: p. 77). Perhaps objecting to the implicit gendering of Bion's definitions of alpha thinking and beta sensations, Eigen also says we can swap them round. Sometimes thinking is a murderous beta attack on feeling, whereas sensation can be alpha work in its own right. He gives Toni Morrison's fiction as an illustration saying she is a "sensation genius". Alpha work is the unconscious, processing or dreaming our sensations into usable feelings and thoughts. "When rhythm stops" says Eigen, "The psyche stops breathing" (Eigen, 2004b: p. 75), and this rhythm or breathing of the psyche is at work between trauma and recovery, establishing a rebirth of the self in relation to unknowable experience.

Eigen points to Winnicott's idea of the creativity at stake in approaching madness or "X". This madness is the most personal, private, and yet unknowable core within us. Touching upon this mad uncommunicable "true self" can make us feel real and it is also why breakdown in therapy can often be a breakthrough. This is true, only up to a certain extent, because a total breakdown is an ideal; an impossibility. Madness is a sublime experience in the sense we can approach it but never totally become immersed. Our mad "true" selves are non-communicable with, because they arose at a point where the personal self was beginning to form, thus our mad selves are the experiences and affects, those traumas and passions that occurred before we had developed an apparatus to house and experience them. Indeed, trauma raises the early defences against this hidden core being interfered with. The question, for Winnicott is, "how to be isolated without having to be insulated" (Winnicott, 1982: p. 187). I want to suggest that the raw passions of this true self are exactly like the hidden material of our dreams; a madness that can't be known, but can be translated into forms that make them communicable in a manifest sense.

"We do not know what X is" writes Eigen, although we can't experience or know it:

> We postulate it as a certain fact, yet also as a reality we grow around, with, through. It may be viewed as an ideal pole or limit, like total chaos or nothingness. It determines a vector of experience, a sense of something breaking through, something collapsing, associated with unbearable, unthinkable agonies. (Eigen, 1999: p 176)

Rhythm is then involved in the move towards this breaking of the self and its recovery; a rhythm that makes raw and painful experience more readable and digestible. In order to grasp the nature of the rhythm that Eigen describes between destruction and rebirth, or between trauma and recovery, we have to understand the uncanny doubling or dissociation that exists in relation to the "true self".

As Eigen himself suggests, there is a schizoid mechanism to the true self where a fragment of the un-integrated ego is detached. This ascetic "megalomanic" ego part, unfettered from collective embodiment within the rest of the ego, establishes a kind of crystal gaze that Eigen calls "electrifying" (Eigen, 2004a: p. 8). Winnicott's true self becomes, in this analysis, irremediably split between, on the one hand, an "active seeing stillness" which hallucinates and observes the more spontaneous "id" instincts that readers are familiar with. Eigen acknowledges that the crystal gaze is not strictly speaking part of the true self, as it is not integrated with the repressed body-life of the rest of the ego's structure, and so it can be involved with "self—falsification in order to fit in with others" (Eigen, 2004: p. 8).

And yet this doubling between an early unconscious perception and repression is persuasive and is in accord with Sándor Ferenczi's ideas of telepathy and the "clever baby". In his famous paper "Confusion of Tongues" Ferenczi describes how altruistic self-division in the face of sexual trauma splits the ego into a clever baby who thinks, but can't feel, and a hysterical subject closed off from representation who converts feelings into physical symptoms. The clever baby is the clairvoyant and masochistic part of the ego that telepathically identifies with and imitates the intrusive adult or other.

As a traumatised split off fragment of the ego; this baby is a "guardian angel" that watches over the hurt and feeling self. Healing this split between the clever baby and the mad hysteric is what Ferenczi attempts through the telepathic transference. His idea being that it is only when the clever babies (belonging to both analyst and patient) can unconsciously communicate with each other's mad affects, that early experiences can be processed. Ferenczi emphasises that some portion of the ego remains repressed in the mutual telepathy of the analytic session. Perhaps the creativity of the wise baby depends on this reclusive self being protected? We could also say that the clever baby is evidence of an aesthetic and perceptive unconscious intelligence that communicates. Ferenczi sees primal repression as a form of "imitation magic" whereby the ego is initially formed through a masochistic surrender to the external world. In this primordial splitting,

> I am frightened of the dog, I become the dog. After such experience, the ego consists of the (undisturbed) subject and the part that has become the object through the influence of the trauma. (Ferenczi, 1995: p. 113)

Becoming the dog or becoming our mothers, is perhaps a first magical sublimation whereby the ego disappears and reappears to become the powerful object it fears and desires. Such traumatic mimicry is repeated we are told, creating memories and then speech; but I suggest that provided the object in question is not too terrifying this mimicry also makes way for more generative and telepathic translations between an unconscious perceptual ego (the clever baby with its crystal gaze) and the repressed passionate Id. Arguably in primitive splitting, telepathy is very near to repression which is precisely why Ferenczi saw the telepathic transference as so essential in processing raw and repressed passions. Jean Laplanche suggests that translation follows repression of the enigmatic signifying breast, but without some initial, primitive receptivity and reading of the breast (or the dog), repression and the ego would not come to exist, and so we have to see telepathic translation and repression as interlinked entities: the inevitable two sides of how the dynamic unconscious works.

Rhythms of the "true self", or what Eigen calls "psyche-music", makes up the first unconscious identifications and translations of the ego and its objects. We can think of this telepathy and translation occurring between clever babies, reading each other's repressive bodies in the analytic session. But we can also think of this rhythmic, telepathic reading as a crystal gazing that happens in our dreams. How are we to understand this uncanny doubling of the "true self" as if it were a dream, with the inviolable and transcendental observer in the corner of one's mind, watching as Anna O famously said, "all the mad stuff going on"? Dreams as Freud has described them are divided into the part of the self that observes and represents the dream and the part that does not observe, but experiences. Arguably, a dream experience is actually a rhythm between the dream content and the unconscious observing ego; with the unconscious perceptive ego processing the dream material, so giving it form. Repressed instinctual wishes of the dream will be disguised symbolically by the unconscious perception of this hidden observer, and yet it is perhaps hard to tell with dreams what is covered over because contents are forbidden and what remains unintelligible because the translation is still too condensed. Thus unconscious affects are given their more primary forms through this dialogic rhythm that exists between the self and it's other in our dreaming minds.

An early unconscious reading occurs in the infant, a perceptual mimesis, but as Freud tells us, this can only come about if there has been a prior experience of satisfaction. The baby hallucinates the original feed reproducing the perception, which then becomes the fulfilment of a wish. Freud writes:

> Nothing prevents us from assuming that there was a primitive state … in which wishing ended in hallucinating. Thus the aim of this first psychical activity was to produce a 'perceptual identity'—a repetition of the perception which was linked with the satisfaction of a need. (Freud, 1901: p. 566)

In dreams there is a re-perception, a mimesis of perception (we could call it a translation), satisfying the wish by recreating and fulfilling earlier experiences of gratification. Through dreams we unconsciously read our own traumatic desires and satisfy them! Without dreams we cannot experience reality; our night dreams are an example of how we utilise the days residues and forms together with our instinctual wishes and affects that unconsciously might go back a very long way.

The dream day is similar in that we have to dream our way into reality. Processing our affects, the actual experience of the world and or objects has to be done through dreaming, because it is through dreaming that our passionate affects can be unconsciously perceived, communicated, and elaborated, into forms that build and embody the ego. Unlike the dreams we travel by at night, which are an essentially unknowable narcissistic retreat, daydreams involve actual objects and others. In the night dream those realities exist, but they are remembered, imagined, and re-performed through our unconscious perception. Freud remarks that dreams and telepathy are mutually exclusive because in dreams we are repressing and distorting the unconscious, whereas in telepathy the unconscious is descriptive, a more straightforward communication between the ego and the internal or external world. Telepathic communications are,

> treated as a portion of the material that goes to the formation of the dream, like any other external or internal stimulus, like a disturbing noise in the street or an insistent organic sensation in the sleeper's body. (Freud, 1922: p. 207)

I suggest, however, that there is an internal unconscious reading that occurs in our dreams alongside repression, where the ego is unconsciously scanning and reading its own non-personal materials. And so, just as Winnicott says, there is no such thing as a baby, because a baby always comes with her mother, so there is no such thing as a dream without the materials and forms that spring from the non-human object and other. Of course these forms and objects are virtual ones, but what is so interesting about our night dreams is that this virtual function of the dream other is taken over by the most personal albeit unknowable part of the ego.

Although Winnicott talks about the ethics for psychoanalysis in respecting and not invading the personal repressed true self, I want to suggest another way of thinking about this, which is to suggest that the true self has to be dreamt into being. Because the repressed true self as the most inviolable part of ourselves is both the most personal and the most impersonal, it cannot be invaded, but it can be telepathically translated (although only in part), through a relationship with a non-personal other, such as the analyst. We can think of Christopher's Bollas' notion of the "unthought known" as this unknowable self which finds its form through the transformative maternal object but as I am arguing in this book the "true self" is always arrived at through a process of telepathic reading. An elaboration of our spontaneous instinctual self between the early ego and its objects, that is unconsciously perceived and dreamed into being, and into our bodies.

Without this unconscious reading of our passions we remain divided between a mad subjective ego which has withdrawn from the world and a mass of painful affects that like Bion's beta elements are unavailable for feeling or thinking by the ego. We can, as I have suggested, think of Eigen's electric gaze as belonging to what Ferenczi called "the clever baby"; that wise, but essentially mad and detached part of the subjective self we regress to in times of trauma. Interestingly Ferenczi says that access to the primary repressed bodily self, what Winnicott would call the "true self", cannot be accessed by the individual on her own and neither can it be accessed in analysis, as long as the analyst seeks to understand such material through conscious interpretation. It is only when the analyst can sink down into his own unconscious streams and complexes, only then can the clever babies with their electric perceptions belonging to analyst and patient, telepathically read each other's dissociated and repressed affects.

For me this is also a function of the dream. Dreaming the self is how we arrive within time, within our bodies and within our egos. Or to put it another way, this dream is a rhythm between self and other, which is first virtual and then actual. We are used to thinking of memory as coming after a perception, but as Henri Bergson tells us, this is an illusion. Instead, memory and perception take place together, like two streams. The stream of perception springs forward as our actual consciousness, whether that is a consciousness of an internal or external object. The stream of memory takes us back to the dream or virtual world that surrounds us. So consciousness is always selective in that we have to limit or select from our dream world to begin living in an actual way. The unconscious is our virtual or dream past that is both general and shadowy; and it is the ghosts of this virtual past that suggest our more embodied actual life. Memory and perception are not the same and just like the hypnotiser suggesting the hallucination, the virtual memory suggests and provokes the sensation which grows stronger and stronger. Meanwhile, in the background playing the role of a puppeteer is the virtual image.

It is tempting to ignore the virtual ghosts of our memory when we are immersed in reality. As Bergson says, "We have no need of the memory of things whilst we hold them in themselves" (Bergson, 2002: p. 145). Our virtual memories are useless practically and often not available to rational reflection. Nevertheless, they are the accompaniment to all conscious perception. Behind every actual perception there is a virtual memory as a mirror double. This dream double keeps step with real perception, just like a dancer following his partners moves, giving to "each of its stages the aspect of the 'already seen', the feeling of the already known" (Bergson, 2002: p. 148). What is this, if is not Freud's description of the uncanny?

Thus our memories are always shadowing our perceptions and memory takes it shape, and is filled out as it were, by the perceptual moment in present time. Bergson calls this a "memory of the present" which is made up of "the past in its form and of the present in its matter" (Bergson, 2002: p. 148). We can see how this doubling creates a dance between dreams and reality, rather like a moving mirror stage. In normal circumstances we are not aware of this duplication because all our focus is on the action of the present. Only when we have a weakened attention to life does this doubling become apparent, something that happens when we are perhaps very introspective or in extreme cases, mentally ill.

Bergson describes this moving mirror passing between memory and perception, as the difference between being an actor or a spectator in a theatre. Becoming conscious of our duplication between memory and perception, we feel split between two people, one is the actor who simply plays his part automatically and the other beholds and watches himself play. It is the perceptual self that independently watches the performance, while the dream or virtual other is seen playing in an automatic or mechanical way. So the first, perceptual self is the one rooted in reality whilst the perception doubled with memory "makes us believe we are repeating a part we have learned, converts us into automata, transports us into a stage-world or a world of dream" (Bergson, 2002: p. 149). Bergson goes on to say that this virtual double is often encountered in moments of trauma:

> Whoever has experienced during a few seconds a pressing danger, from which he has only been able to escape by a rapid series of actions imperatively called for and boldly executed, knows something of this kind. It is a duplication rather virtual than actual. We act and yet "are acted". (Bergson, 2002: p. 149)

Rhythm and the relationship between memory and perception is unconscious; we only become reflective of the distinction between our virtual and actual selves at moments where we are most depersonalised or where the ego is at it's most disembodied. We can also see this as the primordial splitting between a clairvoyant clever baby and its repressed passionate affects. Duration or lived psychological time in Bergson's work is the interrelation of unconscious perception and memory which actualises and embodies our attention to life. But the ego's duration can also be understood in the translation work of the true self; the way the virtual dream can be unconsciously read, translating our split off affects into forms of a more collective embodied ego.

The splitting of the true self in trauma is protective, we retreat into a dream self where the body and what we feel is left behind. Many clients who have been sexually abused in childhood describe themselves in such a dissociation; hovering above themselves looking down on the child that is being hurt. I don't think therapy work in trauma is about getting the client to re-experience the event; this is often tantamount to subjecting the patient to re-traumatisation. Rather, it is the enabling of a dreaming telepathy between self and the virtual other within the transference that can translate elements of the trauma, without repeating the event. And this, it seems to me, is how we can think of the difference and intrinsic connection between our dreams by way of the night and those that embody us through our waking day. At night we withdraw into a dream world where our actual relationship to the world and to our bodies is left behind, and yet I suggest we still engage in an unconscious processing of our libidinal ties with the other, through the virtual forms that dreams carry. However unknowable or virtual and uncannily other our dreams are, they become through the dream day, more awake. Dreams, if you like, that have an attention to life, rather than repose away from it; something in other words that we can translate into an actual relation with objects in the world.

It's as if our subjective narcissism that we retreat to at night, in our dreams, is the way we process and enlarge the ego without the necessary limits the world of reality imposes on us. In the day we continue that dreaming in another way because the body and time are hopefully what we wake up within, and in this more awake dream our attention to life is fed by a more relational narcissism that can be equated with object love. Thus, in our more wakeful dream day, the virtual dream other takes the form of actual people or objects in the world who can elaborate our bodily egos in new ways.

Love is what fills and shapes our egos and makes ourselves and the life we inhabit feel alive and real. As psychoanalysis continually tells us, love is an achievement arrived at fairly late in the day for the baby. If we pay attention to what Freud tells us results from psychosis, which is narcissism, then we also have to distinguish a narcissism that signals our retreat from elaborating our passion in relation to objects and a relational narcissism which is identical to object love. In psychosis and extreme states of trauma we eschew not just our bodies and the external world, but a libidinal relation to the dream other, which will narcissistically and lovingly build and shape the self. And yet, for this love-making of the ego to work, we can't just dream on our own as it were, we have to allow another person to become our dream other. We have to submit or surrender to how the other person or object will dream and elaborate us. Our deep ego shaping response is then the evolvement of our loving selves in continual elaboration through another.

Trauma and death

In trauma this love work of the ego is abandoned and we find ourselves within a dream where our subjective self and the more collective bodily ego are completely estranged. I can give a really clear example of this in relation to my own experience. In July 2005 I suffered an extremely traumatic experience, whilst coming home from my analytic supervision, when I sat down next to a suicide bomber on the tube. The bomb only partially exploded and the "would be bomber" was thrown onto the floor, we were at the time still travelling between stations. I knelt down next to the man who was lying face down on the floor where he had been thrown by the explosion. My initial thought was that he had been shot, but then I became aware of the wires sticking out of his T-shirt and a sick-like material oozing from his rucksack. The other people in the carriage were all standing around and looking at this physically strong young man splayed out on the floor; one woman was crying hysterically but the rest of us were frozen in shock. I remember someone saying that his breakfast was coming out of his rucksack and whilst watching myself I said, "We have to get into the next carriage" but my voice seemed to be coming from some place outside of me. And yet, we seemed to stand looking stupidly down at the man on the floor for an eternity. Eventually we started walking to one end of the carriage and one man behind me said; "there is no need to rush", and I thought, "whose rushing?". We seemed at the time to be talking and walking in slow motion. The whole experience for me, as I remember it, was like a dream. I saw myself acting and talking, yet it was exactly like Bergson described, everyone seemed to behave like automata. There was the perceptual me, with my crystal gaze watching from the ceiling of the carriage and then there was a sort of puppet me being acted out in the drama below.

Once we got to into the next carriage we turned and watched the man through the window; pulling himself up and then down on the hand-pulls dangling from the ceiling, just like he was at a visit to the gym. I don't remember feeling any sensations, although clearly I was terri-fied out of them. What I do recall, is the rocking of the train, backwards and forwards, and that rhythm is always with me when I remember and look back. The rocking is of a piece with the dream memory and the dream self that I escaped into. Perhaps the rocking of the train came together with a rhythm in me, and in my mind, trying to ward off the awful reality trying to penetrate it.

So the virtual self, our dream double, can be both an evocative object like my dream of Lyme with its sandalwood smell that sends me on so many free-associative journeys. Or it is the hideout from a traumatic reality, where we retreat from our attention to life, as in Bergson's dis-cussion of the moving mirror—with me on the ceiling of the tube train carriage, watching myself. What are the differences between these two rhythms and memories, one pleasurable, the other frightening and traumatic?

In the first the virtual other is mobilised by senses, forms, and objects, there is dissociation and free-association, unbinding and binding to forms that are both imaginary and real. In the Lyme Regis associations, the evocative objects such as sandalwood and the granny teeth steps are bound into a personal memory, indeed a history that stretches back beyond my parents to my literary ancestor. The elaboration of personal memory seems to come about in the way I bind these memories as a loving part of myself. These are in distinction to the parts I can't love and make into me, the "granny teeth steps" that don't remind me of my brother, but of the those bullying aspects of my granny my mother seemed so unable to confront, sealing my lifelong hatred of Jane Austen. That is until I am able to re-read her, rhyme her and bring her to life with the Lyme of my loving memories. And of course "grannys teeth" also suggests my grandmother's fierce personality and domination of the family. Her law has always been a rather unyielding Oedipal injunction that was perhaps harder for her children to remake because it was so austere.

Love shapes the ego, and embodies our different selves, narcissistically in relation to the world. But in order for this ego love to work, in order for the ego to be built and shaped with enough plasticity for it to receive and bend, contract, and extend in relation to reality; it has to dream, and be dreamed, by a virtual other. It is no exaggeration to say that we come into embodied being and life through our first rhythms of dreaming our passions in relation to the world. And yet, these first rhythms of the young infant, as it dreams the wind on her face, or the rocking arms of her mother, or being held by a father's singing voice, are dependent on a passive surrender to those external forms. It is as if in order to dream our bodily selves into being, we have to first allow ourselves a passive receptivity to the unconscious other. Through "imitation magic" we unconsciously read and allow ourselves to be dreamt into being by the virtual object. This yielding then becomes a more active and libidinal dreaming in the ego, growing the self, or shrinking it; creating all the necessary spaces in which it can reside.

We are created and recreated in the rhythm of our dreaming selves; an unconscious reading that takes place between our subjective and bodily ego; and between the ego and its virtual other. In my early rhythms of Lyme, my loving self rests on a relation to a dream other, that I can unconsciously read, and translate, and yet my rhythms and the living passions attached to them arise from my sense of my mother's blue-grey eyes, and my father's smile. Another not so loving memory of my childhood in Lyme is of watching my older sister jumping on the bed, and me jumping onto the bed to join her, and being hit over the eye with a Ponds cold cream jar. My first memory of being hated, and perhaps hating her back, that has to be placed outside of me and my preferred, loved self.

And of course that hate has continued to haunt and inhibit me, but whatever the ambivalence of my familiar self and the rhythms that feed it—the trauma I experienced on the train is something else. Because this trauma is frozen in psychological time; the images of the bomber are empty not enigmatic signifiers. They evoke nothing and go nowhere; there is no movement between inside and outside; no reality that can be brought into being, read, and transformed by my dream self or my dream objects. For the virtual or dream self to be creative it has to have an exchange with reality and that means it has to work at constructing and re-creating both internal and external objects. Freud's reality principle does not really mean we swap reality for our dream worlds. It is rather that there can be a dreaming exchange between the pleasure seeking self and the reality objects that we encounter.

Rhythms of the personal and non-personal self

One of Freud's principle insights was that the mind provides a sheath or clothing for the body; and this is also one of the core ideas behind this book, that our passions and affects are in search of forms borrowed from another. It is precisely these passionate forms that establish our loving selves within the growing shapes of the ego. Narcissism is the name of this rhythm, or pattern, where the unconscious is our starting point, founded in relation to the other as a non-personal object; an excess of ourselves and the world which we then introject and personalise. In this sense we can talk about the mother being at first a non-human object for the child. Primarily, she is as much a tree, or an animal, as a human presence. Psychoanalysis has been so concerned with the development of the meaningful self that it has seemingly repressed and forgotten how much of the unconscious falls outside of the arena of the personal self. We are born into a world before we arrive in it as meaningful human subjects and yet the creativity of our earliest and more primitive selves is not often acknowledged in psychoanalysis. There are exceptions, and it is perhaps Winnicott's influence that has most enabled psychoanalysis to understand an unconscious that lies outside the boundaries of the personal ego.

Freud has been known for his invention of psychoanalysis and a dynamic, repressed unconscious. This is the unconscious of our individual subjectivity: our personal developmental history. Yet there has always been another story of the unconscious lurking behind Freud's meta-psychology and this is the story of our unknowable selves, an unconscious that is virtual; one that has never been known as such. Freud's virtual unconscious is situated at the very beginnings of life, stretching out to the environment and landscapes that surround us and backwards into what he saw as our phylogenetic evolution and history. So much of psychoanalysis has been indebted to Freud's ideas of an internal psychic world, and with repressed, internal mental conflicts. And so much of psychoanalytic practice has been about revealing how those internal psychic conflicts are generated by the repression of libidinal wishes and instincts that lead back to early childhood. However, the repressed unconscious tells the history and story of a human self, whereas Freud also saw the very early unconscious existence of a child as primitive to the point of being non-human or animal.

In Freud's view the personal self captured by the psychological ego, is not there from the start. In *Civilisation and its Discontents* he makes a point of stressing something we take for granted all too easily. "Normally, there is nothing of which we are more certain than the feeling of our self, of our own ego." (Freud, 1920b: p. 65) But, Freud continues, this certainty that we have an autonomous self "marked off distinctly from everything else" is deceptive. For the ego is continuous with the unconscious Id and serves as its "façade", we are reminded of Winnicott's false self, which faces and adapts to the world. Thus the ego develops over time, but the baby cannot "yet distinguish his ego from the external world as the source of the sensations flowing in upon him" (Freud, 1920b: p. 67).

So it is only when the mother's breast, so desired, is withdrawn, reappearing only when the infant yells, that the object first appears. Subject and object are created together, and in his essay *Instincts and their Vicissitudes* Freud describes the various ways, through identification, introjection, and projection that the individual subject, the psychological self is fashioned. The instinct responsible for this fashioning of the ego or self is the pleasure principle. The ego separates off from the mass of sensations that surround it by binding and fashioning pleasurable instincts narcissistically to itself and making the unpleasant, part of a threatening outside world. The pleasurable life drive is how we arrive at a place of self-love and how we bind others to us as part of that loved self. And this libido (or what Freud called sexuality) is directed towards both the self and the world; it is how we develop and progress.

But Freud also posited the existence of a death-drive as something in conflict with the pleasurable life drive. In opposition to the pleasure principle, the death-drive is not libidinal, but remains associated with the more primordial self-preservative instincts such as hunger. The death-drive is unbounded, leading back beyond the organism to pre-history and inorganic existence. Love and the libido directed towards objects and the ego interests were for Freud a later occurrence. Hate, comes first, and

> derives from the narcissistic ego's primordial repudiation of the external world with its outpouring of stimuli. As an expression of the reaction of unpleasure evoked by objects, it always remain in an intimate relation with the self-preservative instincts; so that sexual and ego-instincts can readily develop an antithesis which repeats that of love and hate. (Freud, 1915: p. 139)

Where we hate, we find the outside world and where we love, resides our ego. Freud's luminous paper, *Beyond The Pleasure Principle* attempts to link polarities of the life and death instinct with the oppositions within object relations, of love and hate. He exclaims, "if only we could succeed in relating these two polarities to each other and in deriving one from the other!" (Freud, 1920a: p. 53). Jean Laplanche has famously re-read Freud's opposition between the life and death drives, making the compelling argument that the death-drive is simply the unbound part of sexuality, the unmanageable part that the ego cannot bind. "The death-drive does not possess its own energy," says Laplanche, "Its energy is libido. Or, better put, the death-drive is the very soul, the constitutive principle, of libidinal circulation" (Laplanche, 1985: p. 124).

Freud's death-drive has been his most controversial idea, most hotly disputed by psychoanalysts because it posits an ultimately biological force, driving subjectivity. Lacan has also tried to re-read Freud's death-drive otherwise arguing that it signifies the alienation of an imaginary ego, which is always based on its distance from biology. For Lacan, the death-drive is the mute, non-representable breakdown of the ego's imaginary psychic unity and as such it is always linked to the emergence of desire that "must remain in a fundamental relationship to death". (Lacan, 1992: p. 303). For Lacan the death-drive comes in the shape of the real or we could say the "id" shattering the unified ego. And this is a good thing, provided that the deathly shattering of the narcissistic imaginary ego, the beyond of the pleasure principle, is mediated by the signifier taking us forward to desire, underpinned by the Symbolic. Otherwise the imaginary is just demolished by violence that we simply experience as unbearable trauma.

Lacan's reading gets rid of Freud's biological death-drive, and yet I wonder at what is lost by trying to fit the death-drive within a purely psychological explanation of the subject? I would like to read the so-called death-drive as both a virtual form of the unconscious and a return of a repetitive, perceptual real. Like Freud and Laplanche, Lacan posits a primary masochism or Jouissance as the motivating force of the death-drive, one that moves us beyond the imaginary structures of the ego and narcissistic ego. For Lacan, desire, and the way out of being bound to the imaginary is Oedipal—through language and culture. Lacan's thesis is essentially a description of the birth of the psychological self as a socially transpersonal subject. But we can also think of the psychological self as being born out of, and potentially open to an unconscious that is trans-human. In this sense, the death-drive is the "real" of our passions which break up the personal ego and lead us towards a "virtual" non-psychological other. We can see that this virtual other exists as both a brutal unknowable difference and a potential uncanny sense of being that moves us beyond the purely psychological self. Lacan and Laplanche, despite their differences, confine their investigation to a psychological and human subject, dependent for its existence on the scene of representation. And yet the rhythm of Freud's death-drive points beyond the realms of the human ego and the subject, towards a virtual non-psychological unconscious.

I want to return to Freud's question of how we relate the life and death instincts to the love and hate within the object relation, in the particular way that Freud describes the first object relation as being created. Freud understands the self as created in opposition to the external object and world. The pleasurable life instincts are attached, for Freud, to the sexual libido and they bind us through love and representations, through our affects and ideas, to internal and external objects. The destructive instincts are tied to the self-preserving instincts of the narcissistic ego, but Freud also says that early on "a portion of the 'ego-instincts' is also of a libidinal character and has taken the subject's own ego as its object" (Freud, 1920a: p. 61). Primal narcissism is sexual, although there is still a remainder of the so-called ego instincts which are not part of a libidinal structure and remain aligned to death. No longer able to put the ego and sexual instincts into opposition, Freud then argues that the new battle is between life and death, which takes place within the ego itself,

> the libidinal (ego and object) instincts and others which must be presumed to be present in the ego and which may perhaps actually observed in the destructive instincts. (Freud, 1920a: p. 61)

Some objects are allowed in as part of the rhythm of the loved self and the rest are alien and deathly. The death-drive for Freud is what cannot be held and shaped within the loveable ego and so affects and passions which can't be symbolised as part of me, or part of the "me and you" are projected onto the alien outside, associated with a traumatic real of the maternal body. This is why Lacan says that the passions or jouissance in relation to the real must be taken up by the Symbolic order. And yet I want to suggest that the death-drive represents the affects and passions that can't be shaped or formed into bearable feelings and thoughts. As such there is nothing intrinsic about the death-drive, it is a rhythm that becomes stuck within an ego that can't find a form to dress and carry it. But as a component of a non-human and virtual unconscious that is not part of the self, the death-drive is simply what is unknowable; unbearable because it is unknowable to the loved self. And so a beyond to the pleasure principle does not have to be destructive if we can find a way of unconsciously dreaming and reading our relationship with the non-psychological maternal object.

What are we to make of Freud's continual insistence on the polarity between the life and death instincts? The duality of drives he never seems to give up on. We can after all explain everything by Freud's description of libidinal narcissism. If the ego can in a libidinal sense take itself as its own object, then what need have we of a separate death-drive? Freud's ideas of destruction turn up again in an essay written five years late entitled *Negation*. Here, Freud takes up the discussion began in *Instincts and their Vicissitudes* on the construction of the ego in relation to its object. He reiterates that the pleasure principle operates in early life, by introjecting everything good and spitting out anything bad. The distinction between subject and object "does not exist from the first" but is brought into being along with thinking (Freud, 1925: p. 440). Because, at first all the subjective presentations we experience as infants are of a piece with so-called reality, and all our perceptions are repetitions of that original presentation, then something has to happen to make that presence distinct for us. Through thinking we repeat and re-present something that has once been perceived as a subjective reality. So thinking, like language, is moved by rhythm, one that has a particular pattern and force; as Freud says the finding of an object in reality is a re-finding of it. We have to rediscover the object in order for it to really exist out there in the world.

Winnicott would say we have to use and destroy the object so that "she" endures as something real. The rhythm of unconscious dreaming where we re-read our objects and our desires becomes transferred to what Freud calls judgment and the reality principle. We select new dream objects in reality and bring to action and life, a world outside of us. This judgment or selection originally distinguishes between internal and external worlds and whereas affirmation leads to Eros and the binding of our internal pleasure, "negation—the successor to expulsion—belongs to the instinct of destruction". So death, for Freud, unbinds and expels. It is destruction that marks what is different from the compulsion of the pleasure principle, set up as Freud describes by the symbol of negation. Negation, then, is a kind of doubling where the image is taken in place of the reality. And it is here we can see Lacan's more positive interpretation of destruction and negation as a Symbolic substitution leading to the movement of the signifier.

Negation and destruction can lead us away from the imaginary narcissism of the ego towards language and the world. But there is something that is missed out if we just see this conflict of life and death work, and the accompanying opposition between subject and object as all there is. We need our hate to keep our love alive, but this ambivalence rests on a previous unconscious dreaming where we transform and give plasticity to our egos; shape our body egos if you like, through the virtual forms that come from another. The unconscious perception or reading that happens every night in our dreams is arguably set in motion by the forms we take from life: they turn up in our dreams in distorted forms. But we can't really know about these dreams, they are too unconscious; only when we move this dreaming into the world, can we begin to start making this unconscious reading with other non-me, non-psychological objects. Negation as a positive destruction and use of the maternal object can only work well if we have enough of a dream drive to process the non-psychological forms of that object in relation to our love and passions. Thinking without this telepathy becomes too violent or not violent enough; thoughts fly but there is no exchange or conversation. If this opposition becomes too stark and libidinal parts become too withdrawn from the object, then what Freud calls a "defusion" of instincts takes place, "a negativism which is displayed by some psychotics" (Freud, 1925: p. 239). We can see here, how psychosis is not just a withdrawal of sexual libido from the ego and its objects, but an inability to dream that sexuality in relation to another. Without the unconscious telepathy of being able to dream our desires into reality, the negation of thinking becomes a negation of life; an autism where perception of the world breaks down because it has become too delinked from the dreaming ego.

How can we think about this in relation to the clinical transference? Famously, in *Remembering, Repeating and Working-Through*, Freud notes how what is repeated and acted out: the symptoms in the session are precisely what cannot be consciously remembered. Through symptoms and the rhythms of repetition the analyst ascertains what has happened in the past, not because the patient actually remembers but because he acts it out, in the consulting room. Now Lacan sees these symptoms are those aspects of the real that have to be reconnected with Symbolic functioning, and separated from the preferred reminiscences of the ego's imaginary maternal relations. And yet it is hard to see from this, what's in it for the ego. Or to put it another way, if symptoms are looking for not just fantasy relations with the analyst or other, but a real experience, then in analysis dissolving the preferred imaginary ego has to go together with a retranslation of that ego, in relation to the virtual forms of a more non-psychological unconscious that reside outside the self. So it's not simply a bypassing of the imaginary ego as in Lacan's account, but a remaking of the ego; destroying old familiar forms as a way of re-creating them within different designs that inscribe us within the real objects of our everyday world. The early ego had a relationship to the mother, we hope, where real and imaginary worlds came together in an unconscious reading and dreaming of that mother's non-psychological forms. Return to this early telepathic ego enables our dream drive to move beyond the sterile opposition of life and death, to a place where the loved ego can bear the necessary destruction of itself, surrendering to future forms of being that exist in relation to another.

Freud notices how the unbound rhythms in the analyst transference are the return of an automatic past in the present, a past that "could never have been 'forgotten' because it was never at any time noticed was never conscious" (Freud, 1914: p. 149). And he contrasts those unbound daemonic rhythms that elude secondary processes with the pleasurable repetitions in children's stories and games. Rhythm becomes a way of binding both pleasant and traumatic experience together. Young children love to have their favourite stories and games repeated with a view to mastering them and Freud's famous account of his grandson's game with the cotton reel making the reel disappear and return is also an account of how the child masters maternal absence and enters Symbolic language. Chucking this object about, throwing it away and pulling it back are all the ways that the child desires this non-psychological mother; a desire that is before the mother has become a loving and meaningful presence for the child.

But we can see the game of the reel as precisely one that allows the child to play with his mother as a non-psychological object or thing that he can move inside and outside, between the me and the not-me. Just as the young child reading will have a relation to words and objects that at first mean nothing, but eventually become a part of his meaningful loved self. Learning to read from our mothers does not simply come about because we eventually just start to understand language; rather in being close to the mother and reading with her, we are able to take her gestures, her responsive body and voice, together with the forms in the book—fairytales, adventures, poems, as a living model for our emotions. I don't think we can enter Symbolic language without this unconscious reading or dreaming of a maternal form and it is the telepathic dream forms we get from the mother (and arguably the pre-Oedipal father) that allow us to move our rhythms from dreams— towards language.

Beyond pleasure and death; A third rhythm

Language might carry the unconscious as in Lacan's ideas of the Symbolic, but the unconscious is more invested in the image that is both hypnotic and poetic. The hypnotic end leads back more passively in sensual dreaming; whereas the poetic side of the image is more active and carries dreams towards language and representation. The example of free association illustrates this point. Dreams are communicated by language through their interpretation and through conversations between analyst and analysand, who both participate in free association. However, it is primarily the dream image that is integral to the unconscious. The patient lies on the couch and dissociates from real life and then associates with the dream image. This rhythm that unbinds itself from reality and then binds itself to the dream image, continues as the first dream image is followed by another association and then another. Sometimes the associations are recent events, sometimes they are distant memories. The whole scene of free association thus moves in rhythm backwards and forwards between past and present, and between dreams and reality. Moreover, as Bergson has already acknowledged, dissociation comes first, so unbinding (that radical hypnotic rhythm) is primary, followed by association and fixation of the image. My free associations to Lyme Regis begin with my ability to creatively dissociate and then associate with images from my dreams and my memories; but I am also in rhythm with the present affects and feelings that actualize those memories. The smell of the sandalwood summons up the dream image of my grandmother's summerhouse; the grey sea-light through my window brings my mother back to me, through the matching colour of her eyes.

It is the rhythm in language that makes it move. Language carries the unconscious image, more or less rhythmically, and connects and carries our dream images on their libidinal travels towards real objects. Without language, appetite remains unsatisfied, but there are other, arguably more familiar rhythms, that can transport our dream images realising them within affectual and emotional encounters. Voice is one such rhythm. Before the time my father tried to teach me physics—the molecular structure of an atom as I remember—(unsuccessfully) at the age of six, he taught me to read. But before he taught me to read, I remember him singing to me, and his song and musical voice are the rhythms I prefer. Art is another form of dream travel. Me and my daughter are wandering sleepily, hung over from the heat of New York, amongst galleries of contemporary photography or classical paintings. The images please us differently and as Esmé starts to explain to me why one photo of the American West called "Moonrise", by Ansel Adams, is so technically brilliant, I start to see it differently. Emerging from the shadows, the images of this artwork come to life, made vivid not simply by my daughter's description, but because we are suddenly there together, astonished by the lights of a sky striped with cloud, moving above still Mexican landscape.

Dreaming this beautiful photograph into a lived experience is arguably an unconscious reading and perception that moves not just between me and the still landscape in front of me, but also between me and my daughter. Why can't we see the unbound rhythms of our virtual past not as a death-drive, but as a dream drive? Whether or not the dream drive becomes elaborated or stuck, is contingent, and this contingency lies precisely in its ability to unconsciously read our loving selves into life in relation to another. My virtual dreams of Lyme Regis are an elaboration of my personal ego, precisely because they are found in relation to a personal history and real evocative objects that I can visit and encounter in the world. On the other hand, my virtual dreams of the bomber on the tube train can't have any such exchange. What dream would I ever want to have that would make this event more real? And anyway what sort of conversation (even in fantasy), can you really have with someone who sits or stands next to you with a bomb in his backpack? Imitation magic here, would be in its most mad dog impersonation; the ego's adaptation through complete repression or splitting. Trauma instigates a withdrawal from the world: a retreat into a secret dream "other".

Does the real meaning of the death-drive, rest in that particular rhythm when conversation between our dream and real selves is seemingly over? Can an ego exist without a familiar object? Or what kind of war results between the personal ego and it's virtual other when the imaginary and real are so set up against each other? Is the death-drive, in fact, an uncanny doubling, where we are returned on the one hand to a solipsistic world that is defensively personal, in opposition to an external and internal objectivity that is non-psychological, not potentially mine, and not ever mine because I reject it?

Freud is categorical, the ego is a dependent being and is both dependent on the super-ego and a slave to the id. Desperate to be loved by both, the ego has according to Freud much in common with the analyst. He or she is always trying to get the recalcitrant id to bend to reality and by dressing up as a representative of the world, the ego (and the analyst), tries to win the id's love. But the ego is also submissive with the super-ego. Through the repression of libidinal instincts the ego fuels the aggressive death instincts that have become part of the superego. And then the ego starts to fear death and loss of love by the very super-ego, she has in a sense created. Giving up the object, through fear and dread, goes together with the withdrawal of love (from the other and the self). Death wishes for Freud are akin to this terrible dread of the object, this fear of death that can emanate from an external danger or an internal instinctual threat.

The death-drive is a withdrawal from a dreadful world that is indistinguishable from the super-ego, but this unconscious guilt is also a retreat into an increasingly fragile ego, whose dream world and reality sense are incapable of fusion; incapable, that is, of being dreamed together. But the death-drive can't just be a dream escape from a sadist whom has usurped the role of a reality ego, or, can it? What is Lyme Regis for me, if it is not some dream escape into what is, after all, some suspiciously ideal fantasies of my childhood? But Lyme remains a place in the world, and by that I mean somewhere between dreams and reality; it is both a rhythm and a space, where and whereby my ego can live. And where it can love, as opposed to my dream escape on the tube train where a loving exchange with reality is impossible. In the carriage, all that is left of reality is the mechanical remains and repetitions of the real. The automatic ways in which we all stood around the bomber lying on the floor, saying nonsensical things, or sleepwalking away into the next carriage.

Or another way of thinking about this is how id and super-ego take over, putting the imaginary and real (or the body and mind) into a violent non-compromise; nothing can ameliorate the stark opposition between the aggressive unmanageability of our passions, and the punishment dished out for having them. The ego, we could say can no longer help, and when it can no longer help it ceases to live. When I knelt down to help the man on the floor of the tube my ego lived, but when I stood up, it had fled. In its place was my dream escaped self, up on the ceiling of the carriage looking down. And completely detached from my memory or dream self were the repetitive mechanical movements of my body, moving like a puppet with strings.

The death-drive when it turns up in analysis is by definition, something that cannot be helped by the therapist or the ego. Freud describes in *Remembering, Repeating and Working-Through*, the experiences that get acted out and repeated in the transference precisely because they cannot be remembered. These bodily re-enactments of past experiences are unavailable to the patient in any conscious way and Freud notes the difficulty when the analyst's interpretations do not fit any recollected memories. This is then the unconscious that has never been conscious. But I don't think these repetitions are deathly simply because they can't be represented within conscious mental representation and language. In other words acted out repetitions of our traumas in the transference aren't helped by meaning; what possible meaning is there to my experience on the tube? For these unconscious and automatic repetitions are the passions we can't feel; they are excessive. Beyond not just pleasure but the ability of the ego to provide shape or form to them, these rhythms are unbearable because they simply too unknowable. It is within the unconscious scene of reading that the dreaming ego can give form to these unknowable passions, but only if it surrenders to the virtual nature of what lies beyond the boundaries of the self. And this is the paradox that confronts us, because we normally only desire what is familiar, what the ego recognises as its most personal passions—and so what is impersonal is often seen as a difference that is too unbearable. To have courage in our desires means to bear our hate and frustration, because frustration is arguably inevitable in the search for novel experiences. We have to be bold in our ability to try out what is new even if we don't think, or can't possibly imagine that this new object or style will ever suit us.

Freud quite rightly says that the ego has to get the wishful unknowable id to love "him", but this can't be a one-way street. In fact, the ego and id have to love each other, without either being subsumed. For the love between the ego and the id tends to be possessive. The ego pretends that the id is his personal property or else he simply starts hating it; projecting "it" outwards, as an enemy to the loved self. So the ego has to learn to be interested in the non-psychological parts, the "it" factor, that is carried by other people and external objects, and it is a matter of luck and chance whether those unfamiliar objects can become dreamed into the right kind of experience that makes the ego elaborate its forms of feeling and being. My father's attempts to pass on his meaningful love of science in my young life were a spectacular disaster that haunted me through school years, in various ways. Consequently, science has always remained an "it" for me, and never an "I". But my father's ability before that to be a singing man was something different, and it is that rhythm which led me to read.

Because the virtual unconscious is distinct from the personal and psychological self, it can't be captured by meaning or interpretation. And yet this non-psychological unconscious arguably exists in relation to the repressed and unrepressed; as both an inside alien, or as a potential for what we can be in relation to the external world and objects that surround us.[1] As such it is contingent and accidental whether our virtual selves can be elaborated, or sent into violent retreat. Just as contingent events can both traumatise us, or be that wonderful surprise that beckons our desire into being, the death-drive, as a virtual unconscious, is only destructive if it remains cut off from being able to dream its way to reality. Freud realised that traumatic neurosis turns up in our nightmares as a return to a frightening situation that cannot be bound by the ego and he comments that "this astonishes people far too little" (Freud, 1920a: p. 13). Dreams,

Freud reasons, cannot simply be wish fulfillments if they carry this repetitive and destructive trauma that continues to frighten and undo us. So, wish fulfillment is something dreams learn; it is not their original action:

> It would not be possible for them to perform that function until the whole of mental life had accepted the dominance of the pleasure principle. If there is a 'beyond the pleasure principle', it is only consistent to grant that there was also a time before the purpose of dreams was the fulfillment of wishes. (Freud, 1920a: p. 33)

Before we learn to desire with our dreams we have to unconsciously read them. And without this telepathic reading and forming of our affects and passions there would be no ego filled up, or bound with pleasure, and no positive destruction of the maternal object. In order to come through murdering our primary relationship to the mother she has to be a mixture of the impersonal forms we can both hate and break, in order to recreate the house of felt passions that constitutes the personal self. The rhythm between destructive breakdown and recovery that Eigen talks about as being central to therapy is surely linked to this. If negation, and the thinking and symbolisation that follow it, are to be productive then I suggest a kind of telepathic, maternal, and dreaming form has to be in place to allow that movement into the Symbolic to occur. We can't just substitute the relationship of the maternal body with a system of signs. Before we are able to sign and signify our bond with the mother we have to be able to dream her. And this involves a dissociation and association of forms in the unconscious, a reading of our unknowable passions or the "it" factor inside us, in relation to the non-psychological forms that are offered by the early maternal object.

Conclusion

By way of conclusion, I want to return again to Freud's Book of Dreams where he suggests that our first system of thinking is the establishment of a "perceptual identity" where an imaginary mimesis of perception "is linked with the satisfaction of a need" (Freud, 1901: p. 566). The hallucination of our wishes must have had a basis in something real that has satisfied us previously. Winnicott says something similar when he says that reality cannot be arrived at without illusion, the baby has to be able to hallucinate the breast at the point where the real breast is offered. Where these two things intermingle we have the illusion necessary for acceptance of reality:

> If they overlap there is a moment of *illusion*—a bit of experience which the infant takes as *either* his hallucination or a thing belonging to external reality. (Winnicott, 1984: p. 152)

Illusion, intuition, and the unconscious reading of our instinctual selves in relation to reality is what informs the ego and brings real experience into being. Primary and secondary processes, or our dreams and reality, are not sequential: they are in rhythm with each other. The spontaneous true self (our most hidden reserve) can only be realised and embodied by the ego, when it is unconsciously read and translated beyond the familiar pleasures of our knowable self. Affects breaking out of the ego's shell move in a rhythm drenched in trauma, always tinged with manifestations of hate and death. Until, of course, we learn how to use that rhythm to read our passions in relation to more non-human forms that exist outside of us. Illusion, then, is more, perceptively and unconsciously more than an ideal.

We could say that illusion is the re-perception and actualisation of our memory and desire. Thus illusion and the reality that accompanies it, is always a relation and a translation between our personal egos and a more virtual life; an unconscious reading and receptivity that is intrinsic to all living symbolisation and myth. And by symbolisation I don't mean within language, but the putting together in the unconscious (what Freud called free association) of affects and thoughts and cultural forms. There is a rhythm of life and love that takes me back to my familiar ancestor and Lyme Regis, and there are the rhythms of death that end in the untranslatable events of July 2005. And there is a third rhythm that arrives in time and with the body, in our ability to unconsciously read and translate our raw passions. However, this third rhythm begins, suggests and beckons us, from the dream other existing unconsciously inside, and as the virtual world that surrounds us. It is only when we can creatively dissociate and surrender to being dreamed by this desirable alien other, that we are in touch with the forms that will shape our affects into new possibilities and loving selves.

Notes

1. See my article with Steve Pile, "Telepathy and its Vicissitudes: Freud, thought transference and the hidden lives of the (repressed and non-repressed) unconscious" *Subjectivity* 3(4) pp. 403–425, where we argue that on the one hand, telepathy as unconscious thought transference brings to light the secret repressed unconscious that is the corner stone of Freud's theory and practise. On the other hand, it also leads away from this crypt-like space of the repressed unconscious to illuminate non-repressed thought transference—an unconscious sharing of thoughts and affects between individuals enabled by a lack of repression.

CHAPTER FOUR

Symptoms, 'sense and sensibility'

Thus neurotic symptoms have a sense, like parapraxes and dreams, and like them, have a connection with the life of those who produce them.

—Freud, 1917a: p. 257

There is a moment in Freud's essay *The Sense of Symptoms* where he describes the trivial and futile ceremonies of everyday life that make up the repetitions of the obsessional character, and he exclaims "certainly this is a crazy illness" (Freud, 1917a: p. 259). The obsessive is crazy and yet his symptoms have intelligence, as well as an extreme sensibility. Symptoms for the obsessive are displacements and substitutions, one prohibition after another, one ceremonial and then another. So symptoms for the obsessive person are always far removed from their original form. Like dreams, symptoms are a cover story; they are the melodramatic parts of our character that speak up for our repressed and secret sexuality. Seemingly so immediate and compulsive these symptoms are characters that both hide and carry our desire.

Symptoms and character

There is sense and non-sense to our symptoms; we are always divided between the ego and sexual impulses. We repress our sexual wants according to the dictates of the ego who gives voice to the reality of restrictions in any given society. Our symptoms in the face of this repression are the real distress of suppressed sexuality. Although this deprivation makes us suffer, it would be no good, in Freud's view to just ignore our super-ego and regain the satisfaction we have forgone, because when we ignore our repressions then it is the ego's turn to object and we simply enter into the strife of a different set of symptoms. If our passions express themselves in revolt at the fierce beliefs of the ego, then this conflict between what we feel and what we think can't be resolved by simply giving into our wants, because our emotions and thoughts don't coincide. Freud writes:

> If, on the contrary we were to secure victory for sensuality, then the sexual repression that had been put on one side would necessarily be replaced by symptoms. (Freud, 1917b: p. 433)

In this never ending conflict, one party is always left wanting and so happiness is always elusive because the contradictory suggestions of what is in our head or our hearts is never in union. If this is so, how can we really understand what makes up our temperament or character? When it comes to the unconscious it seems we have many different characters, but how do we recognise and distinguish what they are? Are characters made up of passion or sense? Are they imaginary or real, derived from instinct or identification? If, personal character is our pre-ferred and distinguishing traits, the ones that are up front, so to speak, on the stage. Then what happens to the other more unknowable char-acters we would rather not notice, the ones that we have deliberately forgotten or foreclosed? And then there are also the characters, or the parts to one-self that remain waiting in the wings; a kind of understudy for our future selves who have no idea what, or how they will be, and if they can act.

Freud tells us that the clues to someone's character are both manifest and mysterious. We can know someone by his or her symptoms, their outward display of neurosis or illness. And in analysis, we can know someone by their resistance, the ways they repeat, rather than remem-ber their pasts through the transference.

Freud writes that:

> What we describe as a person's 'character' is built up to a consider-
> able extent from the material of sexual excitations and is composed
> of instincts that have been fixed since childhood, of constructions
> achieved by means of sublimation, and of other constructions,
> employed for effectively holding in check perverse impulses which
> have been recognised as being unutilisable. The multifariously per-
> verse sexual disposition of childhood can accordingly be regarded
> as the source of a number of our virtues, in so far as through
> reaction-formation it stimulates their development. (Freud, 1905:
> p. 239)

So, in therapy we can't take people's more obvious characters at face
value, because characters in Freud's book, are never completely who
they, or who anyone else thinks they are. A young man turns up for
therapy, a charming man, an academic, whose work and home life are
being wrecked by his obsessive conscientiousness and guilt: his concern
for being dutiful and solicitous to his students, colleagues and wife.
Tracing his symptoms back to his home life as a child, we discover all
the ways he has defended himself from his Oedipal conflicts. Repression and then sublimation of his feelings of longing, fury and competition have constructed a character, a preferred self that is self-contained
independent and hard working. As a child, this man had avoided fierce
competition with his brothers and schoolmates by withdrawing and
being the best scholar. The favourite son of a depressed mother, this
man had spent his youth looking after her needs, by being as good and
undemanding as possible. His father had escaped the mother's depression (and been a major cause of it) through his career and work.

Love and desire, as Freud tells us with the obsessive, has been experienced in the past as dangerous because it is mixed up with hate. And
so it was with this seemingly gentle and agreeable man. His rivalry
with other academics and pleasure with his wife were things he escaped
from because he found it hard to bear the paradox inherent to love for
other people, or his ongoing desire. Where we love, we also hate, and
my client wanted to keep his love clean, as it were, unblemished with
jealousy, frustration or disappointment. Obsessive in the way he spent
all his time on lecture preparation, he could never finish the research
articles that would establish his career. He was in trouble with his rather

volatile wife because he always found his conscientious work routine, got in the way of coming home, having sex or anything more intimate with her, and yet these were not obvious symptoms of being ill. Most academics supposedly doing their jobs properly would no doubt fit this picture. This man's charming and hardworking character had also got him a long way in life, his teacher's praise, a good education, scholarships, friends and girlfriends.

So, when this man allowed himself some pleasures, his ego entered into the scene as a fairly conscious guilt that guillotined his desire with pointless work routines, espousing obligation and duty. Like a hangover from an illicit bout of drinking, this man's sensible symptoms came racing to the fore, the day after he won some new found intimacy with his wife, or made some headway with his research, making sure his more creative and passionate self was packed away under the superego admonishments of sacrificing his pleasures to the rules of work and pleasing others.

Refusing to be done away with, however, his more secret and unconscious sensibilities and passions arose in opposition to his highly prized rational and thoughtful self, being far more sexual and stubborn in their fixation. Freud tells us that symptoms create substitutes "for the frustrated satisfaction by means of a regression of the libido to earlier times" and earlier loves (Freud, 1917c: p. 365). In the face of repression the libido seemingly submits, but then escapes out the back door, to those earlier moments when wants were more easily satiated. What happens in this escape story is that our prohibited passions withdraw from reality and then run off home, shrouded and guided by fantasies that become more and more unconscious the further back they go. Freud writes:

> From what are now unconscious fantasies the libido travels back
> to their origins in the unconscious—to its own points of fixation.
> (Freud, 1917c: p. 373)

And of course conflict with the more sensible ego becomes inevitable, as it was with my client, who would spend his life, running from work to home, in a frenzy of activity. But when it came to real sexual intimacy with his wife, his unfinished work was always more pressing, and anyway she was hysterical in her expression and refusal of her own wants. This hysteria coupled with his constant escapes made her far too demanding and furious to really fulfil his needs. In the face of his wife's demands, my client could not assert himself and following in his father's footsteps he escaped into his career. If he managed to find space in his day, for his very real creative potential in research, then he would immediately take off in the opposite direction, into endless emails or surfing the Web, so that realisation of this desire and his potential also became an increasingly elusive reality. And yet the real dilemma for this man was not, as he preferred to think, the never ending tasks of his university job, for his obliging personality was also a cover character act, for the insistence of his desires that constituted something quite different, a competing character that was ferocious in its demand for love and acknowledgement.

This man's "crazy" behaviour, in our society, is quite normal, and it defines many people's work and home life routines. If this man's conflicts had not boiled over, if his research career and marriage were not in the balance, it is doubtful if he would ever have showed up at the therapy door. So, when it comes to our character or what we call the personal self there is always a battle between the powers of the ego and of desire. Having a character that can work for us, is on one hand essential, but if our character ceases to function for us, or is clearly ill, then we come to therapy for help. But characters, like symptoms are never as straightforward, or as knowable as they seem. Characters are on one level, like dreams, in that they have to be taken apart and traced back to their formative beginnings, their perversions, fixations and repressions.

Their sense and sensibility

Symptoms for Freud have sense and sensibility, which are necessarily competing and confusing; they have a meaning and an expression that is always in excess of each other. Affects are always moving and racing beyond their available forms of meaning, just as the meaning of what we feel is duplicitous, hiding unconsciously behind the facade of a preferred character, although constantly showing up in various hysterical or obsessive traits.

Jane Austen's novel Sense and Sensibility is all about secrets and concealments. In a society where personal desire must find an acceptable social form to grace it, there becomes an increasing regulation of both those desires, and the public conventions in which they can be carried. In Austen's fictional world, societal forms are everywhere, hiding or screening more illicit and private desires. And such is the regulation of these social screens, that the truth of one's desire is an unbearable, but also an unimaginable entity. The price paid, as we see with the character Marianne, of eschewing cultural forms is a regression into nervous illness and hysteria. Marianne sees the available forms for her desire as a "feminine" and social masquerade, how the woman has to pass and be passed about in a social and economic market of exchange. Therefore, she resists and leaves the codes and manners of society to others; refusing to play the game she settles for an authenticity that becomes increasingly fixed, as it has nowhere to go. As readers we sympathise with Marianne's sensibilities. When she is asked to join in the flattery of Lady Middleton, Marianne refuses, "it was impossible to say what she did not feel". Such manners are left to her elder sister Elinor, to who "the whole task of telling lies when politeness required it always fell" (Austen, 1969: p. 144). And yet Austen continually shows us that the reality of society can't function without the circulation of necessary screens and lies. Freud agrees, and like Austen he shows us the price we pay if we can't let these two sisters communicate. Marianne wants all outward forms to mirror our inner feelings, and this stubborn desire is always in a stand off from the reality and the social forms that are needed to move it into new shapes and directions. On the other hand, Elinor's sensible ego is far too grown-up, too much a mistress of her unruly passions.

As an older sister Elinor "possessed a sense of understanding and coolness of judgement…she had an excellent heart; her disposition was affectionate and feelings were strong; but she knew how to govern them". The younger sister Marianne, meanwhile, "was eager in everything; her sorrows, her joys, could have no moderation" (Austen, 1969: p. 42). With these two characters, the expression of meaning and emotion is always at odds with each other. Emotions are never reliable expressions of the truth, because meaning is always buried, and so knowledge is elusive; it is always more mysterious and harder to track then we would like. So there is actually nothing straightforward about what we feel, or what we mean, and our symptoms are the expression of this confused relation between our sense and sensibilities. The ego is our character of sense and the libido is one of sensibility. And when both these sisters squabble and are intractable, then we become ill. But because libido is always the most recalcitrant, like Marianne, it is adolescent in its refusal to take any but the most authentic or primary of forms, so then it is the character of the ego that has to be more compromising, it has to bend to the libido's determined will. To say, though, that the libido has a will is to grant it more organisation than Freud's Id in fact possesses. For will belongs to an ego that is capable of shaping our libidinal energy into different wants and wishes.

One way of making sense of this is to see the ego, as Freud did, as a traveller, someone who is constantly on the move setting up camp in different spaces and locations. Life for the ego, in the ruled confines of the super-ego, or squatting amongst the tribal id, is arguably a character in service to more fundamental powers. And so we could say that the ego is a form giver and shape shifter of our desires, but those forms are borrowed by the ego from the world; designs that house or inhibit our passions. We don't just have one ego, but many and they occupy different positions in space and time. The ego can be a sensible character rather like Elinor who pays respect to social authority, borrowing and espousing its forms. Or it can be a more libidinal performance, a passionate character like Marianne that is always seeking a return to primary loves that were less inhibited.

Sociability of symptoms

Symptoms, Freud tells us in his essay *Inhibitions, Symptoms and Anxiety* are different from inhibitions, because whereas an inhibition is simply a restriction of ego function or action, the symptom is something new, "when a function has undergone some unusual change or when a new phenomenon has arisen out of it" (Freud, 1926: p. 87). So, the symptom is a form of behavioural change, something that acts out, or repeats itself in curious and troubling ways. Inhibitions in work or love are a lessening of the ego's function but don't signify, or point anywhere else. Freud gives the examples of an obsessive patient whose repressed rage led to exhaustion and a depressive with melancholia. In depressed states we are often made inert and immobile. Suppression or withdrawal of the libido leads the obsessive to become unproductive at work, endlessly repeating details or becoming distracted. The refusal to eat or an inability to have a good sex life, are also the ego's inhibition, the lack of energy that results from its repression and suppression of libidinal urges. But with the symptom something has escaped from the ego, or perhaps never belonged to it in the first place. The symptom is always beyond the ego, as Freud says, "A symptom cannot any longer be described as a process that takes place within, or acts upon, the ego" (Freud, 1926: p. 90).

Outside of the self, outside of the family, and yet refusing to leave either, symptoms are a way of leaving home and staying behind. They are about how we circumvent the ambivalence of Oedipal loves. However much the ego might experience the symptom as an alien, he or she will find a way to minimise its strange nature and curious form. The hysterical ego or character for example simply divorces her symptoms dissociating them, until she is forced to meet up with them in unspeakable bodily complaints. Whereas, the obsessive will try and accommodate his rituals and ceremonies and so over time they seem, not alien, but an inescapable part of his personal self. Because the symptom is always half way between an impulse and defence, not situated in the ego, so to speak, but always mindful of the ego's presence. This means that the symptom is something we can say that exists between the ego and the world and between people. Symptoms carry our desire and they are, perhaps surprisingly, inherently relational. So it is always worth thinking whom (or what) is the symptom speaking to and for? What kind of relationship is the symptom involved in, and more importantly what is the relationship that the symptom wants to create and construct?

The symptom, then, speaks up for desire, but it also is in a relationship (often a bad one) with the ego. Hysterical symptoms have nothing to say to the ego, they have been summarily dismissed. Whilst obsessive symptoms, on the other hand never shut up, but are always intent on missing the point, like some big cover up. In this scenario of bad communication, there is something, a story or a secret that is constantly starting to speak, but is always left halfway told. Symptoms are stories that can't end or find resolution, so they are a species of wanting where pleasure or satisfaction, or a suitable narrative ending remains elusive. And yet as any couple therapist knows, one partner might seem to carry all the blame, or all the need, so the other person doesn't have to. So it is worth asking how well the ego can adapt and listen to what the symptom is telling him. If some egos are oblivious, then others can hear quite well, but remain harsh and unsympathetic. Because there is always more than on ego at stake, there is the ego we know, and the one that seems to know and rule us, and then there is the more unknowable and hidden ego.

If symptoms seem unintelligible or crazy, then it's maybe because nobody knows how to listen to them, but perhaps symptoms become loudest, when the particular reader, which they are seeking, remains elusive. To achieve a narrative ending, a real reader, as well as the ideal reader is required, if pleasure is to be more than mere anticipation. And so if symptoms are desires in search of a form, or stories in search of a reader, then they need someone to listen and make them feel real and heard. But it is worth asking, here, who or what is the intended reader of the symptom? Arguably it is not the ego but the other that the symptom is addressed to; which is why, on some basic level, the symptom and the ego have such a bad time of it together. Rebellious and yet not able to completely leave, the symptom has to keep repeating its opposition, stuck in a celibate relationship where its desire lies elsewhere.

Thus symptoms are always, as it were, out of step with the manifest ego. They are always reminding us of whom, what, and where else we could be. If symptoms tell us how desire is always unknowably elsewhere they also show us how the ego has to lose its familiar, personal self and place and go travelling. Here the ego has to learn from another, such as the therapist, who can show how the ego's mystery tour can begin. So the question of the symptom should always be—what is it telling me? What kind of relationship is the symptom involved in and what kind of relationship does the symptom actually want? In the beginning Freud saw the ego and the libido as sisterly opposites, but later he realised that the ego was unconscious and libidinal too. The characters of the libido and the more conscious ego do not belong easily together, according to Freud, and although the ego's job is to make sense of the libido's strident early wants, when it can't then the libido sulks and withdraws. It narcissistically takes a holiday and retreats from the ego, into earlier fixations and phases where its wants were more satisfied. But the question here, is who, or what withdraws, or regresses? As Freud eventually realised, it is the ego that makes the libido regress, just as it is the ego that represses.

Symptoms are then our desires and wants on the run, from an ego that is too sensible and serious. The more sensible a character becomes, the more argumentative and outrageous will be the symptoms in response. In this unhappy marriage between our ego and libido, it is our neurotic repressed wants that make the most complaint. Our neurosis is noisy and hard to ignore, for us and for other people. But character formation is a silent, behind the scenes, activity. And so Freud makes a distinction between the development of character, and neurosis, in that neurotic failures of repression, or the return of the repressed "are absent in the formation of character" (Freud, 1913: p. 323). In the making of character, repression does not occur or it is not obvious, it "smoothly achieves its aim of replacing the repressed by reaction-formations and sublimations". Giving the example of a menopausal, older woman who has lost her "genital function" and changed from a loving wife and mother, into an "old dragon" or witch, Freud argues the fate of such women is that,

> They become quarrelsome, vexatious and overbearing, petty and stingy; that is to say, they exhibit typically sadistic and anal-erotic traits which they did not possess earlier, during their period of womanliness. (Freud, 1913: p. 323)

Although Freud acknowledges elsewhere the hysteria linked to various stages in a woman's life, he forgets here the neurotic conflict menopause heralds for women. Giving up the womanliness of being beautiful and desirable, acknowledging the ending of her childbearing years, is a loss, for the woman that has to be mourned and remade. Menopausal women do get grumpy and hormonal, just like adolescents, and yet in both their altered characters seems to go hand in hand with neurotic conflict.

The old woman in Freud's example is a sexist stereotype, but we could say that this woman, where she exists, is not necessarily suffering from character alteration, but from an ego that has become a bit of a bully. Women, as they age, don't have to lose their desire, and become the unflattering caricature Freud describes, indeed plenty of women run out of desire before their menopause arrives. But to keep their desire alive, women, like men, have to be able to shape their unconscious ego and characters to the time and change of life they are experiencing. Perhaps character change and some sort of neurotic conflict are inevitable, that without the conflict, no creative change of character shape can take place. So we need to pay attention, in therapy and life, to the more silent attributes of someone's character by listening to their symptoms, and perhaps the most worrying symptoms of all, are the ones that seemingly don't exist. We worry about our adolescent children going off the rails. But just think for a moment of the adolescents who never rebel, who never go through the necessary battle of losing and remaking their parents or their ego ideals? Or what does it mean for the older woman, who does not react to the changes and limits, which her time of life imposes on her?

Becoming an older woman, and being an adolescent are arguably journeys that are necessarily accompanied by conflict, regression, and hysterical symptoms. Hormone replacement therapy, or drugs, can successfully silence our symptoms, but there is a risk, that goes beyond physical addictions or cancer. The risk involved in shutting up our symptoms is one where the character called our ego won't change, or be mobile enough to mediate or meet our desire. Freud's stereotype of the spiteful "old dragon" is not the fate of all older women, just the woman who can't remake and shape her ego and her character to integrate the vicissitudes of her libido and the losses inherent to life.

Another way of thinking about this, is to consider what kind of symptom, someone's character is? What exactly is being substituted or foreclosed in the manifest character we perceive, in ourselves and others? Freud makes a distinction between symptoms and character in that with the former we are in the presence of neurosis; a symptom is a substitute satisfaction that reminds us we are in the territory of the return of the repressed. Character though is a way of avoiding or replacing the conflicts of repression by defensive forms and sublimations. Like symptoms, someone's character originates in conflicts but surmounts them through formations of the ego that are designed in various adaptive ways. Unlike symptoms, character is an ego that has stopped quarrelling with the id and the outside world and has found some peace or equilibrium. But we can, in another sense, see the preferred ego we call our character as a symptom of what has been foreclosed and denied.

Gender performance

Masculinity and femininity are the character traits that become stabilised over time to give rise to prevailing gender identities in our society. Judith Butler has shown us how we are always performing gender in a melancholic fashion. How, in other words the gender that we unconsciously prefer to imitate is always in character, with for example, our heterosexual identities foreclosing the more ungrievable homosexual loves that are less sanctioned by society. Butler reads masculinity and femininity in Freud's essays on sexuality, not as dispositions, but as accomplishments. They are character constructions. Dependent on various prohibitions, at first, the taboo on homosexuality and only secondarily meeting up with the incest taboo, Butler emphasises how heterosexuality is a consequence of what has been disavowed and refused.

We can see what Butler calls "The force of this accomplishment", as a symptom. Symptoms are not there from the beginning; they are constructed as a solution to desire that has been forbidden. Straight sex might be one of our characters, but it is one that is always a substitute for something else, repressed or denied. Heterosexual symptoms are thus a demand for "the abandonment of homosexual attachments or, perhaps more trenchantly, pre-empting the possibility of homosexual attachment" (Butler, 1997: p. 135). The foreclosure of homosexual passion in this character construction means that such love remains unlived, as an "ungrievable loss" (Butler, 1997: p. 135).

We can think of this denied same-sex passion, not just in terms of the laws and taboos of a society, what it proscribes and excludes, but also in terms of what cultural forms are available to us. For our desires to be expressed they have to come dressed in some kind of recognisable forms which the ego is continually borrowing from another. However, when it comes to early Oedipal conflicts and character, these desires become fixated, leading to separation and a mutual exclusion within our culture between straight and gay sexual desires. Butler writes:

> The oedipal conflict presumes that heterosexual desire has been accomplished, that the distinction between heterosexual and homosexual has been enforced (a distinction which, after all, has no necessity). (Butler, 1997: 135)

Perhaps we can also think of the Oedipal conflict as an arena where the ego and the libido are at odds, a place where what we desire and whom we are becomes problematic because all identity and gender is premised on loss. And the more we suffer melancholic loss, of our father or mother, the more our developing gendered characters will copy and identify with them. Butler describes how gender is constructed through the ungrievable loss of homosexual desire. Her account is persuasive and deconstructs the heterosexist matrix that has ruled psychoanalytic thinking for too long.

Except we don't have to read the Oedipal conflict simply in terms of fixed desires, as an enforcement of the distinction between heterosexuality and homosexuality. We can see it, alternatively, as a scenario of competing characters and symptoms that are at odds with each other, precisely because no final sublimation or silent gender formation has been made. If we see gender identities as symptoms, not just accomplished character formations, then loss and difference become differently situated. As symptoms, our characters are always wrongly convicted of whom and where, they are. And as symptoms, our characters are never just our preferred selves, they are troubled and troubling, always moving beyond the stable ego or coherent gender identity, and pointing to something or someone else they can be. Character as a silent formation and accomplishment of heterosexuality will always be a cover, as Butler tells us, for a melancholic and ungrievable loss. But character as a neurotic symptom is always speaking its desire outside of the available ego, which seeks to house it. Once characters become symptoms they cease to be the foreclosure or inhibition of another form of sexual identity; they start another process beyond the remit of the ego, opening themselves to other possibilities.

There are at least two things that are striking about the distinction between what Freud saw as the seemingly silent forms of established character that have escaped, or replaced repression, and a character that we can see as symptomatic. The first is that with neurotic characters the body speaks, affects are fixated, but they are not in harmony with the ego. They are in a stand-off, with a demand that refuses and outstrips the ego's power to contain. Symptoms show how recalcitrant our passions are, how inadequate the ego forms we have taken to dress this desire up really are. And yet we hang onto our impoverished familiar forms, our masculine and feminine identities, not because they are true or authentic expression of our essence, but because they are a kind of ballast, a structure and sense that can give shape to what would otherwise be too confusing and too unthinkable.

Symptoms of character, hysterical femininity or obsessive masculinity are interesting, not just because they show the various ways our Oedipal desire becomes dissociated or fixated, but because they always reveal the performance and the provisional status of gender identities. Hysteria is a caricature of femininity taken to an extreme, where its symptoms have ceased to have anything to do with the resident ego; they speak through the body, as a process that is on the move elsewhere.

Obsessive masculinity is seemingly more obedient to the rules of the ego. But in the face of these rules that inhibit the ego, the obsessive's symptoms and desires flare up compulsively. Hysteria and obsession reveal just how unstable gender identities are, sick with a desire that is always beyond the available forms of expression. Butler tells us that each of our gendered identities "is haunted by the love it cannot grieve" and this melancholia grounds what Freud sees as the silent character formation of our gendered selves. If this is so, then the hysterical and obsessive symptoms of our gender identifications are an ending of that silence, in that they speak, trouble, and travel beyond the gender truths of the ego. In psychoanalysis these neurotic symptoms are brought as an invitation for engagement, they seek a conversation beyond the self. Recalcitrant and painful as these symptoms may appear, it is through them we face the unconscious conflicts that ground character forma- tion, the voices that won't give up on their lost desires. This noisy refusal of loss seems different from the silent melancholic incorporation of unlived desire that constructs the more stable heterosexual perform- ances of Butler's inquiry.

Gender as genre

Sense and Sensibility is not an obvious text to illustrate ideas of gender performance and character, and yet it demonstrates how the sense and sensibility of the ego, the symptoms and character of our sexuality and gender perform. How sense and sensibility are different forms that reveal the passions, the theatricality, and melancholia that are inherent to the construction of our gendered selves. The two sisters in this novel are both similar and different, they both have sense and sensibility and the difference is one of form. Elinor is described as having had "a deli- cate complexion, regular features, and a remarkably pretty figure". But Marianne was, "still handsomer. Her form, though not as correct as her sister's, in having the advantage of height, was more striking", (Austen, 1969: p. 78). The more startlingly beauty of Marianne is due to its ability to break out of its requisite form and establish a difference. Both sisters find the shapes and fashions for their feelings in their respective lovers. Marianne tells her mother that her ideal man is the same as her, he "must enter into all my feelings; the same books, the same music must charm us both". Horrified at Edward, her sister's lover, for lacking taste and sensibility, Marianne observes that "his figure is not striking" (Austen, 1969: p. 51). Dramatically telling her mother that such a man would break her heart, Marianne insists that passion is important in being able to select and match necessary forms for the self. Edward might admire

Elinor's drawings because he loves her, but this, for Marianne, is not enough, "He admires as a lover, not as a connoisseur," she says, "to satisfy me, those characters must be united" (Austen, 1969: p. 51).

Marianne's view here, might well be Austen's, because she is arguing for the necessary joining of passion and form, a marriage which is, one might say, the overarching message in the book. However, Marianne's sensibility is portrayed as childish and self-indulgent and is often likened to the narcissistic and passionate bonds between mother and child. Marianne's mother and Mrs. Jennings are silly and affectionate and even Lady Middleton casts off her indifferent demeanour when it comes to doting on her spoilt offspring. Form comes from the more sensible Elinor, who not only narrates most of the story, but also seems to substitute for a missing paternal identification in the family. And yet, Elinor is not without passion or love; the reader is shown only too clearly with pictures of the ruthless Lucy or the cold Lady Middleton, the price that is paid when feelings are left out of both societal manners and personal egos.

Where Marianne's romantic sensibilities are stirred by nature, Edward Ferrar's perceives only utilitarian objects. Where she marvels at the grandeur of the hills, he sees dirty lanes. "Remember" Edward says to Marianne, "I have no knowledge in the picturesque" (Austen, 1969: p. 121). Nonetheless, Elinor, who paints such lovely screens, is in agreement with Marianne; excusing Edward she explains that his refusal to appreciate the picturesque is because he does not want to fall in with the affected appreciation put forward by society:

> Because he believes that many people pretend to more admiration of the beauties of nature then they really feel, and is disgusted with such pretensions, he affects greater indifference and less discrimination in viewing them himself than he possesses. (Austen, 1969: p. 122)

Elinor then, is some kind of balance or bridge between the indifferent and rather empty forms espoused by the reserved Edward and the materialistic aspirations of Lucy and Lady Middleton. Marianne's passion means first forms are always more appealing, whether these come from nature, rather than the conventions of society, or her first impressions and loves. Colonel Brandon is written off by Marianne for not being vital enough and so her immediate response to Willoughby when he cruelly declares Colonel Brandon as boring and forgettable is to reply jubilantly, "that is exactly what I think of him" (Austen, 1969: p. 81). Meanwhile, Elinor accuses them both of being unjust and ignorant of the world. The Colonel observes to Elinor, "Your sister, I understand, does not approve of second attachments". Elinor replies, "No, her opinions are all romantic". "Or rather" the Colonel corrects her, "she considers them impossible to exist" (Austen, 1969: p. 86). Elinor agrees but attributes the reason to Marianne's forgetfulness of her father— "But how she contrives it without reflecting on the character of her own father, who had himself two wives, I know not" (Austen, 1969: p. 86).

Gender performance in this novel moves beyond the confines of discreet feminine and masculine characters to become a problematic relation between form and feeling. A masculinity of form accompanies the reserved manners of Edward but it also shows itself in Lady Middleton's cool societal indifference, or Lucy's ruthless designs: her manipulation of social and moral codes. Whereas Marianne's feminine sensibility and her preoccupation with personal feeling is taken to ridiculous extremes, by Mrs. Jennings and sometimes by her own mother. In Willoughby this sensibility is an echo of Marianne's impulsive immediacy, and yet his passion is wholly selfish and lacks sympathy, he is incapable of really considering or empathising with anyone else.

Lauren Berlant, in her fascinating book *The Female Complaint: The Unfinished Business of Sentimentality in American Culture*, asks what it would mean to read femininity like a genre, to see it as a conventional form or expectation that guarantees, so to speak, a particular emotional register or kind of intensity.

> For femininity to be a genre *like* an aesthetic one means that it is a structure of conventional expectation that people rely on to provide certain kinds of affective intensities and assurances (this is to say what we have called the "performativity" of personality usually produces variations *within* a conventional expectation of self-and world—continuity, rather than the mainly providing dramas of potentially frame—breaking alternativity). (Berlant, 2008: p. 4)

If this is so, then we can also say that masculinity is a genre in the same way. In the normative genre conventions that make up psychoanalysis and certain social, historical communities, femininity and masculinity divide up along registers of romantic feeling and enlightenment reason. Nevertheless, femininity does have reasonable and recognisable forms, just as masculinity is a cultural expectation attached to certain assurances of the strong containment of emotional feeling. Psychoanalytically speaking, pre-Oedipal femininity is associated with primary forms of desire and attachment whereas the Oedipal moment ushers in secondary forms and narrative that have been positioned under a paternal or phallic metaphor. And yet no-one could ever know what femininity was, or romantic feeling, or sentiment, or any of the terms associated with our first forms of desire, if they had not also become at some point in our past, secondary narratives. Femininity has to have mixed with masculinity in order to bear its name. If, as Adam Phillips suggests, "It is the aim of our so-called second thoughts to re-describe our desire as sufficiently pleasurable"; then our first romantic desires have to be translated within secondary forms which can move them out of the realm of the traumatic and make them into something we can play with and use (Phillips, 2006: p. 259).

It is worth thinking here the stakes of the transformation of our first desires, the kind of re-description of them that takes place in order to make them into the passive genital femininity of Freud's classical Oedipal complex. If femininity is associated with our primary bodily desires, which are so strong they are unbearable, then what we see in the secondary narrative of femininity is the reversal of this desire into a genre and a gender identity that performs seemingly the opposite. This is perhaps one way we can marry the frightening pre-Oedipal images of femininity in Klein's theory to the so-called normative femininity in Freud's account. And yet if femininity travels from the monstrously terrifying to a benign sentimentality, then masculinity as the name of the father (rather than the body) attached to our secondary forms and desires, must also translate itself into a gender identity that incorporates and embodies feminine sensibility and desire.

For in the genre formation of gender, within psychoanalysis, we are all feminine before we become translated through masculine naming and form. We all desire and romantically suffer like Marianne to begin with; and yet to articulate that desire, to name its terror and longing is to have tied it to a conventional expectation or genre. The question of sexual difference, psychically, is how can we distinguish and connect our passions and our forms? We need to acknowledge difference and the symbolic codes of society to make our desires bearable and to live and perform so-called gender identities. But in order to feel alive we also have to attach to these conventions, the desires that have been tamed and civilised but not extinguished. This conversation of passion and form that we call sexual difference marks how we become human, and yet to see sexual difference (as the difference and connection between feeling and form), as only reducible to heterosexuality is to miss the point that sexual difference goes on *within* each of us, as a psychical relationship. There can arguably be more sexual difference going on within a gay couple than a straight one; sameness of gender identity is no marker of our internal relationship to gender as a genre, and our ability to match our passions with requisite and satisfying styles.

Marianne's conflict in *Sense and Sensibility* is based on her refusal to accept anything but her primary and authentic romantic feelings; she eschews the societal forms, the tired jargon and language of the affected middle classes. Although these societal codes are so disappointing, dried up, and hackneyed, without them Marianne cannot move to translate or re-describe either her desire or her identity. When Willoughby betrays her she is literally forsaken, for she has no way of replacing him, or mourning her loss. Berlant writes "even the prospects of failure that haunt the performance of identity and genre are conventional" (Berlant, 2008: p. 4). Elaborating she says, "the power of a generic performance always involves moments of potential collapse that threaten the contract that genre makes with the viewer to fulfil experiential expectations" (Berlant, 2008: p. 4). These "blockages or surprises", we could call them repressions and traumas, are according to Berlant of apiece with the convention, and not anything radically other: they make up the particular genre's rich diversity. Thus in the soap opera that is Marianne's life, the disappointment she feels with the social manners of her community goes hand in hand with the trauma of her loss of Willoughby. Both of these failures are not only inscribed into a familiar and recognisable love plot, they also meet our desires as readers, because we too, romantically identify with Marianne's desire and her refusal to submit to alien rules and regulations that don't match with what she feels.

This hysteria, shared by the character Marianne and the reader, is fascinating, because what is revealed is not just a performance of femininity but its symptom. Signs and associated traumas, or failures of femininity interfere with the requisite expectations of the one who performs, views, or reads the genre. These symptoms or failures as Berlant says merely add to the richness of the mix, and perhaps it is the very symptoms of gender that ensure its mobility from one genre to the next.

What makes *Sense and Sensibility* more than a soap opera of its time, more, some critics would say, than Emily Bronte's *Wuthering Heights*, is its attention to the subtleties of aesthetics and style. If Marianne's femininity and sensibility lacks these more elaborate forms, then they can be translated the novel argues, into differing genres and social codes. Marianne's illness in the face of her betrayal by Willoughby is, as Tony Tanner describes, one where she "is sick with the intensity of her own secret passions and intensities" (Tanner, 1969: p. 15). Marianne's complaints begin with psychosomatic symptoms of fatigue, indifference and yet they become louder and louder; her bodily fevers speaking beyond the solitary confines of a melancholic ego, finally bringing the attention of others, particularly the watchful and holding presence of Elinor to the fore. It is only when Marianne's symptoms are fully acted out, when the drama of them has reached its climax and she is saved from death's door, that she can repent in true melodramatic fashion. Only then is Marianne able to acknowledge her selfishness and commit herself to the civilities of everyday life; whereas Elinor can finally articulate her feelings and her sorrow. Marianne's hysteria, as a melodrama, has the ability to move and mutate in differing genres and character conventions. In health, Marianne's romantic self is uncompromising; it is not until her feminine sensibility elicits symptoms and becomes sick that it can begin to move in other directions.

Paternal names and sister forms

So what does it mean to say the symptoms of gender, the failures and neurotic repressions of a particular genre, ensure its mobility into different characters and conventions? As Freud says a symptom has escaped the ego; it is a process in search of a relationship that has become in excess of a particular character's or genre's ability to contain it. One Freudian or more accurately Lacanian reading of Marianne's sensibility would be to read it as an imaginary pre-Oedipal arena that needs lifting into the Symbolic through the paternal metaphor. But I suggest, no easy privilege is given to language in this text. As Rosalind Ballaster notes, the reduction of the plot in *Sense and Sensibility* to a kind of intellectual game is shown through the use of alphabetical letters to refer to lovers:

> Margaret lets slip that Elinor's 'beau' (as Nancy Steele terms it) has the initial 'F' and thereafter, 'The letter F-had been likewise

invariably brought forward, and found productive of such countless jokes, that its character as the wittiest letter in the alphabet had been long established with Elinor'. When the sisters arrive in London, Marianne instantly writes a letter and we are told that 'Elinor thought she could distinguish a large W. in the direction'. Austen's alphabet games reminds us that distinctions between persons may be little more than differences of language and form. (Ballaster, 1995: p. xxiii)

As Ballaster reminds us, the forms of the lovers are often interchangeable in the novel. Edward's distant figure riding towards the cottage at Barton is first mistaken for Willoughby by Marianne and then mistaken for Colonel Brandon, by Elinor. Ballaster sees this confusion of forms as pointing to how sense and sensibility are "etymological relatives rather than linguistic strangers".

This seems true. Austen is portraying how sensibility and sense are a difference in kind rather than a difference in category; a difference between first and second forms, between the personal and the more impersonal. Language, however, seems inadequate to bridge this difference between personal passion and a wider world of social practices. The circulation of alphabetical letters in the novel are far too impersonal and unemotional; as a masculine naming of secondary forms they do nothing to mediate the secret desires they convey to a wider audience. On the other hand, the very personal letters written by Marianne to Willoughby are met with deception, with his reply being actually dictated by his wife, "What do you think of my wife's stile of letter writing?" Willoughby asks Elinor sarcastically, "delicate—tender-truly feminine—was it not?" (Austen, 1969: p. 306). Marianne's outpourings of love are not matched by her lover; his romantic style is not an authentic response being steeped in lies and deceit. We can perhaps see the virtual nature of male forms that circulate in this text in a more positive light, because it is their very impersonality, as genres and types, which makes them so mobile and changeable.

Paternal metaphors in *Sense and Sensibility* are either absent, forgotten, or simply inadequate in uniting feelings with form. Rather, it is through the forms of sisterly, same-sex love, that the relationship between passion and wider social figurations is arguably transformed. Marianne's melancholia in the face of the desertion of her first love is hysterical; a feminine sensibility that is quite mad in its refusal to accept loss. I don't think we can see Marianne's sick femininity as simply a lack of paternal identification. What Marianne loses in Willoughby might well be a forgotten father figure, but he is also clearly a loss of sameness, not difference: a failure of her romantic self and sensibility. New forms of desire and love are not given either by the depressed and melancholy Colonel Brandon, as most critics argue this marriage is the most unbelievable ending to the novel. Secondary forms of desire and self are made available to Marianne, when she can receive them, through her identification and love of her sister Elinor. It is this same sex love, albeit familial, that allows Marianne to bear and mourn her loss, creating new shapes in which to fit her desire.

If all character formation is a copy of whom we identify with and can't have, then what is Marianne's feminine identification in search of? The interchangeable male figures and forms in this novel seem to suggest that it is the form of masculinity rather than any innate essence that is desired be Marianne's sensibility, and yet that supposed phallic genre is always on the move. The forms that finally contain Marianne's love come in the book, not by means of a man, or in the shape of a father, but through the sense of a woman and sister. Elinor's sensible charac-ter observes and often criticises Marianne, but above all she loves and matches her, providing a model that holds and returns Marianne's desire in more plural ways. And so perhaps Elinor's and Marianne's love rep-resents a same-sex passion that can incorporate (sexual) difference.

In this scenario Elinor as an older sister, becomes a different sort of mother; a mother who does not just narcissistically invest in her daughter, but can return her passions through an elaboration of them in secondary (maternal) forms. Marianne's sensibility is a symptom of femininity, a romantic and first love that has been arguably melan-cholic, incorporated, and lost, long before she meets it again in young Willoughby. These symptoms and feminine sensibilities, Marianne's passion and affects, are always in excess of her ego, they are always racing backwards in search of first loves, or desperate in their search for available forms, where only the authentic loves, ones that are already past, will do. Elinor teaches Marianne to bear her loss, not with her ser-mons, but through example, for Elinor has the capability to suffer. It is only when Marianne sees how Elinor is able to grieve and continue to love the things existing outside her personal self, that the younger sister can begin to find some future in the secondary practices and customs that await her.

> Your example was before me', says Marianne, 'but to what
> avail?—Was I more considerate of you and your comfort? Did I
> imitate your forbearance, or lessen your restraints, by taking part in
> those offices of general complaisance or particular gratitude which
> you have hitherto been left to discharge alone. (Austen, 1969: p. 357)

It is perhaps worth noting that Austen is not simply judging Marianne's selfish passion, clearly following her elder sister's footsteps requires some sacrifice of pleasure, and yet paradoxically it is the symptoms of Marianne's passion, their stuck refusal in the face of loss, that allows them eventually to find another semblance or style. Characters without symptoms, such as Edward Ferrars, are perhaps even more problematic because these figures are far too resigned to their fate.

The risk of Elinor missing out on love, because of Edward's real inability to be a virtuoso; his lack of fervent pursuit of what he wants, is also evidence of another more silent melancholia, belonging as Butler tells us, within a more harmonious and composite character formation. Marianne's symptoms and Elinor's sensible ego are necessarily at odds, before they can be married. Without Marianne's romantic sensibilities there would be no excess, no symptoms and therefore no passion and loss to be expressed within the willing and suffering forms that Elinor provides. In the gender performance of sensibility and sense, it is only those characters that refuse silent adaptation and fully live, that can eventually find new and vibrant fashions for their desire. If melancholia signifies the silent incorporation and fixing of our gender identity, then is the finding of new forms of gender and character dependent on mourning? And if this is so, then what leads us from melancholy to transience and mourning, and what difference would understanding this make to the ways in which we perform and converse with gender characters in therapy?

From the melancholia of passion to the transience of form

In Freud's evocative paper *On Transience* he describes a walk on a beautiful summer's day in the company of a friend and the poet Rilke.[1] The poet finds it difficult to be moved by the lovely natural world around him because he is troubled by the fact it will not last. Freud protests that the transience of what is lovely does not lessen the value of its pleasure; on the contrary, the precious things in life are those we will one day grieve for. If what we loved was eternal, we would not desire it so intensely. However, if there is one thing that psychoanalysis teaches us, it is that we don't give up objects or our relationships just because they are lost to us. We observe the libido clinging to objects that have departed, even though there are available substitute, and that, Freud says, is mourning. Indeed, what spoils pleasure, and his companion's renunciation of the surrounding beauty, is

> a revolt in their minds against mourning. The idea that all this beauty is transient was giving these two sensitive minds a fore-taste of mourning over its decease; and since the mind instinctively recoils from anything that is painful, they felt their enjoyment inter-fered with by its transience. (Freud, 1916a: p. 306)

What Freud is pointing to here is the difficulty and the necessity of mourning. Suffering and mourning are hard to stay with, but to see our suffering through is essential if we want to be able to love again. Sándor Ferenczi makes the same point when he argues that suffering and what he calls the "feminine principle" is essential in bringing about change and reaching reality. "The drive for self-assertion may be seen as the basis for Freud's pleasure principle", Ferenczi argues, "the drive for conciliation as the basis of his reality principle"[2] (Ferenczi, 1995: p. 42). The pleasure in mothering, a maternal willingness and capac-ity to suffer are for Ferenczi not just the basis for endurance but also at the root of the deepest satisfactions. Freud and Ferenzci are saying in different ways that suffering if we can bear it, can lead to happiness, because once we have the ability, or the maternal form if you like, to carry our pain then we can truly appreciate and receive what the future holds for us.

Our characters and the difficulty in altering them are indelibly tied to mourning, resistance and to the melancholic identification with lost objects. In his essay *The Ego and the Id* Freud discusses how when sex-ual objects are given up, the ego becomes altered, and there is "a setting up of the ego inside the ego, as it is in melancholia" (Freud, 1923: p. 29). Freud wonders if it is only through this process of introjection and the accompanied regression to an earlier oral phase, that the pas-sionate id will let go of its grip on the object. The ego seems here to be re-constituted through the remaining imprints of the object libido after they have been given up. So who we are, our characters from the beginning are never original; they are always second-hand, belonging initially to someone else. We become the people we love, but especially when we lose them. Although, Freud also thinks that this morphing of self can take place whilst the object still exists in reality; observing that women who fall in love many times carry their past loves in their present character traits. Character, here, ceases to be something individual and becomes a palimpsest, peopled by others from the past that are always leaking back, appearing behind the more manifest picture of the self.

Love and identification, it seems, are not separate but simultaneous; Freud admits that there are cases where, "alteration in character occurs before the object has been given up" (Freud 1923: p. 30). We change into the people we love even before they leave us. Think of the intimate bond between twins, or the symbiosis that exists between certain lovers, and it seems such character shifting of the ego in the presence of its objects, is always something of a replacement. We identify with those we love, but this act or performance carries an early oral cannibalism, where the objects we adore are always to some extent eaten to make way for ourselves. So maybe the women, or the men, like Marianne and Willoughby, who become most like their lovers are already preparing for their loss; they have limited future damage, so to speak, by mummifying their chosen object within themselves. In this scenario, character alteration is simply a performance to cover intractable resistance against loss, a way of keeping the people we love forever, and ever.

Character, in other words, is simply the history of all our resistances and our losses. And so our belief in transience therefore becomes important, because transience means not that there are limits to identification and to love, but that reality is by nature, protean and shifting. The people we love, the world we inhabit have to pass and pass on; they can't be endlessly preserved and dominated without considerable damage to ourselves. Without transience we cease to be poets and start becoming perverts, turning everything into stereotypes, the same old ego and the same old satisfactions. Love and character replays itself as the same endless tune. Transience creates the kind of mourning that moves us, and the recalcitrant ego, into being undone. The people we love are unique and so we will always be mourning and that grief goes hand in hand with desire. What saves or distinguishes someone from being terminally depressed is the capacity to grieve and remake our lost loves over and over again. And yet we are all like the poet on Freud's summer walk, in our rebellion towards the transience of life, in the fixations of our desire. When it comes to the transience of love and life, our libidinal desires behave like the poet, who refuses to yield to the uncertain loveliness that surrounds him. Desire, is akin to the romantic poet and Austen's Marianne, in being unable to repress her needs and wait for spring. Although the paradox of this most elusive of figures, is that without the ability to accept her own wintry death, desire shrivels and retreats. And so it is the ego (we can think of Elinor) that must befriend the temper of desire, enabling her to endure the fleeting and fugitive nature that will be her lot. The more the ego can acknowledge the transience of life, the more ongoing will be the life and the symptoms of both grief and desire, and this is what lends variety and vicissitudes to our characters. Without our symptoms we are truly bereaved. The ego is an engine that drives our characters, creating them, fixing them and moving them.

But in order to change our character and bear the loss of the people and objects that we love, we have to rely on the sensible (operational) part of the ego convincing the passionate Id, that it can substitute for what has been lost: "Look you can love me too" says the ego, "I am so like the object" (Freud, 1923: p. 30). Indeed, Freud considers that all sublimation, or character making, only ever takes place, through the medium of the ego, "which begins by changing sexual object-libido, into narcissistic object-libido, and then, perhaps, goes on to give it a different aim" (Freud, 1923: p. 30).

Suffering it seems is character building, but only if we can be sufficiently self-absorbed about it. First forms, our most narcissistic ones, have to be returned to, in order to keep our lost loved ones alive. And as these loved others gradually become worked into whom we are as characters, then new self forms take the place of old griefs. Listen Freud says, to how we have to go backwards and regress; there is a kind of alchemy in our narcissism that enables us to become our objects. Sometimes this happens when we still keep those objects in the external world, but more often than not transforming ourselves into the characters we identify with and love, happens most strongly when they are lost. There is a difference though, between the incorporated forms we borrow from others, which go on to haunt us and live on in our egos, and our ability to make those forms the right fit, as it were, for our desire.

According to Judith Butler, Freud's understanding of melancholia is also a description for the founding of the ego and self. The incorporation of the object within the ego, in melancholia, produces the ego,

> Thus, in melancholia not only does the ego substitute for the object, but this act of substitution *institutes* the ego as a necessary response to or "defence" against loss. (Butler, 1997: p. 165)

Butler wants to challenge psychoanalytic idea that sexual difference is the marker of castration or loss. "Why" she asks, "is sexual difference the primary guarantor of loss in our psychic lives?" To generalise, this structure condemns us all to gender melancholy, repudiating same sex love. And yet, perhaps we can see all heterosexual and homosexual positions as secondary descriptions, only possible once some kind of outside form, a virtual other, has given shape to our animal passions. As Freud says in his essay *Instincts and their Vicissitudes*, the ego makes itself through incorporating and eating the object, but it also creates the external object, through what it refuses and spits out. If sexual difference is understood as the cultural and bodily way we have interpreted the distinction between first desires and secondary forms, then the melancholia of sexual difference is a description of how we all lose, and refuse to lose and bear our primary desires. Homosexuality is perhaps easier to repudiate simply because it is not tied to the conventional expectations of the genre or gender in our society; but of course this is changing. Butler wants to know if "every woman who desires a woman desires her from a masculine disposition" (Butler, 1997: p. 165). The answer, I think, is both yes and no, because all desire has to signify difference from the primal mother, and within our culture the naming of this secondary form of difference is masculine. But the signifier of this conventional genre is only a name, in that the real alterity of our desires rests on the richness and passion involved in the remaking of those genres. Sexual difference as a primary guarantor of loss is not a guarantor of a heterosexual position, simply a marker that some genre making and shape shifting of the ego has to take place.

In *Sense and Sensibility* it is not the letters signifying a masculine naming that provide Marianne with the new forms for her desire but a re-description and a returning of her feminine sensibility, differently, through the same-sex love of a sister. Marianne's melancholy, her grief and pain at the loss of Willoughby as her ideal self and lover, leaves her ego impoverished. But Marianne's melancholia has been preceded and accompanied by an uncompromising stance in relation to social forms. She won't accept the societal conventions of genre or gender, believing her romantic feminine sensibility has been only hers to invent and make, and hers alone. As Ballaster reminds us, Marianne has to learn to take second place, "not only in her family, but in her views on culture and her aesthetic judgments". And this means acknowledging not just current social genres but the historical ones that preceded her, the fact that Marianne's "favourite Romantic writers, Cowper and Scott, were there before her" (Ballaster, 1995: p. xxiv).

Marianne is like the poet on Freud's summer walk, in that she will not accept the transience implicit in the nature that surrounds her. Her version of the picturesque is that it be frozen in time, a beauty and desire that will be everlasting. As she is leaving her beloved home, Norland, she says,

> And you, ye well-known trees!—but you will continue the same. No leaf will decay because we are removed, nor any branch become motionless although we observe you no longer! No; you will continue the same; unconscious of any pleasure or the regret you occasion, an insensible of any change in those who walk under your shade! But who will remain to enjoy you? (Austen, 1969: p. 60)

Within this melancholic speech, the changing nature of reality is resisted and perceived through screens or fixed tableaus, capturing what is loved as an everlasting sameness that can't respond in any living way to its recipient. Pleasure is only to be had through acknowledgement of the transience of life, and this means engagement with cultural and historical forms, so that they can be part of the ebb and flow between desire and reality. Transience and the reality principle walk hand and hand, and Marianne's melancholic romanticism is a refusal of what is in the world in favour of her romantic fancy.

Mary Wollenstonecraft, the famous feminist and writer, was a companion author to Jane Austen in that she also wrote about the sexual politics of sense and sensibility. A more radical critic of romanticism than Austen, Wollenstonecraft thinks the female mind to be corrupted by sensual and sentimental arts:

Let he honest heart shew itself, and reason teach passion to submit to necessity', she writes, 'The passions which have been celebrated for their durability have always been unfortunate. They have acquired strength by absence and constitutional melancholy (Wollenstonecraft, 1985: p. 184).

As a feminist, Wollenstonecraft sees women's alignment with sensibility and desire as coterminous with their subjection, leaving them outlawed from a world of rational citizenship organised by men. Freud would only agree with this in part, arguing that female sensibility and desire are distinct. Female sensibility does render women outlawed, in its hysterical sense, because this is where an imaginary world of fantasy substitutes for the exchange of feeling and form that takes place in reality. This, come to think of it, is an interesting way to view the difficulty that women sometimes have in experiencing their desire. Difficult, not because passion has been unavailable, but precisely because its sensibility has been too strong, or like Marianne it is too romantic and refusing of mediating translations. Marianne's flights of fancy and fantasy are melancholic in that they inhabit a solitary existence, untouched and oblivious to their surroundings.

What can turn Marianne's fancies and our incorporated melancholic objects into a variety of characters that can give creative form to the ego? What has to happen for our passionate and stubborn symptoms to become translated into a plurality of (maternal) forms? If melancholia underpins all mourning, then perhaps mourning is our ability to acknowledge transience, and the mutability of the forms in which we build our future desires. Empty melancholic forms inhabit and haunt the ego, but if these are to become more than fixed types of feminine sensibility and masculine form, more than the simplistic division between Marianne's romantic passions and Edward's pragmatic rationales, then exchange between fantasy and the transient forms of our evolving world have to occur. This is what Freud meant by the reality principle—of Elinor's sense; her conscious and unconscious perception of the ongoing relationship between individual passion and the more collective genres that can express desires and their vicissitudes.

Freud, like Elinor, is a realist, but that does not simply make him an espouser of enlightenment reason. Both a pragmatist and a romantic, Freud understood the necessary translation between sensibility and sense. Strung between a nineteenth century theorist of the libidinal unconscious and a more modernist thinker of the egoist self, Freud is remembered for dividing up the Ego and the Id, when in fact they initially belonged together; indeed, the whole realisation of desire depends on their friendship. The ego is made up of many characters that multiply as we grow and develop. There is the punitive repressive ego, the realist ego, and of course there is, as Freud acknowledged, the libidinal part of the ego and the dream ego. The ego grows out of the id and at first it can't be differentiated, and yet the ego is the capacity, or the brains, organising and shaping our affects into their first forms. If forms are how we express our affects, then our first forms are extraordinary because they undergo a sea change, transmuting from the free flow of id energy to a crystallisation within rudimentary images and representations that make up the early ego. This early unconscious ego that has transmuted from the id, leads Freud to remark in *The Ego and the Id*, that the unconscious and the repressed do not coincide. "A part of the ego, too—and Heaven knows how important a part" he says, "may be Ucs, undoubtedly is Ucs" (Freud, 1923: p. 18). And this, finally, leads Freud to concede another non-repressed unconscious, which begins life as unconscious perception and reception. Indistinguishable from the repressed and yet different, the non-repressed unconscious implies receptivity and exchange between the character of the ego and it's passions.

In the beginning the ego and the id were companions and sisters, like Elinor and Marianne, who unconsciously helped each other. As time goes by, they become divided and oppositional and when the libidinal self confronts repression, she retreats and flees back to a time where she felt more welcome. And so fixation of our affects to a more infantile place where the libido was gratified, rather than frowned on by the ego, is the neurotic solution to repression. Affects, here, are on the move, but not in search of new forms, merely the old; because it is within our hysterical old forms, that our libidinal wishes get some life of their own, albeit on massively compromised terms. In this neurosis, the grown-up ego and the stubborn passions fight it out, and yet it is only through the ego's regression that these two can become intimate again. It is through the dream, as Freud tells us, that the ego manages to go back in space and time and become playmates with the id. It is here, in this fellowship between the ego and the id that new formations and re-workings of desire occur. Thus the id allows itself to be shaped and formed by the ego, just as the ego loses its snootiness, allowing its own forms to dissolve and become reshaped to accommodate and mitigate the desire it has snubbed.

Conclusion

Dreams are the maternal forms, for all their secrecy, that are borrowed from others. They work from outside to in and back again. So, although part of the dream ego's work is to make sisterly friends with the passionate id, it can't allow passions to win. Passions have to learn a benign regression in the service of the ego; like Marianne, they have to acknowledge their dependence on the changing species and seasons of our social landscapes. But such shape shifting in our egos, or our passions, can't take place, or so it seems to me, without conflict, resistance and flight. Character, and for that matter, social life, can only develop through renewal but it is worth noting how painful such regeneration is. What kind of society do we find ourselves in, when that renewal doesn't happen, a place perhaps where no-one grows up? Equally, we could imagine an even worse scenario, one in which no-one can ever regress to childhood. Because however much regression is the seat of acting out and mental illness, the inability to regress to earlier passions and affects, would usher in a total sovereignty of the ego's repressive function, robbing us of our desire, or more accurately our ability to befriend and use it.

And so symptoms—the symptoms of masculinity and femininity—our obsessions and hysteria, are interesting, because they are not reducible to the silent melancholic. In play beyond the composite incorporations of character, our gender symptoms are in process, stuck but also travelling in search of something more relational. Symptoms mark the travel of affects and the unconscious characters of the ego beyond the fixations of normative gender identities. Involved in resistance and yet speaking to another, symptoms show that sense and sensibility are on the move and can offer some kind of exchange—Elinor's and Freud's reality principle. For, the transience of our gender identities is of course dependent on a real, not just a fantasy correspondence, between our passions and the varieties of public convention that give them a voice. This raises some interesting observations for the clinical situation, in that the neurotic symptoms that are spoken, our obsessions and hysterias, want a real as well as a fantasy relationship in therapy, which of course entails conflict, resistance, and flight. Symptoms of gender can't be seen as something that should be just silenced by drugs, or told what to do by the right cognitive behavioural advice. Gender symptoms, in therapy, however mad or intractable, are always a demand to be read, they are seeking a response. Perhaps it is ideally within therapeutic company and conversation that these symptoms, our favourite stories, are not subjected to artificial narrative endings such as "the psycho-analytic cure", but are allowed evolution into more impermanent and changing forms of our desires.

Notes

1. Freud's companions were Freud's friend the writer Lou Andreas-Salomé and her lover the poet Rilke.
2. Ferenczi's "feminine principle" is quite different from Marianne's traumatic romantic sensibility which in Freud's view would be associated with a return of the repressed. The "feminine principle" in Ferenczi's thinking is associated with a primary unrepressed unconscious, which is both receptive and perceptive; an heir to the receptive and mobile capacities of the ego, captured by the older sister Elinor in Austen's novel.

CHAPTER FIVE

All about our mothers: melodrama's maternal form

Melodrama and psychoanalysis are both concerned with the dramatisation of affects in search of form. Indeed, if we are to think of Freudian sexuality as this passionate drive in search of forms that are initially derived from another, then we can also see how sexuality begins as both melodramatic passions and non-personal objects or types, which over time become inscribed as a personal identity we call the ego. The next two chapters explore, in their analysis of melodrama and psychoanalysis, how passions and sexuality move between a personal ego and non-personal other. Significantly though, this rhythm is captured through an early maternal form and aesthetic, rather than the naming of language or the paternal signifier. Pre-Oedipal experience is not simply an imaginary entity that is then broken up through a language of the unconscious and notions of the signifier. For me, there is an imaginative as well as a fantasmatic aspect to the imaginary; one which corresponds with our perceptual senses and reality through a lived mimesis with the mother. In this mimesis sameness is returned albeit differently, in relation to her aesthetic and cultural response—her gestural form. It is the mimetic return of maternal gestures that occurs initially through the non-personal (and virtual) form of the mother which both elaborates the child's passions and builds what I have called a painterly home or being for the ego. And yet it is the melodrama of passions in search of old and familiar forms that stages the dramas of our personal and historical pasts. Therefore to really get somewhere new, we have to go back further, beyond the pleasures of the ego and the personal self, to encounter an older relation to a virtual form of being, which is unconsciously perceived and received in association with the early mother. It is this older relation to a virtual non-personal world where we access the unconscious not simply as a private entity but as an historical force.[1]

As every psychoanalyst knows, the clinical transference has to go back in time before it can move forwards. What constitutes the drama of both the clinical scene and a melodramatic film or literary text, is this return "home" to the old preferred forms and stories of childhood. But the paradox of these first forms is how intensely they are guarded by the ego. For therapy to work, and for the ego to elaborate itself aesthetically and emotionally in relation to the world that surrounds it, we have to allow passionate symptoms their relational search beyond the self. Symptoms run backwards but they are also affects that move forward. As an escape from the ego's boundaries they are in search for new forms beyond the self. Melodrama can help us to understand how affects are in search of forms that only arrive through the response of another. Although because melodrama, like hysteria, is so fixated on its return to primary loves we have to ask how can our preferred Oedipal symptoms move anywhere new? What forms can beckon them into a new rhythm that will lead them beyond the confines of the personal self?

Melodrama is a theatre of the analytic space, a dramatisation of unconscious desires or passions that hysterically plays out an established form of being and characters. Our first forms are not made from language but from things. We spend our lives, as Alphonso Lingis tells us, by giving forms to the forces and the emotions that drive us; and the forms we get are from others:

> One takes ones place in a place another has vacated. One sits in chairs, opens doors, rides a tricycle, one's body catching on how from others. Chairs, doors, tricycles them-selves require and indicate certain postures and movement's of one's limbs. They are not made for one's body in particular, but for anyone of certain age and a certain general size. One makes oneself someone, another

one, by taking on the posture and movement they require. (Lingis, 1996: p. 1)

And the forms we inhabit are always old. The passionate characters that are the melodrama of hearth and home are always past passions, hysterical beings who return, again, and again to stage familiar conflicts in familiar ways. Melodrama, as Peter Brooks describes is our most preferred modern mode of experience, a desacralised "modern occult" where the conflict rages between our repressed desires and capitalist society. And yet melodrama is always in hysterical excess of our societal forms. Played out by the body, as muteness, pantomime, and performance, melodrama is composed of sensations of inner unconscious desire and experience, breaking through, destabilising our more normative, tales of the self.

It is through melodrama we are at our most personal, playing out in therapy and in life, our developmental histories, our particular sufferings and woes, or grievances and hates. There is nothing moderate about these feelings or the characters we lend to them. But these characters are, as it were, our most deeply intractable selves, that are given to us on loan. They did not initially belong to us, and were borrowed, like shoes stepped into, from our most treasured and prohibited early loves. So, melodramatic passions are both something deeply secret and personal, and they are also something completely impersonal; a copy from someone else.

Old forms and hysterical Londoners

Everyone's life, both external and internal is a staged melodrama; a space and a place of characters and forms where conflicts between the personal and impersonal are played out. Increasingly as I age as an academic, I find filling the shoes of my role, an effort. There is always someone, younger or more established, or more published to make me feel not new. But then there is nothing very new about these feelings either, or the character I step into to play at being an academic. I remember my intellectually driven father and dreamy mother and their ongoing drama and conflict in me, the part that feels I need to achieve and compete, and the part that would simply prefer to dream up trees. Because passions overwhelm and undo us, we need to have characters which can give shape to these feelings, to help us behave.

And the most reassuring ones are always the ones we have always known. So, one of the problems with our passions is how in fact we can re-experience them as something different, how we can give them characters that don't just squash them back to the confines of our most knowable, personal selves, and histories. Our passions are always in excess of the forms and characters they are given, by our family and particular culture. Stifled in old clothes that no longer really accommodate or fit, these passions emerge again and again in all their hysterical wants and needs, as escape from the family, or capitalist society proves impossible. And so we hysterically return and keep returning, although our symptoms—bodily eruptions, phobic frights or obsessive thoughts—betray our refusal to let desire remake its old forms.

These forms, our Oedipal characters, are like comfortable old slippers. One might think there is nothing comfortable about the neurotic pain and suffering that accompanies the satisfaction of these battered shoes. But however conflicted these internal actors are, their performance ensures an ongoing identity, a gender and genre that ensures above all our individuality, a possession of self.

The ability of passions to find new modes of being and evolving, means risking the more impersonal objects and forms that have no guarantees of becoming solely ours. We are always, when it comes to life, repeating the risks or traumas that accompany our first visit to school, or ride on a bike. But of course these are not the first; arguably taking these risks depends on having some character(s) in place to fall back on. Perhaps, the first desires are much more anxiety ridden because our characters—the forms we make to house our passions to begin with, belong to somebody else. It is only by passionate consummation: the internalisation of what we desire and the expulsion of what we don't, that character can begin to exist. Melodrama is, as Adam Phillips says, about "transparency, immediacy and first impressions". The first form or character the audience identifies with in a melodrama, "is a true but diminished thing because it cannot develop," and because the first impression or passion is so extreme, it is also experienced as suffering or trauma (Phillips, 2006a: p. 223).

And yet the suffering of desire, its inbuilt trauma, is ongoing, despite some repression, its hunger begets more forms and different characters. Although the repetition and force of melodrama, its rhythm, always seems hell bent on return. Melodrama as our most personal, and passionate characters, seems to know only one way—back home.

Full of nostalgic reminiscences from the past, melodrama behaves as a hysteric, shaping present reality from past fantasy. As Freud says in his *Five Lectures on Psycho-analysis* the hysteric behaves likes "impractical Londoners", who pass old memorials such as "The Monument" to the Great Fire, only to bewail the sad history of destruction, rather than to appreciate how the city has been rebuilt "in far greater brilliance" (Freud, 1910: p. 17). Acknowledging these hysterical Londoners, Laura Mulvey notes how melodrama works as a collective fantasy and form that is not restricted to the individual (Mulvey, 1994). Melodrama has been famously defined by Peter Brooks as an externalisation of repressed desire, Freud's internal psychic drama made public and shared. If this is so, then melodrama must also figure, as the repressed and the unrepressed unconscious. There is an acting out in melodrama, an expression, and transmission where, "Nothing is understood, all is overstated" (Brooks, 1996: p. 41).

Meaning becomes deciphered by the other—the audience—who identifies so closely with the passionate character on stage. Brooks interprets the rhetoric, the painterly language of melodrama, as an unconscious mode akin to the Freudian dream. If melodrama is a dream code of "plastic entities, visual and tactile models held out for all to see and to handle" then it also a dream act that erupts and interrupts, breaking "through everything that constitutes the reality principle" (Brooks, 1976: p. 41). For all melodrama's transparency as the shared unrepressed unconscious, it is still mute and hysterical, remaining repressed and secret at its core. Dreams are not knowable in themselves, until they are transported and interpreted; and so the full psychological expression of melodrama is always suspect. There is always a residue of intensity and force that remains in waiting; a secret self, that as Winnicott says, must not be interpreted. To be a character, is as Christopher Bollas describes, divided into dream experience and a dream text, first and second impressions, or forms: what Freud called primary and secondary processes (Bollas, 1993). If the dreaming experience is characterised by the actor on stage, then it is the audience watching from the upper gallery of the theatre that can meaningfully represent the event.

But a question arises, what kind of primary or secondary process is melodrama? For it seems that melodrama is made up of first impressions, with its bodily gestures and pantomime, and its visual tableaux and muteness. Is melodrama the dream experience, or the dream script? And what is the difference? Masud Khan was the first psychoanalyst to make clear Freud's distinction between a dream experience and a dream text. Whereas the dream text is the remembered dream, which is worked through in the analytic session, the dream experience is "beyond interpretation" (Khan, 1983: p. 83). For Khan, the dream experience is of necessity unknowable; it is simply the lived experience of dreaming and life, that can't be represented. Dream experience does not just take place at night. Everyday life is, as Bollas tells us, made up of slipping into subjective states of simple experiencing; a kind of "day dreaming" where we can lose ourselves in deeply unconscious experience. Allowing ourselves to get lost in these unconscious experiential states where we literally forget ourselves, is an elaboration of our personal self through a formation of the Id.

As a jouissance of our most private and mysterious self that allows us to elaborate objects in a transformational way, this losing ourselves to dream is dependent on the containing presence of initially the mother and then the actual structure of the mind. Bollas calls this early dreamer of being a "simple experiencing self" and yet it is perhaps more correct to say it is a potential self in the sense that this early dreamer is dependent on maternal containment and receptivity for its ability to elaborate objects and future forms of character. If containment feels insecure then, "a child will feel hesitant to release the elements of self to their experiencings: such abandonments feel life-threatening" (Bollas, 1993: p. 53). Echoing Winnicott, Bollas describes an essential ability to the young child's ability to dream and play:

> What would turn up? Abandoning oneself to play, what would happen? Or perhaps more accurately, exactly whom do we become as we express our idiom into play? To be a character, to release one's idiom into lived experience, requires a certain risk, as the subject will not know his outcome; indeed to be a character is to be released into being, not as a knowable entity per se, but as an idiom of expression explicating a human form. (Bollas, 1993: p. 54)

Melodramatic characters seem less developed than this, rather like a dream script that is waiting for the right experience to come along, so it can continue. Like Freud's hysterical Londoners, melodramatic characters are full of first impressions that need elaborating. Psychoanalytically speaking, these characters have to regress in the transference. They have to remember the past as a dream experience, in order to move into their present, and towards their future.

First and poetic impressions of character

What is the difference between being a character that can play and take risks and those first traumatic impressions of character that are too unequivocal to develop? Adam Phillips makes a distinction between the child's ability for nonsensical play and his sexual appetites. When it comes to character what are the parts or actors that act out desire and which ones prefer just to play and what is their connection?

> It is essential to the whole idea of playing, Winnicott intimates, to acknowledge what playing cannot do for the self. You can't eat art. When appetite starts, playing stops. (Phillips, 2006b: p. 33)

Phillips is curious about the measure of desire at stake in playing, and in pleasure. If desire at its most extreme dissolves the organised ego, then what kind of desire is involved in the play that elaborates the ego in new and unplanned ways? I think it is also worth thinking about the different characters involved in the early receptive relationship with the mother. If the repressed unconscious is about our desires, the urgency at stake in what we want and yet can't have, then the receptive unconscious is about how that unknowable desire is communicated or transmitted. The receptive unconscious linked to an early maternal aesthetic is how desire can be creatively played with and elaborated into new forms of character. So, I don't think the repressed desiring unconscious and the receptive unconscious are mutually exclusive because one leads to the other. Having a receptive mother enables us to desire, and to communicate that desire, without it being too traumatic. Perhaps most importantly the imaginative and receptive mother enables us to elaborate a dreaming self in which we can make up our new and evolving characters. But it is not enough for the mother to be simply dreamy; she has to be active enough in her appetites both in relation to the baby and beyond the baby. The mother's ability to feel passionate about her infant has to be mixed with another more nonsensical capacity to play and dream. Meeting the poet in your mother is arguably just as important as engaging with maternal desire. And arguably it is this poet through elaborating the infant's capacity to play, that will mediate and reformulate the melodrama of the child's first passions.

There is much talk today about the neglectful mother who usually works. Or, alternatively the optimal stay at home mother, whose supposedly all encompassing desire to mother outstrips all other passions.

And yet, mothers who stay at home all the time would have to invent ways to neglect their babies, if they did not get bored and distracted. Not being bored, in other words is evidence of having no imagination, no elsewhere. The kind of maternal containment that enables the development of character, the imaginative work of making and inventing forms is always a play between presence and absence. If the loving mother enables the infant to feel alive with desire, then the poet mother is the one that mediates and formulates that passion through play and distraction. I think for a child to learn about necessary distraction, he can't be ongoingly stimulated, he has to have a mother who can imaginatively absent herself through reverie and dream.

And so it is with the therapy session whose very form has passion and the neglect of abstraction and distraction built in. The analyst comes and goes, and so does the patient. Passionate love evolves through the transference. The patient loves the analyst, and the analyst loves the patient, except the therapist has another poetic imperative which is to make that desire as playful as possible, to remake it, abstract it, and repeat it in ever more imaginative ways. Of course the one thing that the therapist can't do is immediately satisfy the patient's transference longings, say in a sexual way, for then therapy would be over. So, one of the fundamental things that therapy is about is not simply the waking up of desire, but the remaking of it. The re-storying of desire in therapy is how we move from sensation to sensibility, how raw hunger and the trauma of our first desires can be re-formed emotionally, perceptually, and aesthetically. And it is of course not the case that the analyst and the patient remain at the same even keel in terms of their appetites or indeed their sensibilities. Therapy sessions have a flavour to them, a colour and a music that changes. Sometimes they are melodramatically charged and conflicted; others might feel more dreamy and contemplative, and the receptive unconscious in the therapist is at work matching and mirroring the mood.

Kenneth Wright has recently spoken about the creative finding of form that takes place between the baby and mother. Following Winnicott's emphasis on primary creativity and Stern's work on attunement, Wright traces how the mother's mirroring and attunement to her baby's affects, reflects back new forms with which the baby can formulate new experience. Arguably we need forms to articulate our deepest feelings and this is what art provides us with. But for Wright, the finding of forms is essential to our first mimetic attunement with the mother. He writes:

The search for holding forms is as basic as the need for bodily satisfaction; the need for the mother's responding face is as powerful as the need for her breast and milk. (Wright, 2009: p. 68)

Unconscious mimesis between mother and child is never simply about a reproduction of sameness. Reflection of new forms, internalised by the child through the mirror of his mother, always contain something of the mother; as Wright says, the mother's "response is like an echo, albeit an echo creatively changed, by its passage through her own sensibility" (Wright, 2009: p. 67). We can perhaps also think, here, of what consequences this has for thinking about the myth of Narcissus and Echo, and indeed for narcissistic states, because of course narcissistic disorders are when a person can't do without the other's total admiration. The reflecting gaze, here, can't contain another person's sensibility; it can't produce any new forms. In the more creative narcissism that Wright describes, some difference is always returned through the sensible forms of the other. And this is also an interesting way we can think about melodrama and character, because in melodrama there is always a hysterical excess of emotion and affect, where that excess inscribed on the body is revealed as on the move. Melodrama, like hysteria articulates bodily affect and in doing so it communicates just how important it is to have a form to structure intense feeling, even though the available form is always belonging to someone else. The mimesis or mimicry of melodrama is always in search of new forms and sensibilities that are found or not found in the response or the non-response of the other.

Melodrama on the move

Melodrama is hysterical and like hysteria it has the propensity to move and imitate other genres, other forms, and characters. Like hysteria, melodrama was everywhere in Victorian society. Arising with bourgeois capitalism as a crisis of modernity, melodrama marks a loss of traditional and sacred cultural forms, thereby staging itself in Brook's description of a personal and "moral occult". Melodrama exerts a pressure or force on post-enlightenment reason, externalising privatised family dramas, hysterically acting them out; revealing them as both oppositional and divided. As Brooks notes, melodrama socially externalises and stages what has hitherto been a private Oedipal drama. And so we can understand modernity as a melodramatic imaginary that as Christine Gledhill says is a shifting modality, migrating into other constituent forms. In a similar fashion hysteria, disappears and appears historically, vanishing from clinical diagnosis in the twentieth century, only to return within the academic debates and trauma theories of more recent times. Hysteria has the propensity to mimic borderline states, traumatic shock and eating disorders, and yet it is also a gender performance of Oedipal sexual difference, albeit in a caricatured form. Melodrama has the same ability to move through history, responding as Gledhill points out to the questions of modernity. The modality of melodrama is always double, always a move of the uncanny, articulating distinctive genres at particular moments and then re-articulating them. In this way melodrama is always restaging the relationship and the response between the imaginary and the real. Gledhill describes how melodrama is an organising mode of genres, identifying with many, but not reducible to one, it moves as a two-way exchange between existing genres and "new signifiers of the real" (Gledhill, 2000: p. 240). Melodrama constantly replays and repeats genre in an exchange with different temporal instances of cultural and historical value.

But if melodrama offers in Gledhill's words maximum flexibility, why is it in another sense so completely one dimensional? This is the dilemma of the hysteric, on one level so permeable in her performativity, and on another level so fixed. In the theatre that makes up the psychoanalytic session we can see the various characters, the narcissist, the pervert, the obsessive, and the anorexic as melodramatic performances, in the sense that they are one dimensional. Perhaps we are all melodramatic, in that we have only one dominant or preferred way of being, a particular exaggeration or symptom that is meant to make sense of all the rest. There is the melodramatic trauma of our first pre-Oedipal desires, where suffering is an excess that articulates itself through the body in the absence of other forms.

We can see how the Oedipal drama of sexual difference is often similarly one dimensional in the sense that the melodrama of this conflict is hierarchically fixed and oppositional in terms of gender, class, and race. I want to suggest that the hysteric articulates an intense performance of affect that is always in search of different forms. To position the hysteric as simply in rebellion to the paternal law of the phallus is to recreate an opposition between the body and language, where you choose one or the other, mother or father. And of course hysterics are famous for refusing exactly this choice. As I have argued,

> To place the Oedipal Complex as a symbolic discourse or moment of exchange from ego to object love is to fix it in some kind of identity, heterosexual, normative. Alternatively, to see the Oedipal Complex as a bedrock of possible mimetic fantasy in relation to mother, father, siblings is to understand how we can regress to these familial fantasies again and again and then transform them into whom we want to be. (Campbell, 2006: p. 42)

I want to return to the dilemma of the hysteric (in both her pre-Oedipal and Oedipal moments) as a melodramatic response to questions of modernity and history, where the articulation of affect is an expression of desire in search of form. Now this, as Adam Phillips has pointed out, is hard to track.

How do we move from desire to play, from the urgency of our first wants to their repetition in a more generative way? For Phillips this move can only be incoherent "One kind of chaos occurs when absorption, or preoccupation, begins turning into appetite and the hope of satisfaction" (Phillips, 2006a: p. 34). Such transition can only take place as a move from internal to shared experience. We can play on our own, but the capacity to play has been dependent on our initial experience of maternal reverie. We regress from our private internal thoughts, through free association, to the desire for someone else. It is curious how in hysteria and melodrama, the form of either our emotions or our thoughts is not something internal; it is not, so to speak already individualised but belongs to someone else. And this is a good thing because without our initial hysteria, our desire in the absence of answering forms, we would never go seeking. The baby, as Kenneth Wright says, might need to be fed, but she also needs the perceptual and receptive response of a holding maternal aesthetic. Within this description it's almost as if the hysteric is telling us, through her staged melodrama, that internal experience, or the so-called individual self, is always a product of a more shared and social unconscious. We have to have many selves, there has to be an orchestra of unconscious characters, so to speak, in order to provide a dreaming experience called the self.

In the repertoire of the unconscious we have both a repressed and a receptive unconscious; we have repressed desire and a telepathic transference which is communicative. Without such a receptive and perceptive unconscious, psychoanalysis ceases to be a sensible mode of retelling our desire; it just becomes a regulation and organisation of experience into relevant genres. Perhaps, this is nothing more than a sophisticated version of cognitive behavioural therapy. As Freud real-ised pretty early on just telling someone his Oedipal story through clever interpretations isn't going to work. Character, and history, as Freud saw only too clearly, are more intractable; hysterically defended we might say, from the dependency onto anything new or different. And yet, hysteria can be worked with in therapy more easily than any other personality neurosis or disorder. So, why is this? I want to suggest that the original desire and hunger for the mother's breast is inseparable from the equivalent need to find a form for that instinctual affect. For, the baby's cries of hunger are not immediately satisfied; there is always a gap between need and its satiation. So, the mother's face, her sounds, smells, and her bodily gestures, become a holding form that responds to the baby's hungry need to eat her. There is the breast that yields milk, although this breast can do nothing to provide the baby's screams with a form of expression. There is also, what Laplanche describes as the enigmatic signifying breast. Yet surely, the mother passes on more than internal alienation? And this is because the unconscious that passes between mother and child is not just repressed, it is also an unconscious that can receptively create. Thus it is the mother who responds to the baby's raw affects through her own sensibility; a mimetic close-up in rhythm with his bodily needs that provides him with some kind of very early organisation of the ego.

Hysteria and melodrama have much in common in the ways they can help us to understand the relationship between the unconscious, history and the re-making of cultural forms. The hysteric and the melo-dramatic character suffer, and their affects are always a bodily expres-sion in excess of the prevailing narrative reality. Linda Williams has developed Gledhill's understanding of melodrama as a protean and shifting modality to argue for the development of modernity as mel-odramatic. Far from being anti-realist, or some displaced subgenre of classic realist narrative (such as the women's film), melodrama eats up and appropriates new realist material all the time for its never satisfied project (Gledhill, 2000: p. 297). Melodrama seeks to fix moral legibility out of a mass of moral confusion and disarray, always trying to assert certainty and virtue at those points where everything is so uncertain. Through a rhetoric of bodily gesture, expression and muteness which is pictorial and metaphorical but never really within language, melo-drama searches for a truth and virtue that lies beyond words. Although

Williams is primarily concerned with mapping a history of American film and culture which has "talked to itself", through a white and black racialised melodramatic mode; many of her observations are relevant to my argument. She emphasises the innocence and pathos at stake in melodrama, juxtaposed with action, where the race is on to defeat time. In melodrama, virtue and innocence are saved "in the nick of time" or they are defeated in the pathos of the "too late". This rhythm backwards and forwards as a "transference" between present and past, is, more often than not, a return to the familiar. Although things seem to going forward they are always in effect racing backwards to recuperate lost innocence:

> The "main thrust" of melodramatic narrative, for all its flurry of apparent linear action. Is thus actually to get back to what *feels* like the beginning. (Williams, 2001: p. 35)

Search we might say, for the ego ideal, is always a return to sender. In hysteria and melodrama the crisis of idealisation, of the sentimental, is always that in the recuperation of the lost ideal we are faced by an inexorable super-ego that victimises. In one sense this is the crisis of the bourgeois individual, where self-mastery and moral certainty are meant to triumph over the otherness of something much more difficult to define. Melodrama, in this description is simply a hysterical externalisation of a normative Oedipal conflict, one where the suffering and expressive female or black body is repressed through a colonial, phallic law. But is melodrama always this same old script? Why can't it also be an undoing of those normative Hollywood ideals? Think of the films of Lars von Trier and Pedro Almodóvar; aren't these melodramas which remake passionate ideals in other ways? So, what makes the difference between melodrama as a tired and one-dimensional script and one in which new experience, we could say the dream experience, can be created?

Melodrama and hysteria, I suggest, are made up of affects in search of form, which can only be found in the response of the other. Linda Williams discusses how melodrama does not necessarily have to contain sensational scenes of pathetic death or victimhood to provoke tears in the spectator or audience. The "idea that each character in melodrama sounds a single emotional note that is in turn simply mimicked by the viewer" is too simplistic (Williams, 1998: p. 49). What matters, she argues, is the "feeling of loss suffused through form" (Williams,

1998: p. 70). Through our tears in the face of this loss, I suggest we respond through our own sensibility—we echo back the loss and pain, the raw articulation of affect in a way which produces more forms, arguably to a history beyond the frame of both screen and the present character/self of the viewer. If, as Williams remarks, we always identify beyond the crying character in a more complex way, I argue that this identification is with a more unknowable loss, located both within and beyond the one-dimensional character on stage or screen. It is in a sense the very superficiality of these characters, as archetypal types with no complex interiority, which allows us to project into them and beyond them. Thus, we elaborate their characters with our imagination, or identify with the aesthetics of the pictorial tableau, the music or bodily gestures, as we allow our feelings—forms of expression.

Melodrama can be conservative and nostalgic or it can lead somewhere different. Like hysteria it has a kind of reserve or excess force that in one culture is simply a return to powerless suffering and victimhood. And yet hysteria and melodrama have the affectual potential in another kind of culture to become something else. Perhaps, what women want, in answer to Freud's famous question, is a dependency that is not a malign regression. They want, in Ernst Kris's phrase "a regression in the service of the ego", a dependency that will lead to different stories and forms with which they can articulate themselves. So many of the women I see in therapy are very frightened of dependency and as a result their needs, sexual and emotional, become very obscure. I don't think we have to see the way Freud understood this dilemma as simply sexist, that is, women don't know what they want because they are too narcissistic. For women, historically, and indeed in our contemporary culture have always been subject to the demand that they conform to being beautiful, ideal, and good. And so moral sentiment for women, their manners of being, how they look and act, is often a regulation of what they need.

Regression to dependence is a real dilemma for women because women are divided between sacrifice and abjection, the ideal and the carnal. Risking dependency, where the only cultural forms available are about being beautiful, or sexy, or good, is sometimes just too terrifying. What women want is arguably a response from the other that will return and echo their desire in forms that enable them to play and remake their hysterical affects. But without the mobility of those affects and their stubborn insistence, there would be no response. Symptoms of depression, anxiety, and hysterical conversion are not simply something to be medicated, or regulated away with the right cognitive behavioural advice. They are the articulation of a suffering that is necessarily ongoing, an excess of the body, beyond the self, that needs to be storied, played, and worked through. And who is to say when this journey of turning affects into form is ever over?

Analysis, Freud eventually realised, is interminable. Indeed hysteria and the melodrama of character might be as necessary to the re-invention of ourselves and our culture, as it is a symptom of our refusal to yield, to any different or future sense of whom we can be. Melodrama is on one level the return of our first impressions: the return of the repressed. Melodrama, I suggest, can also be a way to move those passions beyond the self, through "aesthetics of the ego" which can qualitatively shape and sublimate its passions. For without these flexible aesthetic forms, the daughter in particular, remains in a state of abjection with regard to her mother. As Luce Irigaray has described, passions and melodramas must be elaborated through the painting of colours, sounds, and light in the clinical sessions. For her painting and elaborating the senses in art and therapy is a way of re-presenting perceptions and "building bridges between past, present and future" (Irigaray, 1993: p. 155). Another way of saying this is to say that our imaginative perceptions and senses of reality have to be put back in rhythm with our fantasies. We have to elaborate an "aesthetics of the ego", with which we can shape our passions and map them in conjunction with the world. Landscaping our passions builds connections between the unconscious topographies inside the ego and the virtual ones that surround us through our senses.[2]

Genre

We can think of hysteria and indeed melodrama to be privileged movers of social and historical genres. We don't have to see genre as simply a literary phenomenon, or as some fixed taxonomy and classification of inert cultural objects. Such a view of the universalising laws of literature and culture might have started off in neoclassical literary genres as immovable rules, but in our more modern times, genre is history and whatismore it is history in the making. "Genre is neither a property of (and located 'in') texts, nor a projection of (and located 'in') readers", according to John Frow, (Frow, 2006: p. 102). Rather it, "exists as a part of the relationship between texts and readers, and it has a systemic existence; It is a shared convention with a social force" (Frow, 2006: p. 102). Genre is therefore a practice of reading, it is something we do and as Carolyn Miller argues, genre is a recurring social and rhetorical action. What we learn from genre is,

> not just a pattern of forms or even a method of achieving our ends. We learn, more importantly, what ends we may have. … We learn to understand better the situations in which we find ourselves and the potential for failure and success in acting together. (Miller, 1984: p. 165)

Thus genre is integral to how we engage in the social order; it is the means of access to our desires. And this makes me think of how genre pertains to psychoanalysis. We have the law of the father which is read in Lacanian theory as some immoveable Oedipal injunction or No. We could say that the Oedipal complex in practice is arguably as much about how we read and re-remake the genres of our families and our sexualities, as it is about leaving them as some kind of unchangeable script. I have suggested in this book that our different selves, made, and elaborated through the ego, begin through the unconscious reading and translation of the mother; a figure that occurs and recurs as both a source of real satisfaction and as a virtual, non-psychological other. Genre structures the relationship between our minds and the society we live in through a repetition, a mimesis that begins with the mother and then repeats and translates into ongoing similarities and differences that we perform individually and culturally. But because genre is always being repeated, it is always subject to being read differently through changes to the acts and authorities of reading, but also through the simple action of time. And so with genre, whether that is a favourite movie or soap opera there is always the repetition of the same with the inevitable return of difference.

We like watching "Desperate Housewives" (or at least I do) on television because it is a familiar, but each episode brings enough difference to make it pleasurable. Even so we have to gain sufficient satisfaction from the show in the first place to be able to read that genre in the particular ways that make it the same and yet sufficiently different. James Bond films to me are much of a muchness, because they never really inspired me to identify with, or consume them in the first place.

And so it is with our mothers, that we begin identifying with them as something to consume and then read, but this mimesis is not simply a return of sameness because the mother's response over time returns difference and form to her child, with her gestures. In fact the whole relation of the melodramatic tableau between mother and child, or within the performance of melodrama on stage or screen, is arguably not just a punctuation of narrative but the juxtaposition between the fixed intensity of our passions and how they become replicated as a living form within the reader or spectator. So in this mimesis or play between similarity and difference, form is returned and becomes a new translation of our older and more familiar passions. The melodrama and the mimesis with our initial mother can be more or less generative in unconscious terms, a dead mother produces dead genres and arguably fixed translations of sexual difference. And yet the affects that are mobilised in the reading of melodramas, maternal or otherwise, are always in excess of the forms to contain them and this is a good thing, because it is this remainder and force that drive us forward in the search of new forms to elaborate our desires.

If genre structures what can be known and experienced in relation to our mother and beyond her in our cultural lives, then genre as social action produces that knowledge and reading of the world. Genres perform what Miller calls "exigence" a form of social understanding, "a mutual construing of objects, events, interests and purposes that not only links them but also makes them what they are" (Miller, 1984: p. 157). So a eulogy is the exigence which is the collective and formal response to death, and moreover it codes and carries individual mourning within a wider symbolic system, so producing shared meaning.

Maternal form and genre

We can understand genre in psychoanalysis to mean all the way in which our passions become coded and carried in relation to wider cultural forms. But where Miller calls genre a form of social practice I want simply to call genre a lived expressive form, initially found in the unconscious reading of the mother, where her affectual and social response becomes a kind of exigence that brings our rhetorical forms of the ego to life. Implicit in this understanding of our mother as a genre, is that she connects and is reproducible in relation to other women and mothers. This is of course central to Lacan's understanding of the father's name, the law of the phallus, in that it refers not to the actual father, but to a system of signifiers that are in a sense always beyond him. The collective and public meaning of motherhood is clearly of importance in acknowledging the nature of living genres and the actualisation of our desires. And yet there is arguably something in recent genre theory that can offer psychoanalysis another way of understanding the Oedipal complex, not just as a fixed gender classification; a hierarchy of the paternal signifier repressing and representing the mother's body. For a maternal genre, when it comes to our Oedipal conflicts would be the forms through which the melodramas of our primary passions can be moved and mixed.

For Derrida the law of genre is, "Genres are not to be mixed. I will not mix them" (Derrida, 1980: p. 55). When we hear the word genre, "a limit is drawn. And when a limit is established, norms and interdictions are not far behind". There is no law without the madness of desire and the female element of genre, according to Derrida. Any invocation of genre and the law is brought into being by transgression and contamination of what is feminine, a playing with the orders of genre that smacks of contamination, incest and monstrosity. The casualties, here, are the woman and her daughter, cast forever as the background, contingent event and bodily ground; a shadow that can infiltrate or destabilise the law but can't establish a separate space-time for the woman, or an encounter between the ideal and the carnal. Luce Irigaray sees this as a need for an ethics of sexual difference where the feminine is acknowledged within in its own specific and sexuate language. We can see this female genre as an early expressive maternal form, open to both sexes, in which the ego finds a style that does not partake of the binary oppositions, subject versus object; the inside and outside that is intrinsic to both the law of genre and its desire.

For what if the genres of our ego are dependent on a living maternal form as a primary means of mediation between our minds and the social sphere? What if before the advent of the law, before we access the land of desire with its supposed gatekeeper of the paternal phallus, we have to learn to read our mothers first? That it is the unconscious reading of our mothers that turns into a reading with, and a reading beyond them, producing the libidinal and aesthetic forms of the ego. This, then, is an early and relational narcissism, where an elaboration of the self is a kind of social and dramatic genre doing, and making. In this genre making with the mother, the ego melodramatically and hysterically performs its passions and symptoms in search of a similar form. And it is in the pleasurable sameness and difference with the mother and in the return of her forms that the self finds new styles to dress the ego. Melodrama, for example, morphs into the poetics of narrative realism where both the passionate self and the world outside become reconfigured.

We can see Derrida's law of genre as a constant breaking and transgression against some kind of fixed prohibition, the id versus the super-ego, or the madness of an unspeakable desire with the mother, excommunicated and yet always initialled by the paternal "No" that argues that generational and sexual difference cannot be mixed. Or we can see genre differently, as the ongoing reading and remaking of ourselves in relation to the forms of the mother, who serves as both a virtual type and a living response to the affects of the ego. After all, another way of reading Derrida's law is just to see it as a virtual entity or ideal that is always being formed and unformed in its particular conditions of historical contingency.

Genre, as Julie Rak and John Frow have both maintained, is always a repetition of sameness and difference. Rak follows Judith Butler in seeing gender as an effect of repetition where the performance "generates excess meaning that cannot be contained" (Rak, 2012: p. 30). Like gender, genre is a repetition of the familiar and an excess that is non-identical. But I want to see this excess as not simply meaning, but as a passionate force or a symptom. One that is always in search of a response from the cultural forms and virtual others that lend style, shape and the right aesthetic room for the creation and ongoing genre making of our egos. Repetition of gender, of our Oedipal femininity or masculinity, generates excess because it is performed and read in relation to a maternal form and genre, that will always be internalised as familiar and yet is also contingent on both historical and temporal difference. So a maternal genre might be different from the typological naming or "Name of the Father" in that it does not separate (castrate) the subject from its object, or the body from the symbolic. Maternal genre is never simply a naming of an individual self or type; it moves relationally, mixing affects with new forms; not so much the organiser of our repressed desires, as an earlier unconscious aesthetics of the ego, moving continually in rhythm backwards and forwards between passions and forms and between fantasy and the world.

All About My Mother

In his essay "Psychoanalysis and the Aesthetic Subject", Bersani argues for a similar account of a virtual unconscious, which constitutes not psychic depth, but a "continuation of a specific syntax of being" (Bersani, 2010: p. 148). Fantasy for Bersani is not a substitute for reality, or a developmental failure, but a sign of "an extremely attentive, highly individuated response to reality"; one which is not necessarily the product of repressed impulses, but situated on the threshold between "an invisible (and necessarily hypothetical) inner world and the world present to our senses" (Bersani, 2010: p. 148). Winnicott describes this simply in a notion studded throughout his writings, of the threshold between the fantasy and the real breast; the importance, here, being that these things occur simultaneously for the young child and allow him to move between them. Within the arena of early maternal care, passionate fantasy and the virtual forms of the non-psychological mother become mimetically replayed. Moving between fantasy and the world, the child mixes corresponding forms and affects in a dramatic realisation of reality.

The film *All About My Mother* is a melodrama and Bersani reads this film through a series of what he calls "loopings" or exchanges between the imaginary and the real (Bersani, 2004). And so instead of a Lacanian and fantasmatic structure of desire that subtends identity as a refusal of a connection with the world, Bersani persuasively argues that this film moves and plays outside the realms of the paternal law of desire and identity. Subject/object divisions, the male gaze and objectified femininity are all replaced by a playing and correspondence of forms that are not a defence against being in the world, but constitute openness to the intimacy it can offer. This film tells a story of lost fathers and sons, and of many mothers. Most of the men in the film are also women and this transexuality is played out in relation to Manuela, who as Bersani remarks is "everybody's mother". Loss in this film, Manuela's loss at the beginning of the film of her son Esteban, and her son's loss of his father Lola (who is a transsexual), is not a prerequisite of desire but of a kind of relational play which establishes new forms of intimacy and connection. In the light hearted party scene where Huma and Agrado (two transsexuals) visit Manuela who is looking after the HIV infected, pregnant Nun Rosa, the penis gets passed around in conversation as a subject of fun, sensual satisfaction, and hilarity. Not "something to be made fun of, but rather something to have fun with" remarks Bersani, and it is through his reading of this film we can see the phallus changing shape into something less powerful and castrating. Instead of the phallus that decides male and female identity, this more "naturalised" penis is a changing shape (more a body ego, than the symbolic), that moves both gender relations and relations between the women:

The many recurrences of the penis in this party of "women" says Bersani, "help to dephallicise it", as a castrating sign and object:

> Lola's penis, it's true, is at once an anomaly and a menace (she is, as Manuela says, not a person but an epidemic), but she can scarcely be said to represent phallic power and authority. And Agrado is anything but a phallic woman; she rather embodies the agreeable (as her name suggests) perspective on the penis as an attractive object of sensual and social interest, detaching it from fixed ideas of male and female identities. (Bersani, 2010: p. 78)

For Bersani there is an aesthetic subjectivity in Almovodar's films that does not so much challenge the law of the phallus as play beside it, and the stakes of the playing before and at the side of the law are different. After all, the search for a lost paternal identity is not abolished by this film. The grief over the dead son and his lost father are an absence which is not resolved or repaired by Bersani's aesthetic subjectivity and the relational intimacy between the many "women". Perversion in this film appears not as a short cut to desire, ruling out exchange with the other, but as an embodied form of play acting, where desire seems to run aground, and is then returned again through the humour, affection and sociability of the various "women". It is no fantasy that the transexual women in this film have a penis, but a reality. And yet where psychoanalysis places such perversions as erotic and hostile, enacting a disavowal of symbolic separation from the mother, in this film Manuela is the maternal figure and form which continually separates and then returns, to care for the other characters.

As a rhythm of living form, which unconsciously disappears and reappears, Manuela is the mother who leaves and refuses to stay with the different women in the film, only to return to them at a later date. Her care, we could say, is not unconditional, her presence is limited. When Rosa asks to be mothered, Manuela responds, "You have no right to ask me to be your mother. You already have one even if you don't like her". She finally agrees to take Rosa in only when the Nun finds herself pregnant and HIV positive. Manuela also becomes the personal assistant and understudy to Huma, the well known actress her son had tried to greet for an autograph before being killed by a car. But as soon as Manuela secures her position of looking after Huma, she rapidly replaces herself with Agrado, the friend she has rescued from her masochistic activities as a prostitute. And Manuela finally finds Lola, not to care for him, but to pass onto him the living story and photograph of her/his son.

All About My Mother mixes genders and genres, its aesthetics shapes intertwined with the familiar passions of a domestic melodrama; a theatre of the internal world that is staged in rooms, houses, and of course an actual theatre. The mimesis between what is fictional and real is played out in the film, with the moveable and matching roles and references to *A Streetcar Named Desire*. As a maternal form, Manuela is the train's rhythm taking her backwards and forwards between Madrid and her past in Barcelona, a movement between different spaces and times. The figure of Manuela also becomes crucial in providing the other characters with the necessary holding forms for their feelings as the melodramas in Barcelona, on stage and off, are played out.

At the beginning of the film we see Manuela giving her seventeen year old son his birthday present, Truman Capote's *Music for Chameleons*: a collection of short stories, both fictional and non-fictional, revealing Capote's painful childhood desires to be a girl. This is the clue that the son Estaban also wants to change shape to become a woman. His desire to elaborate this wish through the art of being a writer has a preface, one that has to be read to him by his mother. On receiving the present he says to Manuela, "Read me something like when I was little". And through Estaban's response to this reading we learn that he has begun writing a story about his mother. In the melodrama of *All About My Mother*, there is a maternal form embodied by the figure of Manuela that is read and re-translated between her and the other characters. Instead of a fixing of passionate forms into split oppositions of rigid gender and moral polarities, *All About My Mother* recreates melodrama's passions into new aesthetic forms. Manuela is the suffering maternal protagonist who refuses to be sacrificial; it is her loving lies and deceit, rather than her moral virtue that wins through.

Authenticity in this film is a creative sense of the self which has nothing to do with being original or singular, but captures the ability of passions to find the requisite imaginative forms to shape them. When Agrado finally gets her star role on stage, she proceeds to tell us her life story; the personal history of her performance; paid for through gender changing surgery: her silicone breasts, jaw reduction and almond eyes. Agrado insists to the audience that she is very authentic, meaning that she feels most at home in the "self" she has performed and artistically helped to create. And yet Agrado's melodramatic performance needs aesthetically sculpting and I would argue that it is only fully realised through the unconscious reading and holding of Manuela's intimacy and love. Agrado says to the audience and to us, "Because you are more authentic, the more you resemble what you've dreamed you are". Authenticity, here, is not the place from which we start, it is who we can become; a re-imagination of the self between dreams and reality.

At the end of the film when Manuela finally re-encounters Lola at Rosa's funeral, she passes on to her/him the notebook and photograph of his son Esteban. As Lola reads, s/he weeps at the expression of this son's longing to know him as a father. Bersani notes how the close up of Lola's face pulls us mimetically in as spectator's to witness his/her tears, and then pushes us away through a staged tableau, as Lola's hands with their long painted finger nails half cover her face. "Everything is real and everything is false", says Bersani, wondering if this close-up makes the choice between fantasy and the reality irrelevant. But there is also something more to this, because through the close up we are mimetically transfixed by Lola's tears, they arrest us precisely because they are frozen in time; a repetitive and repressed past or melancholy that can't be re-imagined in terms of current reality. I think Lola's close-up shows us the fixity of our familiar passions, the melodramatic split between fantasy and reality, which is then brought into motion and a new rhythm with the maternal form of Manuela carrying her son's stories. It is this living form which returns the same old rhythm and transference of melodrama in a different key; one that does not simply carry us back to the preferred fixed forms of our past, but moves these passions within a new pulse of experience.

If the performance in this film, the many parts and theatrical re-plays, make up the dream script, then it is the maternal form of Manuela that moves beyond representation to create a future that can't be known but can be lived, as a dream experience. The film closes with another close-up of a woman's face (who is also a man), that of Huma, leaving her friends to go on stage. As she turns to address both them and us (the audience) with the words, "I will be back"..., we know that our passions, however painful and tragic will be returned, and yet we don't know how they will develop, in their encounter with the changing maternal forms and social bonds of Almodovar's many women.

We move in rhythm from our bodily affects, to maternal form, to language and then back again. The suggestion of these forms interacts with our melodramatic passions. Oedipal femininity and masculinity, the division between subject and object are the fixation of our passions; their flight back home to familiar places. And yet these old melodramas and fantasies can be made to move again within our unconscious reading of lived form that is found in the ego's relation to its virtual other. As Bersani tells us, the non-fantasmatic imaginary in *All About Our Mother* is an aesthetic subjectivity which reaches out to reality. For me, this imaginary is the artworks of an ego in its relation to a maternal form; one which is found initially in the similar (but not identical) mimetic response of the early mother.

Thus the aesthetic play of relational intimacy between Almodovar's women is a reading and working of unconscious maternal form that helps carry and re-shape the passions of the protagonists into new experiences of intimacy. What I want to add to Bersani's cogent argument is the significance of the non-personal mother in this film in returning passionate forms, and our role in reading her in similar but different ways. Within the attunement and a playful mimesis with the early mother an unconscious correspondence and creation of forms aesthetically structures the ego's early being. The imaginary of this egoic being is not just fantasmatic in Lacan's sense, but exists in accord with reality, in a recreational exchange occurring before the symbolic moment of castration and subjectivity. So, in psychoanalytic terms the early mother has a non-psychological function as a form and genre that moves in rhythm with our passions, disappearing into unconsciousness and reappearing like the character of Manuela, as it reworks desire within new forms of being and relationality. Almodavar shows us the rhythms at stake in unconsciously reading film as a living and dreaming form (or screen) which aesthetically replays and moves our Oedipal melodramas in relation to the changing genres of a shared sociability beyond the self.

Conclusion

In the clinical session, this maternal form is in operation within the unconscious correspondence between analyst and client, elaborating the melodrama of the sessions in ways that don't just revisit the preferred, seemingly timeless passions of our past, but also return us to the historicity of our futures. Unconscious reading of maternal form goes hand in hand with the erotic transference; it is the essential ingredient in kneading, mediating, and reworking the transferential past. Therapy, I suggest, is not simply a matter of disabusing people of their imaginary fantasies; it contains something real, in the artistic and unconscious reading of our mothers. What is the question of the mother as a genre in, *All About My Mother*? Bersani writes,

> "Mother" is both present and already lost everywhere; its presence in its lostness, the unlocatable and unsettled nature of its referent and attributes. Repeatable being—being that continuously fails to be unique—creates a hospitable world of correspondences, one in which relations no longer blocked by difference, multiply as networks of similitudes. (Bersani, 2010: p. 80)

In the melodrama of life and in the clinical scene, we encounter the stand-off between our familiar passionate fantasies and a world which we can't relate to in pleasurably different ways. And it is the unconscious reading of lived maternal form which can help move and recreate those passions; mediating and transforming the relation between the mother's body and the paternal symbolic (or between the carnal and the ideal). This transference of work and play is not so much the naming of desire, or the father, as a mixing of it, with new aesthetic and social possibilities of whom we can both love and be.

Notes

1. See my "Rhythms of the Suggestive Unconscious" *Subjectivity*, 6.4: 29–49, where I argue for a suggestive, virtual and non-psychological unconscious as a historical force that is present both within Freud's and Henri Bergson's work. This virtual unconscious is distinct from the repressive personal unconscious in the sense that is a non-repressed suggestive landscape that both surrounds us and runs through us.

2. The plasticity and fixity of the ego is discussed by Freud in different contexts. In *Mourning and Melancholia* he describes the ego as split and raging against itself, whereas in *The Ego and the Id* the ego is unconsciously perceptive and a projection of a bodily surface. We can think of the ego as a shape-shifter whose shapes and forms are both fixed and moveable in relation to the virtual worlds of reality. See Jan Campbell and Steve Pile's *Space travels of the Wolfman: Phobia and its Worlds* in *Psychoanalysis and History*, 2010.

CHAPTER SIX

Sympathies beyond the self in *Daniel Deronda*

I n the famous opening lines of George Eliot's *Daniel Deronda*, we are introduced to the question of Gwendolen Harleth's moral virtue:

> Was she beautiful or not beautiful? And what was the secret of form
> or expression which gave the dynamic quality to her glance? Was
> the good or the evil genius dominant in those beams? Probably the
> evil; else why was the effect that of unrest rather than of undis-
> turbed charm? Why was the wish to look again felt as coercion and
> not as a longing to which the whole being consents? (Eliot, 1999:
> p. 35)

Gwendolen raises these questions in Daniel Deronda's and the reader's mind. And of course, then as now, the question of a women's virtue is a sentiment on which society relies and turns. Are women beautiful, or do they just appear so? And what does being beautiful as a woman, or a man, really mean? In *Daniel Deronda*, Gwendolen's charm and good looks are surface phenomenon. They are at odds with her rather narrow and personal sense of what exists beyond the self. George Eliot writes dubiously of her supposed heroine:

> Could there be a slenderer, more insignificant thread in human history that this consciousness of a girl, busy with her small inferences of the way in which she could make her life pleasant?—In a time, too, when ideas were with fresh vigour making armies of themselves, and the universal kinship was declaring itself fiercely. (Eliot, 1999: p. 159)

Gwendolen's narcissism, her preoccupation with her personal self, is part of the sheltered existence of the Victorian, white, middle-class woman. Eliot presents this "Angel in the House", as a paragon of beauty, but necessarily one of questionable virtue. Indeed, Gwendolen's ignorance, her inability to be curious of anything outside of her own private enclosed sphere is her biggest flaw. And yet, Gwendolens's narcissism is also nothing more or less, than the agency of Freud personal ego. One that recognises and represses everything loved as the owned self, where what is not claimed as being similar is excluded as a hostile other. So, in many ways Eliot's question "Was she beautiful or not beautiful?" is also a question for our time, when modern capitalism's demand for the personal, self-regulated self seems increasingly to relegate real possibilities of a sympathy for anything beyond self, as at best conflicted.

In Lauren Berlant's view there is nothing either simple or clear about sympathy or compassion, they can be judged ethically as neither good nor bad, "just that they derive from social training, emerge at historical junctures, are shaped by aesthetic conventions, and take place in scenes that are anxious, volatile, surprising, and contradictory" (Berlant, 2005: p. 7). For Berlant and the writers in her recent volume entitled *Compassion: The Culture and Politics of an Emotion*, compassion is "an *emotion in operation*. In operation, compassion is a term denoting privilege: the sufferer is *over there*" (Berlant, 2005: p. 4). As Neil Hertz has pointed out, George Eliot refuses to feel compassion for her heroines' stupidity and the best advice he can give to those characters on the end of the narrator's sympathy is to "Duck" (Hertz, 2005: p. 87). In *Daniel Deronda*, that refusal culminates in the cruel abandonment of Gwendolen by Deronda at the end of the novel. And yet arguably sympathy for Gwendolen is complex; indeed, it is the complexity of Gwendolen's character that shapes our sympathy as readers, giving it different forms, at different times, within differing perspectives and contexts. The idea that suffering is always placed at a distance, personified by somebody else, when it comes to the question of how society imagines its sensibility, makes melodrama arguably central in understanding how passions circulate. How passions evolve or don't evolve, within sensibilities that are historically inscribed. And yet as Freud describes so well, the culturally inscribed passions of the super-ego often militate against the more primitive sensations of the unknowable id. Some emotions, after all, are newer and less socially trained than others. Melodrama instigates an unleashing of the most ferocious super-ego in all of us; an unleashing of passion and drive that the most reasonable ego, (inherent within ego psychology or literary realism) simply can't manage or resolve. In this chapter, I want to consider the unmanageable passions intrinsic to melodrama, and how they circulate within both literature and psychoanalysis.[1]

Melodrama and vision

In her essay "Silly Novels by Lady Novelists" Eliot spells out the melodramas that silly women write, full of starring heroines, "usually a heiress"; dazzling all and sundry, beautiful in mind and morals, and surrounded by Rakish men falling about in "impotent confusion at her repartees". This heroine suffers terribly of course at the hands of evil baronets or the wrong husbands and yet whatever misfortunes or

> vicissitudes she may undergo, from being dashed from her carriage to having her head shaved in fever, she comes out of them all with a complexion more blooming and locks more redundant than ever. (Eliot, 1963: p. 303)

Eliot's contempt for melodrama is a familiar sensibility. What literary scholar today chooses the emotional sentimentality or outpourings of Dickens and D.H. Lawrence over the more aesthetic impressions of Woolf or Joyce? And yet melodrama is at the heart of the great psychological novels of Henry James, acceptable here because of its tempering through a deeper, we might say a more repressed, aesthetic literary form. Great writers, insists Eliot content "themselves with putting their experience into fiction, and have thought it quite sufficient to exhibit men and things as they are" (Eliot, 1963: p. 304). And this belies the passionate and ideal forms that pepper Eliot's own literature; passions that finally break out into the melodrama of her final novel *Daniel Deronda*. Eliot's realism, we could say, is more, much more than a kind of faithful copy of the real world. Her novels don't just merely repress or manage passions; they re-imagine passionate ideals in relation to reality.

And just like Freud's reality principle where reality means an exchange between fantasy and the real, a reconfiguration of our ideals and dreams in terms of the world, so in Eliot's fiction true sympathy is evoked by attention to the reality of the object along with a more imaginative reconfiguration through its more virtual powers. In other words the ideal attributes of the object are inferred imaginatively in images that both meet and supersede what is materially given. Eliot's work has been seen as a marker of literary realism, as a faithful mimesis or window onto the world. And yet reality is not just found in Eliot's novels, like Winnicott's transitional object, it is also actively and imaginatively made. George Henry Lewes, Eliot's lover and life partner shared many of her ideas about art and literature. In *The Principles of Success in Literature* Lewes ponders on the vision integral to literature; a vision in which perceiving the object is always, as Freud said about the mother's breast, a re-presentation. For, the breast/object carries with it the suggestions of the original experience, without which the infant would not be able to infer that the actuality of the object in front of him was the right fit for his hunger and desire. Similarly then for the reader, perception, Lewes writes,

> as distinguished from Sensation, is the presentation before Consciousness of the details which once were present in conjunction with the object at this moment affecting Sense. These details are inferred to be still in conjunction with the object, although not revealed to Sense. (Lewes, 1898: p. 29–30)

Without some form or mental vision of the breast, arguably it would be a continuing mystery, or so enigmatic as to be a complete alien. And for this vision to be apparent, the breast or the work of literature must remind us of earlier and actual satisfactions. In order to desire an object, it has to carry virtual powers of suggestion. These suggestions of the real remind us of the sensations previously encountered. As Lewes says,

> The apparent facts disclose the facts that are unapparent. Inference is only a higher form of the same process. We look from the window, see the dripping leaves and the wet ground, and infer that rain has fallen. (Lewes, 1898: p. 30)

And so we don't just copy nature or the objects we encounter in any literal way, we actively imagine them and this is achieved by the ability to fit our experience and passions to the virtual images generated by the object. Through the virtual powers of the other we "render the invisible, visible by imagination" (Lewes, 1898: p. 30). But what has this theory of aesthetic realism got to do with melodrama?

Daniel Deronda was Eliot's last novel, but was not seen as an artistic success. Rather it has historically been seen more like a first underdeveloped penmanship. Initially the novel of promise, after her runaway success with *Middlemarch*, Daniel Deronda excites and then disappoints its critics, because of its melodramatic excess, or as Henry James opines, the novel's simplicity, its manifestation as a diagram rather than an imaginative picture. Because our passions and affects are always in search for available forms and types with which they can express themselves, then literature becomes a living form of reading old passions in new, imaginative ways. And melodrama is central to this enterprise, because it is a manifestation of both the failure and the success of being able to re-imagine our passions. Melodrama is the vehicle, or cultural form, through which raw passions meet virtual types and becomes fixed in familiar senses as the same old genres, or become liberated into new aesthetic possibilities of whom we can be.

Gwendolen's passions

I want to consider the circulation of Gwendolen's sensations and her sensibilities, the question of her moral virtue, in relation to the sympathetic attunement extended to her by the narrator, other characters and us as readers. If compassion is an emotion in operation, so too is hysteria a melodrama of affect on the move, arguably in search of differing responses. The question of Gwendolen's madness has of course been one that divides psychoanalysis from more so-called historical genealogies of trauma and sexuality. And yet, it is the relationship of melodramatic form, in particular, what I call an unconscious maternal aesthetic, that can read the Freudian unconscious and lived history together.[2] We are made aware of the habits of Gwendolen's mind, of her narcissism, early on in the novel, when we learn, "it had been taken for granted that she knew what was admirable and she was herself admired" (Eliot, 1999: p. 40). The portrayal of Gwendolen as a "spoiled child" who has always believed "that her destiny must be one of luxurious ease" is also a picture of Narcissus kissing her reflection in the mirror and chasing any sorrow away:

> Her beautiful lips curled into a more and more decided smile, till at last she took off her hat, leaned forward and kissed the cold glass which had looked so warm. How could she believe in sorrow? If it attacked her, she felt the force to crush it, to defy it, or run away from it, as she had done already. Anything seemed more possible that she could go on bearing miseries, great or small. (Eliot, 1999: p. 47)

Gwendolen's miseries are born of Freud's family romance, her play of being "the princess in exile", and her "inborn energy of egoistic desire", originally located in childhood displacement with the loss of her father, and her mother's depression (Eliot, 1999: p. 71). The horror at her family's financial ruin is thus a later repeat of this cruel disappointment, adding further fuel to Gwendolen's desire to replace her relatives with those of "higher social standing" (Freud, 1909b: p. 239).

Grandcourt arrives as the wished for "Lord of the Manor" and yet his coldness in many ways simply matches Gwendolen's mirror image. He has married her quite literally, for her appearance, and in order to acquire a wife that he can master as belonging to him. Like Grandcourt, Gwendolen's "confidence lies chiefly in herself" she feels "well equipped for the mastery of life" (Eliot, 1999: p. 69). And yet their marriage is not just a triumph of the bourgeois conquering ego, it is also a perversion in the sense that it is something that cannot alter, or permit exchange. Grandcourt is the epitome of evil mastery, a coloniser and a serpent, the "white handed man with the perpendicular profile" and a propensity to exterminate rather than persuade "superseded proprietors" (Eliot, 1999: p. 656). In the face of this perverted ideal, Gwendolen's hysterical rebellion comes to the fore. Before her marriage Gwendolen won't have anything to do with suffering, especially her mother's, insisting "mine is only a happy nose" (Eliot, 1999: p. 57). Such determination to be happy is part and parcel of her refusal to feel, or depend, on anyone else. When Rex makes love to her, the perception that he "wanted to be tender made her curl up and harden like sea—anemone at the touch of a finger" (Eliot, 1999: p. 113). With dawning clarity, Gwendolen cries out to her mother, "I shall never love anybody. I can't love people. I hate them" (Eliot, 1999: p. 115). Her terror of dependency and love manifests itself in clinging to a mother whom she has never seemingly needed in the past:

> She said brokenly, 'I can't bear anyone to be near me than you'.
> Then the mother began to sob, for this spoiled child had never
> shown such dependence on her before. (Eliot, 1999: p. 115)

The melodrama of *Daniel Deronda* is one that puts pressure on the real, staging and dramatising Oedipal sexual difference and the bourgeois individual ego, in all of its hysterical opposition and Manichean conflict. Eliot's critique of the Oedipal sensibilities that regulate Victorian society and marriage illuminates this conflict. A struggle played out, not just over the woman's moral virtue (the question of Gwendolen Harleth's innocence or evil), but through a much more dynamic conflict and movement between passions and their available aesthetic sensibilities. As readers, we are made aware of Gwendolen's "unusual sensibility" early on—her hysterical attack when a secret panel in her house opens suddenly, revealing the painting of an upturned dead face and a figure running from it outstretched (Eliot, 1999: p. 26). Death, then, in place of sorrow is a repression that becomes unlocked: the horror that is the heart of completely egoic character. Feeling in a bearable form can only exist through the sympathy of another, and perhaps it is only by suffering our passion that we can get beyond to the nonpersonal potential that lies outside of the ego and within the other.

Daniel Deronda has been much criticised for being two stories, being as Frank Leavis remarks, a great story about Gwendolen Harleth and a terrible one about Daniel Deronda (Leavis, 1962). If the characters of Deronda, Mirah and Mordecai are simplistic and idealistic, nothing much more than a melodramatic type or diagrammatic sketch, then this also allows these characters, Deronda's, at any rate, to function as potential forms. As an unknowable and non-personal type, Deronda functions as a virtual other to Gwendolen; a possible sympathetic form that can echo and return to her, possible forms for her passions. If our death drives are affects in excess of any available representation, then Freud informs us, our life drives are the possibility of returning and exchanging those affects with reality, And to exchange them, there needs to be an available and responsive form. In the novel these responsive sensibilities are hardly carried by the signifying phallus, the white perpendicular Mr. Grandcourt. Rather, it is Deronda whom embodies a sensible and sympathetic response to Gwendolen, when she finally can admit her need for love and affection:

> You said affection was the best thing, and I have had hardly any-none about me. If I could I would have mamma; but that is impossible. Things have changed me so- in such a short time. What I used not to like, I long for now. I think I am almost getting fond of the old things now they are gone. (Eliot, 1999: p. 500)

Character and melodrama always take us back to familiar faces and forms. In this novel the first encounter between Gwendolen and Daniel is followed by a flashback, where we trace the action of Gwendolin's escape from Grandcourt. But of course Gwendolen is racing to defeat time, to get back to "the before" of her suffering, where she can recuperate lost innocence. If the encounters between Gwendolen and Daniel can be seen as therapeutic encounters, and arguably they can; then Gwendolen's pathos, her suffering, is a hysterical repeat not simply of her current unhappy marriage, but of something much older and too painful to remember. Anything coming back to life, hurts, and the form Daniel offers Gwendolen is acknowledgement of her pain as necessity:

> Take the present suffering as a painful letting in of the light' said Deronda most gently. 'You are conscious of more beyond the round of your inclinations- you know more of the way in which your life presses on others, and their life on yours. I don't think you could have escaped the painful process in some form or other.' 'But it is a very cruel form', said Gwendolen, beating her foot on the ground with returning agitation. 'I am frightened of everything. I am frightened of myself. (Eliot, 1999: p. 500)

How do we know, as Berlant asks, what constitutes sympathetic agency? When is sympathy really an aesthetic agency and response that can generate new forms? Or when is sympathy simply a more conservative compassion which is no "more than a demand on consciousness, more than a demand to feel right"? (Berlant, 2005: p. 4). It is worth thinking just what kind of analyst Deronda would have made and the answer is probably terrible, just as wooden and prudish as he appears in the novel. Not like Freud, certainly, who might sometime have fallen short of being a sympathetic poet, but nevertheless always espoused his own intrinsically literary forms.

More archetype, than newly embodied sensibility, Deronda seems stuck in some intellectualised and transcendental version of the good, dishing out clever pre-Oedipal interpretations, when what Gwendolen needs is a returning of her forms to her; a mimesis that echoes her, not language that alienates. In a Victorian society where sexual difference represses the maternal body under the phallus, a normative Oedipal form simply offers one route out to the world. This one-way mirror, as Luce Irigaray suggests, can do nothing to connect carnal and transcendental, for the woman. Because what women need is to be returned through their mother's gaze in relation to a maternal aesthetic that is always more plural, always more playful than the dominant Oedipal account can achieve. Returning the daughter her desire in aesthetic forms that can play and reproduce is the function of a two-way mirror that can embody a maternal aesthetic. And surely the daughter is not the only child who needs this poet of a mother? Arguably everyone needs a poetic retranslation of their Oedipal story, in different guises and characters. So, is this dilemma really any different today? For some contemporary cultures the Victorian forms of sexual difference that regulate women to a separate sphere need little translation. In western culture women have their sensibilities defined by the market; their passions and their bodies are traded for the literal sameness of economic exchange.

Unfortunately for Gwendolen, Deronda as analyst and substitute mother is less of a poet and more of a prig. Too certain of his religious and cultural views, he is unable to make his ideas into a more dreamy experience. Deronda's response to Gwendolen is intellectual and mystical. Although at times Deronda displays a many sided and flexible sympathy, his sensibilities lack passionate force. Liable to fall in with "that reflective analysis which tends to neutralise sympathy", he ends up telling Gwendolen to keep her feelings to herself (Eliot, 1999: p. 500). Urging her to find her own form for her feelings he says, "Keep your dread fixed on the idea of incurring that remorse which is so bitter to you. Fixed meditation may do a great deal towards defining our longing or dread.... Try to take hold of your sensibility, and use it as if it were a faculty, like a vision." Gwendolen whispers back:

> But if feelings rose—there are some feelings—hatred and anger—
> how can I be good when they keep rising? And if there came a

moment when I felt stifled and could bear it no longer'—She broke off, and with agitated lips looked at Deronda, but the expression on his face pierced her with an entirely new feeling. He was under the baffling difficulty of discerning, that what he had been urging on her was thrown into the pallid distance of mere thought before the outburst of habitual emotion. It was as if he saw her drowning while his limbs were bound. (Eliot, 1999: p. 501)

His compassion invites guilt and reparation but does nothing to return her desire. For Deronda, as a man, or as Gwendolen's therapist, can only do sympathy without desire attached, and his failure to be Gwendolen's dream man is telling. Telling her to be good, when what Gwendolen wants is not Buddhist meditation, or educative talks, but for Deronda to implicate himself in her desire. As a lover of lost causes, Deronda remains a super (egoic) man, whilst she, on the other hand, needs him to perform and form and return her passion, so she can make her affects into the right dream experience.

Dreams and melodrama

As Michael Booth puts it, melodrama,

is a dream world inhabited by dream people and dream justice, offering audiences the fulfilment and satisfactions found only in dreams. An idealisation and simplification of reality, it is, in fact, what its audiences want and cannot get. (Booth, 1965: p. 14)

As a dream world, both ideal and simple, melodrama dramatises the violence and the clash between good and evil. But melodrama is never simply wonderland; it is always in tension with the real, as a modality that is constantly re-organising its cultural value. Dramatising the gap between the dream experience and its textual meaning, nineteenth century melodrama stages affects that are in excess of the available representational forms. In order for melodrama to be more than sentimental, wishes have to be made to work. Dream wishes escape back, but they work forwards and yet how to do they work?

I think we can see dream work, not just as repression, or the interpretation of an analytic session, but as the translation of our instinctual needs into the unknowable forms that are borrowed from someone else. This dream work turns wishes into a bearable dream experience.

Dream wishes, according to Freud, are our instinctual demands turned into hallucinations, or fantasies of what we believe will fulfil our desire. If the baby, wishes for and hallucinates the mother on her own, dream work takes two. Real exchange with the mother, the test of her, is then both the real satisfaction she brings and her presence as a wished for object. Because as Freud says, however good the mother, something necessarily goes wrong with our first dream wishes, and that is a good thing, because without this initial disappointment, without this first trauma or melodrama, we would never go looking for reality. The child has to find the mother, over and over again, and what makes this game, the Fort Da game, so important is that it keeps the child going in his searching. Before the child finds language, there is arguably an earlier version of this game, where the mother attunes herself to her baby's affects, mirroring back forms, which enables the baby to begin to structure his needs. Mirroring, as a maternal reflection of aesthetic form, is not feeding and it is not sameness; it is a mimesis, which echoes desire and returns it as being both the same and different.

Mimesis between the child and holding mother generates internal forms, as a kind of dream experience that operates both inside and out. Christopher Bollas talks of evocative and transformational objects that might begin with the mother, but then extends to everyday life, through which we can dream ourselves into being. Losing ourselves inside this simple dream experience, so we can elaborate internal forms, is dependent on maternal containment. And yet if the mother's attunement is simply just an ability to empathise with her baby's needs, then her response, however poetic, or playful, is perhaps always going to be slightly out of reach, a bit too ideal to respond to the baby's force of demand. For the mother has to desire, to love, and hate the baby; just in the way that the baby desires, loves, and hates the mother. Freud was unequivocal about this: free association and dream-work lead to repressed desire. Desire might have to dress up as a dream, in order to get what it wants, and that costume or play might make those passions more bearable and shareable, or more elusive and mysterious, but the dream, or the poem, or the returning smile of the mother are what carries the desire, they can't replace it.

Melodramas beyond the self

Melodrama, knows this, and so perhaps it is not surprising that in so much melodrama, wishes abound in a dream script but there is not much dream experience. Everything turns on the repression and expression of tortuous passions. Reception and sympathy, meanwhile, are often left to the audience or the spectator. We emotionally respond to Gwendolen's suffering, in the face of Grandcourt's indifference, and Deronda's school-masterly sermons. It is through our form of emotional response that arguably her story gets shaped. Grandcourt is the quintessential villain of domestic melodrama, individualistic and unfeeling. We are told that Grandcourt's passions are of the "intermittent flickering kind", and that there is no question of Gwendolen really loving him (Eliot, 1999: p. 169). At best, she says, "he really is not disgusting" (Eliot, 1999: p. 358). Gwendolen's hysteria and her malign passion are evoked through the stark imperviousness of her husband. His complete mastery of self, his unavailability is, if not attractive, convenient for Gwendolen as his characteristics mirror her own determined self-reliance. Gwendolen's childish desire to please herself, her desire to get back to the time before she was displaced and disappointed, is of a piece with her refusal to depend on another. Grandcourt's villainy and Gwendolen's narcissism match, because they both believe intrinsically in the certain power of their egos, and yet, as Gwendolen meets her double her suffering begins, she starts to want all the things she had forgotten she wished for.

Melodrama dramatises the struggles between super-ego and id, and between good and evil; it expresses and transposes an internal scene, as social experience. It shows us all the ways in which a culture behaves, how its sympathies are always in tension between passions that are out of control and a more sanctioned sensibility. As circulating affects and passions that are in excess of shared language and culture, melodrama exposes contradiction and exerts force on established codes of morality. In nineteenth century melodrama, innocence has to develop into recognition of moral virtue; narcissism has to be exchanged for the right ego ideal. Melodrama and hysteria break out when moral virtue and the ego ideal are found to be floundering, or at risk. And morality is re-established through recognition of the good, the heroine's virtue. This virtue is agony, a kind of passionate self-immolation, which precipitates choice. And so in Henry James's novels, heroines, in true hysterical fashion, make a final sacrifice to maintain the dominant culture of manners. Isabel Archer's decision to return to her dreadful husband and Milly Theale's death are both a resurrection of a shared ego ideal. James makes us see this, but he also makes us see the terrible passions that are left behind, un-translated: the "unconscious moral abyss".

The paradox of passion is that it undoes the ego, exposing the ultimate separation of the individual from shared experience. It is in our suffering that we discover the radical disjunction between our desires and a world that might bear them. And yet if passion marks a break from social existence, it is also the nature of passions, their immediacy and transparency that make them shareable. Passions, bring the lie to the personal ego, in the sense that they are always in motion, betraying the ego's mastery, dissolving its preferred forms. And it is passion that is always on the move beyond the confines of any form of ego or object that might seek to contain it. Eliot's Gwendolen Harleth is different from James's heroines in the sense that there is no individual resolution or choice available to her. Gwendolen's hysteria is more threatening, more working class we could say, than Isabel's or Milly's, because for Gwendolen the necessary ideal that will give a form to her suffering lies in the shared response of someone else.

Peter Brooks argues that psychoanalysis can explain melodrama; the analyst after all is there to interpret and explain the hysteric. And yet hysteria and melodrama refuse any explanation in terms of the individual ego. Melodrama shows us, most strikingly, how the unconscious is always the terrain of the social. The force of melodramas affects, of the hysteric's passions is that they are always in motion and in search of a more sociable and shared form to their feelings. Melodrama leads us beyond the personal self to our potential being in the response of the other. In Thomas Elsaesser's marvellous expression, melodrama "punctuates narrative" with its music, its colour, and emotional polarity. Melodrama, like hysteria "bubbling all the time just below the surface" is what moves the story along; its rhythm is what moves feeling and meaning from one person to the next (Elsaesser, 1987: p. 53).

The super-ego or art as a question of form

The character Deronda, who is also perhaps a double for author and narrator, operates as a potential respondent to Gwendolen's needs and wishes. Gwendolen is a master of herself in so many ways, but she is an amateur when it comes to singing. If music and song can return and reflect passions to the self in differing forms, we learn that Gwendolen has missed out on this important imitation of Art in early life. Murdering her sister's canary because of its shrill singing, Gwendolen grows up to be told by Herr Klesmer that she has not been well taught:

> You produce your notes badly', he says 'that music which you sing is beneath you. It is a form of melody which expresses a puerile state of culture—a dangling canting, see-saw stuff—the passion and thought of people without any breadth of horizon. (Eliot, 1999: p. 51)

This wound to an exceptional sense of "self", is later reinforced by Daniel when he urges Gwendolen to take up singing again under the tutelage of her rival, Miss Lapidoth. Everyone, he reminds her, can benefit from this "good model of feminine singing" as a "little improvement on the ordinary style" (Eliot, 1999: p. 491). Gwendolen objects, "I don't feel able to follow your advice of enjoying my own middlingness". All one can do, Daniel responds is to try, but Art must be the reserve of those excellent at it. Feeling ever more insignificant Gwendolen asks, "But then if we can't imitate it?" Only as an act "of private devotion or … study" is Daniel's rejoinder. Practising art, it seems, is for the few and not the many (Eliot, 1999: p. 491).

What are we to make of this? To be excellent at singing in public is arguably an ideal that will give Gwendolen, passion, breath, and horizon. Like the wished for admiration and love she so desperately wants from Daniel, it will remake her ego ideal and her passions through the forms reflected back from another. Scornfully, Deronda rejects the idea that art can be such a vehicle for the social enlargement of the self. Gwendolen wants Deronda to be her own ideal lover, to reflect her passion with an answering love that, will in turn, make it like art, so she can take to the stage, as it were, with her singing. And yet Daniel refuses her this, referring her in the cruellest manner to her most unobtainable feminine ideal. Be good, Daniel's compassion tells Gwendolen, and be guilty, but don't allow your passions the aesthetic forms and ideals which will enable them to sing you into the world. Daniel is clearly the kind of man who thrives on women's misery; when Gwendolen accuses him of being satisfied with her wretchedness, he says:

> those who would have been comparatively uninteresting before-hand may become worthier of sympathy, when they so something that wakens in them a keen remorse. (Eliot, 1999: p. 494)

Losing himself in "his vision of what Gwendolen's experience has been, and urged by compassion" Daniel "let his eyes and voice express as much interest as they would". Confronted with this rather sadistic sympathy, Gwendolen slips "onto the music-stool, and looked up at him with pain in her long eyes, like a wounded animal asking help" (Eliot, 1999: p. 495).

Guilt does nothing to alleviate hysteric pain, for Gwendolen it merely strengthens her super-ego injunctions of self reliance. Guilt or remorse can't remake passions or return them as art, or sing them into something that is more sociable and varied. Hysteria as Freud realised, is a communication and story told through the body. And maybe all therapeutic encounters are punctuated through with melodrama, where bodily gestures, silence, musical tone and the rhythm of passion and plot are indeed what moves things along. So much of the clinical discussion about therapy is about being caring, about the competition, of who can care the most, the most quickly, the most thoughtfully and so on. And yet maybe the role of the therapist has to mix sympathy with artistic sensibility. Sympathy and self-reflection do not by themselves recreate passions. Indeed as in Daniel Deronda's case, they position suffering over there, compassion works to save the victimised other. Such reparation, shores up the analyst's goodness (along with her guilt), but does nothing to awake a poetry of ideas and affects that move between self and other.

Ego ideals or the unconscious reading of our mothers

Re-configuration of our passions and our past within present reality, therapy or Eliot's fiction, depends on an unconscious lived form; one which returns and shapes melodrama and the hysterical ego within a maternal aesthetic sensibility. The famous theorist of the melodramatic tableau, Denis Diderot, argues that within the tableau, action is suspended, and whilst the actors remain unaware of this, only the audience has access to what is going on outside of the narrative. And so the tableau is both detached from the action and allegorises it, providing another translation or story, of which only the audience is privy to. The stillness of the staged tableau externalises the character's internal world for the audience, often referring to well known paintings by way of illustration.

As Carolyn Williams points out there is a rhythm to this melodramatic form, between the still staged picture and the action which is set to music underscoring "its alternations between motion and stillness" (Williams, 2005: p. 113). So, we can see the melodramatic tableau as the character's hysterical symptom that is suspended, until the audience can read it back within a more living exchange. Williams points to the scenes of melodramatic realisation in *Daniel Deronda*; Gwendolen's terror of the dead face in the secret painting, or the mutual recognition of Daniel with Mordecai on Blackfriars Bridge. Or, indeed Daniel's rescue of Mirah, when he beholds in her form and face something that might be a mother. For Williams, these tableaus dramatise the interaction between the novel's more particular individuals and "a prefigured type"; and we can see, here, how melodrama acts to reconfigure the realist novel and to create literary vision. A vision achieved through melodrama's ability to reform private passions through a more social and virtual type or other. And yet Eliot is insistent this virtual other must be exceptional like Daniel, who is the ideal Jew. Art is not the vehicle through which Gwendolen can remake herself, but it seems that Deronda as a more living embodied ideal, is denied to her too.

The tableau of Gwendolen's terrified response to the secret painting is staged as a domestic charade of Hermione from *The Winter's Tale*. This Shakespearian story of unacknowledged mothers and abandoned daughters figures a statue-like Hermione who comes to life on being reunited with her daughter. However, in Gwendolen's charade instead of coming to life she remains frozen. Her dread at the dead face and the fleeing figure in the panelling reveals her psychic trauma; one that the audience cannot read or translate within a more aesthetic form. There is a quick fire round of questions in response to Gwendolen's painful, hysterical acting:

"Was it part of the play"

"Oh no surely not. Miss Harleth was much too much affected. A sensitive creature!"

"Dear me! I was not aware that there was a painting behind that panel; were you? ..."

"No; how should I? Some eccentricity on one of the Earl's family long ago, I suppose."

"How every painful! Pray shut it up"

"Was the door locked? It was very mysterious. It must be the spirits."

"But there is no medium present"

"How do you know that? We must conclude that there is when such things happen."

"Oh the door was not locked; it was probably the sudden vibration from the piano that sent it open" (Eliot, 1999: pp. 64–65).

Why can't this melodrama be read by the audience? Is it the dead maternal face as literally un-figurable, leaving Gwendolen subjected to the traumatic "real" of her psychic wounds? Putting this hysterical melodrama back in rhythm with reality and thus unlocking the door to Gwendolen's paralysed passion is dependent, I suggest, on an unconscious reading of living maternal form. This maternal form is the mimetic gestural response of the non-personal mother as a virtual other; a presence to the young child which occurs before the more actual personal mother who is loved in a meaningful way arrives on the scene. I have argued that it is the telepathic reading between this virtual mother and the young infant that aesthetically elaborates the ego in relation to the outside world. Moreover, the telepathy at stake here as part of the transference is the other receptive side to Freud's repressed unconscious, and as such is distinct from "spiritualism" and the school of subliminal psychology associated with Frederic Myers.[3] Eliot is disparaging of the audience who believes in the "spirits" and yet as many critics have noted the "second sight" at play in this novel is everywhere.

There is arguably a form of transference and telepathy akin to hysteria where communication between the ego and its other is dominated by fantasies where "spirits" rule. The solipsism here is the business of a purely personal ego, the work of Lacan's "fantasmatic" imaginary. This seems to be the scene of Gwendolen's terror at her repressed passions. The fleeing figure from the dead face in the panel suggests there is no aesthetic mediation, no painterly forms with which to elaborate these traumatic first impressions. Only with Daniel's search in the second half of the novel for an ego ideal or his uncertain Jewish origins, can we see the supposed sublimation of the individual's personal conflicts and fantasies within a larger historical purview. With Daniel's story we see a different kind of unconscious transmission for the self, associated with a "maternal response" which communicates between the early ego and reality. This maternal form is seemingly returned within the two melodramatic sequences of Daniel's rescue of Mirah by the river, and in Mordecai's spiritual visualisation of Daniel on Blackfriars Bridge. In both these encounters there is a telepathic communication where Daniel's virtual form and figure acts as a living response to the suffering of the other two characters.

Moreover, Daniel's compassion towards Mirah seems oddly that she resurrects for him, not so much his specific mother, but the type of one he has never personally known. Indeed the sense and the virtual form of the mother turns up in *Daniel Deronda* in every melodramatic tableau, providing uncanny significance and second sight not just to Daniel's empathic response to Mirah's suffering, but also to Mordecai's vision of his "prefigured friend". What are we to make though, of the kind of telepathic transmissions operating between Daniel and Mirah or between Daniel and Mordecai? As Eliot says "the sense of spiritual perpetuation in another resembles that maternal transference of self"(Eliot, 1999: p. 548). This maternal transmission is the visualisation of a wider geneaology, specifically of the Jewish race.

Daniel we are told is thoroughly masculine and yet holds a "maternal" response which is highly sentimental; in line with Victorian values of the virtuous self, but arguably incapable of moving any "real" suffering or the imagination of the reader. As the "figure representative of Mordecai's longing", Daniel is the "face of his visions" illuminated against a halo of golden light. When Mirah's timid (but not wounded) look of a "fawn or other gentle animal", moves Daniel's consciousness outside of himself to rest with the landscape, again there is nothing believable for the reader. Everything carries on in a dreamy idealised mode, more like hysterical fantasy than any reality. Freud tells us that the ego ideal lays down the foundations of repressions but also functions as a "common ideal of a family, a class, or a nation" (Freud, 1914: p. 101). However, it would be a mistake to see this ideal as a way out from the ego, or as a form to carry its desires. He writes:

> As we have learnt, the formation of an ideal heightens the demands of the ego and is the most powerful factor favouring repression;

> sublimation is a way out, a way by which those demands can be
> met without involving repression. (Freud, 1914: p. 95)

If Daniel's sentimental response functions as the ego ideal for the
novel, then as such it is merely the other side of Gwendolen's hysterical repressions, featuring either an ideal or abject relation to the body
of the mother. Although Daniel's story poses the question of a trans-
missible maternal form as a visualisation of a forgotten history; its
compassion is one way. Daniel's sympathy and intact male ego locate
the excess and symptoms elsewhere, within Gwendolen's unspeakable passion. So, instead of a melodramatic form that can aesthetically
reconfigure Gwendolen's feelings within a wider, social reality, those
emotions become "shut up" and panelled in. Like the eccentric Earl's
heritage they remain as some archaic remnant of the past. Repressed,
utterly mysterious and thus unavailable to a rhythm which will read
the melodrama in relation to Gwendolen's (and the Novel's) present
or future. Gwendolen's terror is the fear and refusal of the powers of
a virtual unconscious form; one that does not sentimentally transcend
the aggressive forces of love, but suggests them. It is this suggestion
and re-imagination of the "real" that creates the necessary illusion and
vision that is arguably inherent to the success of both literature and
therapy. If Daniel's particular story fails, perhaps this is because of
its open innocence that leaves nothing for us as readers to create and
imagine. Daniel's sentimental response evacuates the real, replacing
melodramatic excess with a spiritual fantasy of not just the self, but the
ego's social ideal of family and nation.

In *The Interpretation of Dreams* Freud describes hysterical identification as enabling. It allows:

> patients to express in their symptoms not only their own experi-
> ences, but those of a large number of other people.... to act all the
> parts in a play single-handed. (Freud, 1900: p. 149)

So this sympathy, "intensified to the point of reproduction" shows the
many paths through which ideas in hysteria move. But hysterical ideas
do something more than just straightforwardly imitate, they also make
inferences. In other words, they are imaginative. Freud gives the example of a hysterical ward of patients who copy each other's symptoms,
but the sympathy evoked between these patients will also involve the
knowledge of each other's histories, that is, shared stories of trauma,

broken love affairs etc. Thus identification, for Freud, is also an act of assimilation, or a resemblance, because it mixes sympathy with the inference of meaning. And so in this scenario, sympathy is not simply a copy, nor a distanced observer; it is an identification that moves between similarity and difference.

If being overly self reflexive and separate (Daniel's response to Gwendolen), positions suffering solely within the other, then hysterical imitation is not just a copy of the same; it offers up a melodrama of parts in which the replaying and resemblance of forms can operate. Freud makes an important distinction in psychoanalytical work (and we can assume he means work for the analyst and the patient), between self-observation and the critical or self-reflexive capacity. Translating the dream and free association can only take place with the relaxing of this critical self-reflexivity, which Freud positions as occupying a "watch on the gates of Reason". Only when this watch is relaxed can "ideas rush in pell mell" (Freud, 1900: p. 103). Allowing our thoughts the chance to regress to a space of dream and hallucination is integral to creative life. As Freud says, dreams "dramatize an idea"; they take these ideas and wishes and mould them into visual and sensory images (Freud, 1900: p. 50).

These dream images or hallucinations are an absurd and nonsensical text and they start in Freud's view, when the authority "of the self has ceased" (Freud, 1900: p. 51). As a private theatre much like melodrama, these symptoms are paradoxically conducted and performed beyond the self. And yet the patient's symptoms, the nonsensical bits of dream text, have to be shared and worked with in the analytical transference in order for dream experience to occur. Without this melodramatic script of symptoms, which are always in excess of the ego, dream experience cannot be staged and shared. It is no coincidence that Freud came to write *The Interpretation of Dreams* after *Studies on Hysteria*, because you need a hysteric in order to have access to the dream. In Freud and Breuer's famous romance tales it is mostly the patients who are the hysterics, and these women are all described as sympathetic but rather too self-reflexive (Freud, 1893–1895). Nursing and restoring their parents has taken the place, for these women, of re-imagining them. Care has become a critical and reflexive self who has kept too close a watch on the gates of reality. Day dreaming, as Freud points out, is different from night dreaming, because day dreaming "is never confused with reality" (Freud, 1900: p. 50). Anna O's daydreams, or the storms in Frau Emmy's head, are dream like hallucinations that can't change into dream experiences because repression and the reflexive barrier of consciousness are still in place.

Characters, types and the dream experience

Wilfred Bion teaches us that emotional experience is akin to the dream. We dream by night and by day, but what turns someone's raw sensations into a lived experience is the ability to dream. Dream experience, unlike daydreams, is able to paint the senses and return them, providing forms and thoughts into which we can fit our untranslatable passions. Freud's hysterics are in search of a form for their affects and the right kind of dreaming experience. Of course, this in turn, depends on their forms being returned, their paintings and thoughts being given back by the analyst. This love is never simply a demand for reciprocity, but for implication somewhere else. Anna O hallucinates her pregnancy with Breuer, and Lucy R becomes obsessed with Freud's smell, his cigar smoke, and yet these women are not so much in search for a return of their love, as for a return of its fashioning.

The private theatre of these most famous hysterics, combines affectual conversions, leg pains, voice clicks or bodily spasms, with nonsense dreams: all the fantastic and absurd images and associations of their "reminiscences". And yet to dream this nonsense into a new sense of being, to make Gwendolen's singing a public performance, or to give Elizabeth von R the dancing power of her legs is to understand that these women's hysterical desire is in search of a form for their feelings, that can only be found in the response of the other. Thus hysterical dreams are not quite dream experiences in Bion's meaning of the term. They exist as private fantasy and as a sentimental excess that lives beyond the self, fantasies that are in motion, seeking out new parts to play, new costumes to fit. As Freud pointed out these hysterical fantasies are bisexual; always playing the man and the women, as heterosexual or homosexual. And as melodrama, these parts which swing between masculinity and femininity, activity and passivity, the villain and the innocent victim, are empty of interior meaning. They are passions but also types, virtual, plastic, and immediately available for our reading, and in this sense they contain the open spaces for the reader to enter into. Just as in melodrama where the emotional response is always from the real position of the reader, not the other characters in the fictional plot, or on the screen. So, in therapy the hysteric, along with their characters and their passions, need elaboration by the analyst, emotionally and imaginatively.

If hysterics are melodramatic types that cry out to be imaginatively re-worked and remembered in the analytic session. So too, is the analyst someone who must allow themselves to be loved and hated, worshipped and loathed, made and re-made by the patient. The analyst, like Daniel, is also a virtual type or other whose response is a return of the patient's passions with form attached. Analyst and patient both read each other telepathically in the clinical session and we can think of this unconscious communication as a maternal aesthetic, a living form through which the ego can construct itself in relation to a virtual other. We know the problems entailed if the erotic transference gets out of hand, and analyst and patient become too passionate about each other. There is, however, another danger of both parties becoming types that defend against intensity or pain. Hysterics, obsessionals, perverts are all arguably schematic typologies that patients too easily get fitted into. But what variety of types do analysts come in? The certain interpretations of the Kleinian; or the Lacanian who does not believe in pre-Oedipal reality are some recognisable characters. Or there is the blank screen analyst who uses passivity and silence not so much to listen as to check out, and the too active therapist who interprets every inch of the "here and now" transference.

The dangers of the analyst being too ideal or sentimental a type is that their compassion or insight positions the suffering and helplessness with the client. Melodrama is something we can sympathise and care about so long as it is happening over there. And if passions get too out of hand then we revert to our preferred characters in our attempt to resolve them. Daniel's compassionate nature is a case in point. One of the failures of Daniel Deronda is Eliot's attempts to position Daniel as exceptional and god-like. Whereas with Gwendolen, we are continually reminded that an exceptional sense of self is always built on a grudge against some slight or suffering in our pasts. In his essay on *Some Character-Types met with in Psycho-Analytic Work*, Freud describes how we won't readily give up any of our childhood pleasures. And because we refuse, then the claim of being an "exception" is actually the neurotic sign, telling of early disappointments. Richard, who wants to be King in Shakespeare's *Richard III* is Freud's example of this exceptional grudge. Slighted by his bodily deformity, Richard vows that if he can't be beautiful or a desirable lover then he will be bad and villainous. Freud takes this explanation further by saying that the audience of the play always identifies with Richard because they know they are like him. Moreover the "subtle economy" of Shakespeare's art is to suggest this hidden blow to Richard's narcissism, rather than spelling it out. Because Richard's wounded sense of self is hinted at rather than being a confessional, then the audience have to unconsciously go to work, so to speak, in identifying with him. A "bungler in his place" says Freud, a lesser poet, would "permit his hero to give open and complete expression to all his motives" and as a result be met with our calm intelligence, preventing "any deepening of the illusion" (Freud, 1916: p. 315).

What are the drawbacks of the confessional in relation to Deronda, we might ask? Why is Daniel's innocence so boring, and where is the subtle allure of his grudge? Completely relegated it would seem to Gwendolen's suffering narcissism, and yet it is Gwendolen's pain that we identify with. It is through her tragic dilemma of wanting to be exceptional and of always grappling with disappointment that really affects us as readers. It's almost as if for Eliot the higher art forms of the realist novel aligned with Deronda's noble character always have to trump the more lowly passions of melodrama. And yet without this low Art, no greater work of literature can exist. Is therapy high literature or a squalid soap opera? It seems that it is the exceptional "analyst" or training who will decide. And so without melodrama there is no ability to imagine and vision our egos in new ways; this has been ego psychology's failure, in its exception to melodrama.

Characters both in literature and life, without sufficient passion to undo them remain curiously lifeless caricatures. The second half of *Daniel Deronda* is seemingly awash with ideal and sentimental types; as critics have noted the characters of Mirah and Mordecai have none of the depth or complexity carried by Gwendolen Harleth. Thus fixed archetypes are arguably really unhelpful in figuring the transmission of affects in relation to the living unconscious of the clinical and the literary encounter. In other words, analysts as well as patients have to able to access their hysterical and telepathic powers in order to negotiate the unbearable passions and their crafting within forms that are not immediately knowable to the ego. Arguably it is the analyst's ability to suffer, to be undone, as well as to be a virtual vessel for his client's affects that really establishes the unconscious identifications and their communication in the clinical session. After all, if symptoms are in a conversation, then whom are they actually talking to? Compassion and the fixed character of the analyst (Daniel's type) simply return those symptoms to sender in a melodrama that leaves us safely sympathetic and aghast in equal measure. The lure of ego psychology is always that we can manage our melodramatic passions away. Thus, we are always in danger as analysts of becoming an audience, like the ones at Gwendolen's play, that can't read the suggestions of the past, or the traumatised real into new living encounters. Shutting up pain with the painting in the wainscot, is perhaps what happens when passions and characters become too fixated, when the audience either relegates its sensitivity to "the spirits", or loses it "second sight" in relation to reality. Restoring this telepathy is the material vision that puts melodrama and reality back in rhythm with each other.

As her ego ideal, the analyst is never quite as available, or as remakeable as the hysteric wants and needs. What would have happened if Breuer had worked with Anna O's pregnancy fantasy in therapy, instead of running for the hills? Or if Freud, for that matter, had recognised Dora's maternal transference and had been able to unconsciously read her rapture in front of the Sistine Madonna? Daniel Deronda tells Gwendolen to be good, to idolise her rival, but to keep her art forms to herself. Freud offers Dora an interpretation of her desire that is unbearable, because fathers, for this woman, lack any artistic sensibility. What Freud's women lack, and Gwendolen is without, is a man or a woman who can become a dream experience, or perhaps engender one. Daniel insists on being a sort of super-ego, on loan to Gwendolen. But Gwendolen doesn't need an alter-super ego; she has a furious one, all of her own. She wonders if her remorse would "have maintained its power within her, or would she have felt absolved by secrecy, if it had not been for that outer conscience which was made for her by Deronda" (Eliot, 1999: p. 844). Therapy, however, is not simply a confessional. As Eliot (or the narrator) says, the people we love and hate the most are "our interpreters of the world". Grandcourt is Gwendolen's melancholy theory of life, "a piece of yellow and wavy glass that distorts form and makes colour an affliction" (Eliot, 1999: p. 74). Whereas, Daniel is more like a priest; offering a cut glass reflection of all her pain and suffering.

There is a difference, Luce Irigaray insists, between an analyst who is always interpreting, and one who can help "paint the senses" (Irigaray, 1993). And melodrama and its double, called the analytic space, can do this, provided the unknowable dream experience becomes both a mirror and a way to what Masud Khan calls "the lived experience" of a person. Gwendolen wants Daniel to be her dream man, and yet as a nineteenth century melodrama, Daniel Deronda refuses this hysterical demand, in favour of restoring her moral virtue. And yet there is a fundamental misrecognition in this refusal, because Gwendolen does not require Daniel to actually return her desire, any more then she needs him as an alter-super ego. If Deronda is too much of a guilty therapist, then the reader can be different. Within the theatre of melodrama, as in hysteria, it is arguably the reader who returns the dream and the forms that enable the lived experience of the characters. It is significant, I think, that there is always more than one reader, and in therapy, both analyst and patient are readers of the melodramatic, dream space.

But the reader of melodrama is not the spectator as onlooker, or a clever analyst interpreting meaningful representations and bits of dream text. The real readers, or spectators, of melodrama, like the readers of the therapeutic space, have to be emotionally moved, not by what they discern but by the unknowable. And it is the ability to search for forms to express our passions, without having to know them, which allows their forward passage. Although a dream experience is by its nature not spoken or shared in terms of its meaning, it is still a secret or mysterious experience that passes between dreamer and real reader, without conscious spectating at the gates of reason. We can read the endings of *The Wings of a Dove* and *The Portrait of a Lady* as the melodramatic restoration of virtue through Isabel's and Milly's sacrifice. Or we can read the endings as simply being unfathomable. Like Peter Brooks, we can see Milly Theale's death or Isabel Archer's final return to Osmond as a moral "abyss of meaning", and yet this unconscious darkness or gap, is precisely what allows the reader her future forms of feeling. So, we can disagree with T. S. Eliot when he says that Hamlet is a failed work of art, "the Mona Lisa of literature" because the only way of expressing emotion in art is by finding an "objective correlative". Thus, Hamlet's character is sentimental; he is a man who is a hysteric, dominated by inexpressible emotion, "in excess of the facts as they appear". Eliot writes:

> In the character Hamlet, it is the buffoonery of an emotion which can find no outlet in action, and for the dramatist the buffoonery of an emotion which he cannot express in art. (Eliot, 1997: p. 87)

We might also say, that it is precisely because Hamlet's emotions are not fully explained or formed as an art object, that his character and the play, become such a catalyst for the reader. The Mona Lisa, for Dora, is enigmatic because she can be anything Dora wants her to be. Similarly, Hamlet, as a play and as a character, is art in the making and not "an objective correlative", because being the latter would mean there would be nowhere for the hysteric, or us as readers to go. Hamlet, T. S. Eliot tells us, is sentimental because his mother is so inadequate. His emotions are always in search and in excess of her ability to be an art form. And so we might say of the other Eliot's heroine, Gwendolen, that her sentimentality is in search and in excess of Daniel and the narrative. In melodramatic fashion her sentiment calls for another genre. We are understandably disappointed as readers at the end of the novel, when Gwendolen is left withered with grief at Daniel's departure. His promise that they will never meet but write letters, is too inadequate as an "objective correlative", or an elaboration of our feelings. Our regret is borne out by Gwendolen's missive, that she "may live to be one of the best of women" (Eliot, 1999: p. 898).

Conclusion

My sentimental response to the ending of *Daniel Deronda* is to find it elsewhere, remake it into different genres. My first response is in my imagination of what can still happen in the endless letters. After all, Daniel does say, quite persuasively, that by his writing, "I shall be more with you than I used to be" (Eliot, 1999: p. 893). My second sentimental response is to turn the ending into an Opera, and make Gwendolen the singing instrument of her passions. Melodrama and hysteria are essential components of psychoanalysis, not just because they stage the force of our passions, but because they also dramatise a movement of affects in search of old and new forms. Melodrama and hysteria might champion the most excessive and sentimental aspects of our psychic lives, or our culture. And yet they are also the means and the motion with which we replay those passions anew, as sensibility, in relation to one another. Melodrama and reality have an exchange value within psychoanalysis and literature; one that is dependent on the unconscious reading of our personal pasts in relation to the virtual forms of a wider historicity. Paradoxically this telepathic recreation of our selves within a living history belongs within the rhythms of melodrama and a maternal aesthetic.

And it is this melodramatic aesthetic, not the more civilised ego which has been traditionally aligned with the Realist novel that makes for literary and therapeutic success. Perhaps Freud would have seen Daniel's story as the work of a "bungler"; surely he would not have failed to see the deep and poetic illusion of Eliot's hysteric Gwendolen? As therapists, we are both bunglers and poets. The difference is in the symptom which can't be known but can be unconsciously read.

Notes

1. Many critics have raised the different issue of trauma, hysteria and madness in relation to studies of Gwendolen. Most notably, Matus, Penner, Tromp, Vrettos, During, Trotter and Stone. In this study I am using a Freudian perspective which understands trauma (externally and internally provoked) as the unbearable nature of passions which lack the requisite ego-forms with which to bear them. Thus Melodrama becomes the focus of this study, because it is both an abhorrent low form and a form of sensibility which is mobile and on the move in search of elaborations beyond the self.

2. My reading of *Daniel Deronda* bears reference to recent readings such as Jill Matus's *Historicising Trauma: The Genealogy of Psychic Shock in Daniel Deronda* and David Toise's *Sexuality's Uncertain History: or "Narrative Disjunction" in Daniel Deronda*, but my project in reading this novel through a telepathic maternal aesthetic is somewhat different. This paper, as will be seen, articulates close connections with the ideas of melodramatic form charted in Carolyn William's essay, "Moving Pictures".

3. See Campbell, J. (2009) "Rhythms of the Suggestive Unconscious" *Subjectivity*, 26: 29-50 where I map out the stakes for a suggestive and virtual unconscious in relation to Freud and the subliminal psychology associated with Frederic Myers.

CHAPTER SEVEN

Rhythm of affects and styles of the ego, in *To the Lighthouse*

*Now this is very profound, what rhythm is, and goes far deeper than words.
A sight, an emotion, creates this wave in the mind, long before it makes
words to fit it; and in writing (such is my present belief) one has to recapture
this, and set this working (which has nothing apparently to do with words)
and then, as it breaks and tumbles in the mind, it makes words to fit it.*

—Woolf, Letters Vol. 3: p. 247

Searching for style means finding your rhythm, and although
Woolf is talking here about recapturing a certain style and rhythm
of writing, we can equally see therapy as a process where styles
of the mind, let's say the ego's style, has to recapture or re-find its lost
rhythm of affects. Affects are always uncannily double because they
live to a large extent outside of the ego's ability to bind or harness them.
Affects are unconscious until they become integrated into the perceptual consciousness of the ego.

So, there are the affects we feel and the ones we remain more unconscious of because we split them off or repress them. If our affects are too
unbearable they are externalised and given to somebody else, or we disguise them by attributing to them cover meanings and feelings. Affects,
as part of our instinctual being, are our primary animal passions, but

they also make up are unknowable unconscious phantasies; as such they constitute the beginning, passage, and the expression of our psychological drives and desires. This means not just that affects move, but they incorporate different qualities and meanings. Affects that begin instinctually become psychological desires through the movement of what Freud called libido or sexual drive. Freud tells us the drives are a borderline concept, halfway between the somatic and the psychical, and so desires move from animal passions to something more intangible and unknowable. And this is because our polymorphous sexuality and our desire are always in excess of any object that can fulfil the fantasy. Richard Boothby speaks most clearly about what is at stake in Freudian drives and phantasies. Because, as he says, phantasy is a character with something to hide, then the unknowable heart of whom we are and what we want, keeps moving us forward, compelling us towards something that is always beyond the reach of the imagination:

> Yet this "something more", this summit of rapture, however elusively at the furthest horizon of desire. It remains ungraspable, like a distant object shimmering in the far off welter of summer heat waves. (Boothby, 2005: p. 33)

In Woolf's novel desire is symbolised by the phallic object of the lighthouse, but as she tells her friend Roger Fry:

> I meant nothing by The Lighthouse. One has to have a central line in the book to hold the design together. I saw that all sorts of feelings would accrue to this, but I refused to think them out, and trusted that people would make it the deposit for their own emotions-which they have done, one thinking it means one thing another another. I can't manage Symbolism except in this vague, generalised way. Whether it's right or wrong I don't know, but directly I'm told what a thing means, it becomes hateful to me. (Woolf, Letters, Vol 3: p. 385)

What is this but a description of desire, and of the returnable, repetitive but endlessly changing form that our desires take? We can't know our desires with any certainty without beginning to foreclose or pervert them. Formed by an intangible line, the movement and time of Lily's vision, her last brush stroke, or the keen, "lean as a knife" ongoing demands of Mr. Ramsay, desire is getting to the lighthouse, through shaping our desire into the requisite forms that can express feeling and build character. Affects create who we are and what we want: they are the potential and the expression of our ego designs. But in order to shape our wants, they have to have form. And yet this relationship is paradoxical in that affects are always a return to form, a return to what is personal and habitual, whilst being at the same time wildly impersonal and unknowable. Emotions that literally make us feel beside ourselves, are the affects that are always more than we or other people can bear.

Making a distinction between instinct and Trieb (or drive) in Freud's thinking, Boothby argues that the desire of our drives has "partially cut loose from its biological basis and re-grafted onto a new supporting framework, the trellis of a symbolic architecture". (Boothby, 2005: p. 34) The mystery of our phantasies and drives, their virtual nature of being more than we can know or imagine is what "separates human desire from mere animal rut" (Boothby, 2005: p. 33). However, I want to qualify this slightly because this makes our desires a kind of one-way street, beginning with our primitive passions in the "garden of Eden", and ending with symbolic representation of what we have mediated or learnt. It's a kind of Mr. Ramsay lesson of life on how to get from Q to R, as though desire and a splendid mind is predicated on forward progression. The development model of psychoanalysis is, come to think of it rather like Mr. Ramsay, demanding we move from pre-Oedipal to Oedipal, always fearing the disgrace and loss of leadership that might occur, if we dally or look back.

And yet desire might seemingly get carried by the straight line from the body to the symbolic, when in actual fact all desire, along with the affects that build and express it, are a return of form; a reversion, in other words, to our past, and a return to the other. Virginia Woolf captures this return of affects and form, in various ways, making us question any straightforward Lacanian or developmental reading of psychoanalysis. There are no straight lines in Freud's thinking, either in a literal, developmental sense, or in a symbolic one. Or at least, these straight lines are, as Woolf says about her novel, simply the time lines that hang the designs of our ego together (provided we have had a normative enough development). But these lines are pretty meaningless and empty without the feelings and affects that accrue to them, and it is our affects and feelings that keep returning us to our bodies and our past: to a sense of unconscious time which is circular and reproductive, rather than linear. Our passions, the body as animal rut, is always what we come back to, even though like the wild and fierce daughter Cam Ramsay they are too unbearable to be knowable, except through their virtual imaginary status as dreams or fairytales.

Maternal form or idiom

In *To the Lighthouse*, bodily passions and the "garden of Eden" are associated with Mrs. Ramsay. As Hermione Lee notes the secret pre-Oedipal language of their mother's "miraculous garden ... before the fall of the world" and the law of the father, is something the children can't forget and long to return to. The novel's task, for Lee is to "make its new language re-embody—through rhythm, images and shapes—that first, vanished language" (Lee, 1992: p. xxxviii). The breakdown of traditional narrative in the novel, the rupture and escape from its Victorian, realist, development timeline, is as Lee tells us a rupture with literary tradition as much as with childhood. And yet it is also a break with how so much contemporary psychoanalysis tends to remember Freud, to put him in alphabetical sequence, to make him into the Realist novel, when like the rebellious daughter Woolf (or Cam?) he was always so much more fierce and experimental. In fact as I will argue Freud's reality principle is in fact an imaginary modernist one, because it is premised on both the necessity and impossibility of finding a break between old passions and new forms.

First passionate affects for the mother are what we keep coming back to, along with the forms from her that shaped them. I have argued in this book for these maternal forms as a telepathic reading, which shapes and sublimates our desires. As the psychic designers of our ego or self, maternal forms style our passions into their ongoing characters and psychological drives. The Lighthouse is not really imaginable for young James Ramsay. It is that shimmering unknowable object over the waves, lying beyond his mother as an adventure, albeit dependent on her for giving it a shape or design. The joy in her words, "Yes if it's fine tomorrow ... but you'll have to be up with the lark", is their secret language shaped and built through her attunement to his affectual needs (Woolf, 1992: p. 7). Daniel Stern describes how attunement is the ongoing tracking of the baby's feeling states, by the mother, who identifies and responds in a communicative way (Stern, 1985). Kenneth Wright adds to this a description of how the mother who is in tune with her baby or child, who is holding it in her mind, responds through returning the baby's feelings in symbolic and pre-symbolic ways (Wright, 2009). Wright does not mean Symbolic language but uses Susan Langer's ideas of non-verbal, artistic form to explain how the mother tunes herself in to the child's affects and returns them symbolically. Perhaps it is only when our feelings are contained adequately by an object that we can feel them. Identification between mother and baby is not simply mimicry, but a passionate attachment that returns the child's affect through a maternal sequence which is also different, because it has been "transposed into a different sensory modality, or exaggerated and made more emphatic" (Wright, 2009: p. 23). Thus the child's love is ongoingly returned, mediated, and moulded by the other's form. More, than this, the self begins its life literally through these uncanny silhouettes belonging to the other; the spirits and shapes that are more or less usable for the artwork of the ego.

When James hears his mother's voice he is joyful because it means the longed for adventure will take place. And so, as he sits on the floor cutting out pictures from the Army and Navy catalogue, these inanimate objects become ignited, brought to life, by the feelings he breathes into them. He endows the picture of a refrigerator, as his mother speaks, with heavenly bliss.

> It was fringed with joy. The wheelbarrow, the lawn-mower, the sound of poplar trees, leaves whitening before rain, rooks cawing, brooms knocking, dresses rustling—all these were so coloured and distinguished in his mind that he had already his private code, his secret language. (Woolf, 1992: p. 7)

The intuitive promise from his mother, her telepathic ability to join him in with what he wants and to make it feel real, crystallises his passion into feelings, which in turn, bring the everyday objects he is cutting out, to life. These evocative objects of everyday life can only return us to a transformational maternal aesthetic, if the alchemy of that first passionate tie has generated the forms we need, to turn our passions into a range of feelings. The impersonal shapes that James cuts out of his magazine are illustrative of the ones returned by his mother, through which he moulds his body ego. Personalisation of the magazine objects, and the arrival at a sense of place and an internal space, is something that happens to James, though his mother's ability to voice and co-create his feelings. Interestingly, it is not just the semantic meaning of Mrs. Ramsay's words, "Yes, of course, if it's fine tomorrow", but the rhythm and timing of her response, to that virtual something that James is striving to imagine. His father's tell the truth stance, meanwhile, is not empathic or in time with his son's desire. Mr. Ramsay's interpretation of the weather as he stops by the drawing room window, "But, it won't be fine", is an example of how meaningful interpretations, however true, are often useless in helping us experience lived reality. Mr. Ramsay can only forecast the real weather; he is unable to read the emotional weather,

> He was in incapable of untruth; never tampered with a fact; never altered a disagreeable word to suit the pleasure or convenience of any mortal being, least of all of his own children, who, sprung from his loins, should be aware that life is difficult; facts uncompromising. (Woolf, 1992: p. 8)

But of course reality is unbearable, and ultimately unliveable, unless we can temper it and work it through putting it into some kind of rhythm with our imagination and desire. This makes me think of the fallacy in psychoanalysis that there can ever be the right interpretation. As Winnicott says the therapist is engaging in returning what the patient brings and any interpretation, however accurate, is false, if it is offered at a point where the person can't bear to hear or receive it. If there is a true interpretation it is one that also has to be made up along with the client. Reality in other words has its point of view, and in order to make that view of the world creative, we need both our desire and imagination. The caricature of Mr. Ramsay is of course his sidekick and student Charles Tansley, whom no-one likes; someone in particular the children don't like. For Tansley, is an academic with an autistic point of view, which does not allow for subjective-objects; he is like Andrew Ramsay's description of his father's work. When Lily asks Andrew what his father's books are about he replies, "subject and object and the nature of reality ... just think of a kitchen table", he says by way of illustration, "when you are not there." And just like Lily's subsequent vision of a bare, scrubbed kitchen table, we can see Charles Tansley as a copy, minus creative form. With his mimicry of Mr. Ramsay, snuffing out James' remaining hope with a clap of his hands, and telling him the wind is due west; "There will be no landing at The Lighthouse tomorrow" (Woolf, 1992: p. 11).

"Odious little man", thinks Mrs. Ramsay, her children are right he is a "miserable specimen" and so she defies her husband by saying to James, "perhaps you will wake up and find the sun shining" (Woolf, 1992: p. 19). But of course the trauma, James's disappointment and hatred of his father, for failing to read the right weather, is sealed: "Had there been an axe handy, a poker, or any weapon that would have gashed a hole in his father's breast, there and then, James would have seized it" (Woolf, 1992: p. 8). And so all his mother can do,

> is to admire the refrigerator, turn the pages of the Stores list in the hope that she might come across something like a rake, or a mowing machine, which, with its prongs and handles, would need the greatest skill and care in cutting out. All these men parodied her husband, she reflected. (Woolf, 1992: p. 19)

I want to suggest that we can see Mrs. Ramsay as a representation of unconscious passion and a maternal aesthetic. But rather than seeing her as a Jungian archetypal figure, we can see her as a figure of the id and a maternal idiom which shapes desire and gives form to the ego. In Freud's view the id and the unconscious ego are connected. As Christopher Bollas reminds us without maternal idiom the birth of the self remains elusive. For him, the term idiom stems from the Freudian id; a concept which he thinks has been passed over (Bollas, 1995: p. 44). More particularly, it corresponds to Winnicott's notion of the true self, placed halfway between the id and the ego. So, idiom is an "intelligence of form" that carries the instinct, but of course the ego's forms come initially from the object, before they are incorporated into the self. Idiom is then internal form communicated unconsciously between two people. At first, mother and child, but also in analysis this unconscious elaboration of psychic form happens between analyst and patient, creating what Bollas calls a deep sense of self or "separate sense". Mrs. Ramsay can be seen as both a personification of the id, and a more non-personal maternal idiom potentially of use to the other characters.

With James we see how this virtual, maternal idiom is returned to shape his passions, in the magazine objects and through the fairy tale of *The Fisherman and His Wife*. However, with her husband Mr. Ramsay, we see a version of another more fixated mother child relation, where passions and intellect are divided. For if Mrs. Ramsay figures as an archetype of unconscious lived form, Mr. Ramsay is the repressive, personal ego. The insistent "I", Mr. Ramsay is all brains or all passionate demand: the division of the overly repressive ego, where unconscious affects remain at the level of bodily drive and the necessary form is simply detached. In this "one way mirror", between the body and the symbolic, he drinks Mrs. Ramsay dry with his "beak of brass" wanting sympathy until, "there is scarcely a shell of herself left". Mrs. Ramsay's sympathy, the meeting of her husbands' emotional demand is straightforward. She must simply give him what he wants. Her words are less a virtual form, through which Mr. Ramsay might artistically shape what he feels, and more an instant breast-feed:

> Filled with her words, like a child who drops off satisfied, he said, at last, looking at her with humble gratitude, restored, renewed that he would take a turn; he would watch the children playing cricket. He went.
>
> Immediately, Mrs. Ramsay seems to fold herself together, one petal closed in against another, and the whole fabric fell in exhaustion upon itself, so she had only strength enough to move her finger, in exquisite abandonment to exhaustion, across the page to Grimm's fairy story, while there throbbed through her, like a pulse in spring which had expanded to its full width and now gently ceases to beat, the rapture of successful creation. (Woolf, 1992: p. 44)

How are we to read this illustration of Mrs. Ramsay, as the throbbing pulse of life and creation; a fabric of affect restoring the "fatal sterility of the man", or Mr. Ramsay, to his senses? I think there is a reading of Freudian form and affect in *To the Lighthouse* that enables us to read the normative sexual difference theory of psychoanalysis and gender differently. One in which we can see affects as rhythms, in search of forms that are always housed by another. Affects are fundamental to life; they are pulse and rhythm of who we are. They are both the quantitative building blocks, the raw energy of what Freud called the drives and yet they are also the qualitative effects and intelligent feelings that emerge from the drives, and in this latter sense affects are inseparable from the representations and object relations they also create. And yet affects or passion, without mediation or form, are simply terrifying; an excess to the ego, unbearable in their appetite: Mrs. Ramsay as divine "rose- flowered" rapture say, with no story of her attached. For in the mother-child relation, depicted by Mrs. Ramsay giving succour to her husband, he has not grown up. He should be living a post-Oedipal life instead he has gone backwards and set up his wife, as his ideal Oedipal mother.

For Luce Irigaray this "one way mirror" is the phallic economy of psychoanalysis, a transcendental solution of the Oedipal complex, where the woman and mother remains the bodily ground, or object of exchange which grounds a masculine and symbolic subject (Irigaray, 1991). In this "phallic" economy, form is simply a detached masculinity or Mr. Ramsay's metaphysics "imposed on top" of vegetable life. Affects remains with the woman, until they can be lifted into meaningful language and representation of a masculine ego. And of course, Woolf's androgynous writing critiques this normative sexual difference: the straight sex of literary history. The aim of this essay is not to return to this much rehearsed feminist debate, but to focus on how maternal form operates in Woolf's fiction in a way which enables us to understand the relation between both time and affect in Freud's writing. Mr. and Mrs. Ramsay are in a fixated Oedipal relationship that is all wrong because they are grown up; their Oedipal forms need to be more re-made and more incomplete. One way of thinking about the Ramsay's Oedipal marriage is to see it as the normative narrative of sex that still passes for some as psychoanalysis, where language and knowledge lie with the man and the mother is consigned to the passionate, primitive body. But of course this is a perversion or narrowing of the Oedipal scenario, a fantasy that can only exist, in a sense, for the very young child. In order for the child to grow up, to make her way from mother to father, or from the mother to a lived experience in the world, the child has to have enough forms from the mother, so she can be similar and yet different.

Mr. Ramsay and his wife can't share the fairy stories she reads to her son, James: "No they could not share that, they could not say that" (Woolf, 1992: p. 75). And because he lacks this valuable telepathic form; Mr. Ramsay is stuck being brave in thought, but "so timid in life". We all need to remember how much we loved our mother, but we also need to remember how we left her. As the incestuous object of desire, Mrs. Ramsay is a window onto the garden of childhood that must be followed by walking through the door. And yet as a perfect, rather than good-enough, mother, Mrs. Ramsay keeps on opening the windows and shutting doors. The explanation and perhaps warning is in the fairy story of *The Fisherman and His Wife* which is a parable of the destruction you will invite if the world is just filled with the want for, and the wants of, a wife and mother. Mr. Ramsay features in the novel as both a splendid mind and a failure—the fisherman who can't stand up to his wife. He is the ego in its masterful defence, and unsuccessful attempts to brook the demands of a more triumphant id.

> He should of been a great philosopher, said Mrs. Ramsay, as they went down the road to the fishing village, but he had made an unfortunate marriage. (Woolf, 1992: p. 14)

These remarks about the old Mr. Carmichael could equally have been made about her husband. *The Fisherman and His Wife* is a tale of what happens when we seek a defensive narcissistic solution to our Oedipal desires; when we don't acknowledge the passage of time, remaining in a place where everything is perfectly matched and no discordance occurs. In this symmetry, the throbbing pulse that encloses Mrs. Ramsay and her husband as two notes (one high and one low) strikes together, and time stands still. It is only after this resonance dies that she detects "some faintly disagreeable sensation with another origin" (Woolf, 1992: p. 44). For Mrs. Ramsay does not want to feel better or finer than her husband. His abject dependence jars on her, when she reflects it is he who should be the most important. And it is this flat note that makes her triumph hollow, for it deprives her of what she desperately needs and can't bear—a man who can contain her feelings.

With the exception of old Carmichael, the characters in the Lighthouse all adore Mrs. Ramsay, as their most revered and incestuous object. She, in turn, desires and wants for all of them. And yet one of the most intriguing things about this wonderful book is how it traces the vicissitudes and problems with women's desire. Our energetic and economic passions are always searching for forms in order to become different feelings. These forms returned in the mother's mirroring to the child, is part of a mimesis that reproduces sameness and identification in ways that are significantly eccentric or varied. Through the mother's gestures, the idiosyncrasies of her voice or smile, our feelings are born, in the form of a virtual other that is also us. And this it seems to me, is different from a fully fledged desire where the maternal object has been fully substituted. Children, Freud writes, "like expressing an object-relation by an identification: 'I am of the object'. 'Having' is the later of the two" (Freud, 1938: p. 299). I can only desire the breast when I am no longer being it. All desires carry the trace of a primary identification, and as Freud always acknowledged the mother is never completely given up. But if desire is how we forget our mother and eroticise her body, then maternal form is how we identify with, and begin to, substitute our mother, whilst she is still there. Maternal idiom is a processing, according to Bollas, an operational unconscious of the "unthought known", whereby the child or analysand use the maternal object to elaborate new feelings and ego states. Receptive, rather than repressive, this generative unconscious is involved more with being than doing. And yet as I have argued, the receptive and repressed unconscious are complementary. Whereas the repressed unconscious seeks to avoid the prohibitions of consciousness, the receptive unconscious elaborates the ego and the affects, phantasies or ideas that are part of this self-experience. Both of these areas of the unconscious return to consciousness, but with the receptive unconscious, the unconscious is revealed as "acts of self enrichment rather than paroled particles of the incarcerated" (Bollas, 1995: p. 74).

Without this double movement of the unconscious, it seems to me, Freud's work cannot be fully appreciated. Perhaps it is in Freud's understanding of telepathy that we see this working most clearly. As me and Steve Pile have recently argued, when it comes to the question of telepathy and the unconscious, we can see that for Freud, the repressed and the non-repressed operate together, one bringing and discovering hidden material, one transforming that hidden material by the hypnotic and telepathic transference onto another. So, rather than seeing the repressive and receptive areas of the unconscious as distinct areas, we can understand that one leads to the other. Unconscious telepathy, operating through a maternal idiom and intelligence, in the clinical transference, is a pre-requisite to enabling the communication and expression of repressed unknowable desires. The unconscious transfer of our passions, whether these are travelling towards the maternal object, or emanating from it, are simply unbearable without the right fitting glove or clothes to dress up and design what we feel. Without its own designs and styles, its own fashion sense, the ego is truly bare or bereft. That is why whether we see our unconscious affects as enigmatic signifiers transmitted from another, or as just our mysterious instinctual repressed life without maternal forms to carry them, our desires will always remain foreclosed or in a state of abortion.

A daughter's need of maternal spirit

As a kind of dream, maternal form is on the way to desire. Ensuring the travel of our passions between mother and father, maternal form is related to the body, supporting and connecting body schema and image, linking what Lacan would call the real of our passions with the imaginary. Maternal form is pre-linguistic: the lived form of the body that enables us to elaborate and carry our passions. It is the mimetic double, initially borrowed from the mother; but then fashioned for ourselves that allows our passionate affects to move. And so maternal form is the rhythm and shape derived from the early gestural response of the mother, that travels backwards and forwards in relation to her, and then beyond her into language and the symbolic. A bodily symbolic, this maternal lived form is the way, or the style of our desire, but one that also maintains a close relation to being, elaborating our passionate tie with our mother, without destroying/having her. So, these forms from the mother are not as frightening as the nakedness of passion, they are more of a help, a friendly port in the storm. And whilst this unconscious messaging and telepathic form is an intrinsic part of communicating and unconsciously processing all desire, perhaps it is especially important for women, who feel the most internal violence, the most need for their own double when it comes to forgetting their mums and entering into desire for the world. Maternal form, here, is like a spiritual shape or companion, a soul mate; something to fall back and rest on, when the mother becomes missing. As a virtual maternal figure or form offering more evolved affects, the character of Mrs. Ramsay is liberating, but as a more direct expression of passion for the Oedipal mother we can never leave, she is simply terrifying. The difference, perhaps, between a relationship to the ego ideal where sexuality enters into the conversation, and one where repressed excessive passion becomes split off as a maternal super-ego.

In the traditional Oedipal story that has been much critiqued and mocked by feminist criticism, the division and mastery of the phallus over the maternal body seems impossible to erase. Whereas in Virginia Woolf's "androgynous writing" Oedipal relations and patriarchal literary history are reworked to include the feminine; a feminine aesthetic that partakes of the rhythmic body but also joins the masculine in relation to questions of writing and form. Of course these feminist politics of sexual difference are "old hat" in both literary criticism and psychoanalysis, but I want to return to them in this essay because I think they can give us a new understanding of how we perceive the relation between affects and form within Freud's work.

If sexual difference in psychoanalysis is not simply straight sex; if it is more than the heterosexual difference between women and men (where the body of one complements the mind of the other), then, perhaps we can see femininity and masculinity as genres. Sexual difference becomes the affects and forms of our internal worlds, or as Bollas sees them, the interlocking maternal and paternal orders of a receptive and repressive desire. As genres we can see masculinity and femininity as passionate modalities that move, evolve, go backwards and get stuck. And yet if we see Mr. and Mrs. Ramsay as versions of these modalities, then there is no straight line that leads from mother to father or from pre-Oedipal to Oedipal. Indeed the very dependence of Mr. Ramsay's need for his wife, a demand that makes him a fisherman rather than a philosopher King, is the lack of storytelling and painterly forms through which he can symbolically recreate his passion. Desire is doomed to take us back to our very first forms of love, and without recreation through maternal form those desires become fixated as inexorable demands. Back with his mother, the fisherman's wife, Mr. Ramsay blunders and flounders in search of the ego designs that won't just sit on top of vegetable life, but will transform him into a prince.

But perhaps the most interesting passions in search of maternal form or spirit in this extraordinary novel about creative minds are the ones belonging to the daughter. *To the Lighthouse* has often been read as a quintessential Oedipal story, which of course it is, but one that is sprung not so much from the sexual difference between a man and a woman, but the sexual difference inherent within the mother-daughter relationship. Search for maternal form is an issue for the daughters in the novel, because although Mrs. Ramsay can elaborate and pattern it for James through telling fairy stories, she withdraws from the necessary regression to dependence that would issue it in for herself. And this leaves her own ego curiously undressed, for Mrs. Ramsay is not one to wait for the return of her desire. Like the Beouf en Daube, "everything depended on things served up the precise moment they were ready" (Woolf, 1992: p. 87). Waiting for dinner was out of the question, in case of spoil. The necessary shaping of desire that comes with a maternal response is missing if that particular mother is unable to wait or is neglectful in her attention to her own dress. Mrs. Ramsay is beautiful but as we keep being reminded, her clothes are shabby. In the ceremony of the jewels, when her children get to choose her necklace, it is her daughter Rose, who is allowed to "take up this and then that" because it is what Rose likes best, "She had some hidden reason of her own for attaching great importance to this choosing of what her mother would wear" (Woolf, 1992: p. 89). And as Mrs. Ramsay tries to divine some "quite speechless memory one had for one's mother at that age", she is conscious of feeling sad:

> like all feelings felt for oneself, Mrs. Ramsay thought it made one sad. It was so inadequate, what one could give in return: and what Rose felt was quite out of proportion to anything she was. And Rose would grow up and Rose would suffer she supposed, with these deep feelings. (Woolf, 1992: p. 89)

Yes, Rose will suffer from her passion that is not so much unrequited, as being returned with no sustainable form with which to mould it. Without the necessary shapes, the right clothes to fit her feelings, Rose will always be at the mercy of deep feelings she can't quite translate. Like Lily, Rose is the casualty of the "rose flowering rapture" of her mother's desire. For, as Lily astutely perceives, Mrs. Ramsay is the "loveliest of people" but not quite the perfect shape that is apparent. Trying to move the clods of blue and green paint on her palette into some semblance of movement and desire, Lily realises that the clothes or the glove that is supposed to fit Mrs. Ramsay and so shape Lily's passions, is twisted. What was the "essential thing" Lily wonders,

> by which, had you had found a glove in the corner, you would have known it for its twisted finger, hers undisputedly? She was like a bird for speed, and arrow for directness. She was wilful, she was commanding (of course Lily reminded herself I am thinking of her relations with women, and I am much younger, an insignificant person, living off the Brompton Road). She opened bedroom windows. She shut doors. (Woolf, 1992: p. 55)

Mrs. Ramsay's passions are arrow like, direct and unmediated and she is short-sighted with Lily, cares "not a fig for her painting" (Woolf, 1992: p. 16). Like Rose, Lily is at the beginning of the novel another flower that can't blossom. Or, perhaps the significance of these flower daughters is that whereas Rose is destined to go through life worshipping and admiring her mother's beauty, feeling need for her that will never be adequately represented, Lily perceives more depth. She strives to uncover what lies beneath the painter Mr. Pauncefort's view, the green and grey pictures "with lemon coloured sailing boats and pink women on the beach" (Woolf, 1992: p. 17). The fashion of Mr. Pauncefort, not unlike Mrs. Ramsay, is for "pale, elegant and semi-transparent" art. For if Mrs. Ramsay's rose flowered beauty is there for all to see and admire, it only goes so far. She only appears beautiful. Mrs. Ramsay captures the rosy appearance of love, but not the dark and double side that is part of its essence. She is ideal but too distant. Unable to tell her husband she loves him or to return Rose's deeper feelings, Mrs. Ramsay is wilfully unaware of love's ambivalence. As Lily realises, in order to really make art and life sublime you have to look beneath the fashion for pastel, or rose tinted colours. For "beneath the colour there was a shape" (Woolf, 1992: p. 23).

And all symbolisation of lived form when it comes to a mother returning a child's love must include an acceptance of hate. Winnicott understood this, perhaps more clearly than any other analyst. The idea that the child's use of the mother as an object is always ruthless and that without this acceptance of hate, the ego, can't properly love or find its continuity, style, or shape. Lily's passion, her desire to fling herself at Mrs. Ramsay's knee has to be reduced, because Lily is no longer a child, and there is no way back to her mother's lap. Lily sees the purple passionflowers, the violet jacmanna, as more honest than Rose petals in portraying mother love. Tempering this passion through her painting, Lily pays tribute through the purple shadow that represents Mrs. Ramsay reading to James. But "no-one can tell it for a human shape" protests Mr. Bankes, and Lily replies that there has been no attempt to capture the likeness. The picture "was not of them, she said, or, not in his sense" (Woolf, 1992: p. 59).

For, the form of feelings between mother and child is a virtual entity, distinct from the passion of the real thing, or different enough, at any rate to make those feelings transferable, reproducible in art form. The purple shadow of Lily's painting is an attempt to capture the lived experience of what she feels (what the child feels) for Mrs. Ramsay, in a way that the pretty appearance of the pastel paints or the violet passion of the jacmanna simply cannot. Such lived experience between mother and child is both shared and patterned by the particular forms it takes. In the clinical situation, Wright tells us, "this does not involve describing or explaining but generates "reflections" or "forms" ("subjective objects") that in some way embody the essence of the patients experience in its living reality" (Wright, 2009: p. 35). And of course this is Winnicott's transitional structure, where children need to both find and create their reality. A place in the therapy, inside the mother's reverie, eventually inside the self, where the child or patient can be held; where their subjective affects are returned to them in forms that enable their affects to be experienced as lived and in the world. Within this interplay mother and child, writer and reader and the artist and her spectators translate instinctual passions within the telepathy of a created unconscious invention.

Woolf's fiction, in a very real historical sense, can be linked with Susan Langer's theory of Art and her and Wright's more contemporary psychoanalytic ideas on a non-verbal symbolic form that not only mirrors feelings, but gives birth to them (Langer, 1953). Langer's suggestion that Art is the creation of forms, symbolic of human feeling, is a development of Clive Bell's and Roger Fry's concept of "significant form". Whereas Bell and Fry promote a disinterested contemplation of the aesthetic emotion and its object, the work of art, thereby focusing on the formal properties and relations inherent to the art piece itself. Langer transforms their view by suggesting that the significant form of art moves or speaks to us because it symbolically mirrors and creates feelings. Art, in other words, is a primary and symbolic expression of the living form of human feelings. As I discussed in chapter one and two we can link this idea of a primary symbolic form with Bollas's understanding of a maternal aesthetic and the "unthought known". Although Kenneth Wright is critical of the way in which the unthought known makes the mother and the work of art a nostalgic object, thus "downplaying contemporary therapeutic possibilities as a repository of needed form" (Wright, 2009: p. 151). We can, nevertheless see maternal form as the telepathic transference, rooted in unconscious memories and unconscious perceptions. This therapeutic transference is never simply a here and now phenomena, it is a ghost or spirit that moves between present and past.

Rhythm and Freud's unconscious tree of affects

To the Lighthouse allows us to see particularly how a primary symbolic maternal form operates as a telepathic reading of our affects and

Woolf foregrounds for us the importance of rhythm as part of this telepathic sublimation and movement of our passions. Ella Sharpe was an early psychoanalyst who was interested, like Langer, in a primary non-discursive symbolisation. For Sharpe there is something primal about art, before we can write or conceptually think—we scribble. The early cave dwellers carved on the walls of their caves and danced, inscribing, imitating, and copying the dead whom they have slain. Sharpe argues that in a similar fashion, we incorporate, and magically introject our early parents. Art mirrors cannibalism as "a sublimation rooted in the primal identification with the parents" (Sharpe, 1950: p. 135). The ego's safety, and then its sublimation, depends on it externalising, shaping, and moulding into the outside world, those hostile incorporated paternal imagos:

> All sublimation depends on the power of the ego to externalise the incorporated imagos into some form, concrete or abstract, which is made, moulded, and controlled by the ego in a reality world. (Sharpe, 1950: p. 136)

The artist is thus able to access these primary sense perceptions in his work. As Lyndsey Stonebridge acutely points out, what is significant about Sharpe's account "is the way she refuses to relegate art to the status of a symptom or substitute formation" (Stonebridge, 1998, p. 84). Art is not a symptom of the repressed unconscious, but a part of early unconscious perception where rhythm enables the development and sublimation of the drives. However, Sharpe makes of the ego's sublimation, a goal of restitution of the terrifying unconscious mother, hence her emphasis on identification with the early phallus, as a way of repairing evil towards that mother. And yet I am unhappy with the emphasis on repairing the maternal object in Sharpe's account. Surely the power of her analysis of early unconscious rhythms, is that they are a sublimation of the maternal body, once they have been freed from the confines of the ego's familiar shell? The ego in this scenario is not safe, but splintered or undone, retied and undone again.

As I have argued in Chapter three, there is third rhythm beyond Freud's pleasure and death principles, which arrives with our ability to telepathically dream and read maternal forms beyond the self. It is this dream drive and rhythm that enables us to unconsciously read the non-personal, primary maternal forms, which by definition exist before and beyond the repressive ego. Ella Sharpe captures some of this sense through her ideas of metaphor. For her "metaphor fuses sense experience and thought in language" (Sharpe, 1950b: p. 155). Metaphor is phonetic and "can only evolve in language or in the arts, when the bodily orifices become controlled" (Sharpe, 1950b: p. 156). This connection and translation of the body into speech, is predicated on what Sharpe calls "outerance" and so metaphor here, is not simply a replacement or substitute for what is absent, but directly expresses the rhythmic movement of the body. Metaphor, in other words, is the association and connection of the body and sexuality to language which continues shaping the body's affects into differing spaces and registers. And so if metaphor is a reading of the body rather than its abstraction; then in its primary, maternal and non-discursive rhythms, it also becomes the way we unconsciously and telepathically dream ourselves and the world around us into life.

Language that is not bound to affect can't be used in therapy. The energy and rhythm of our affects moves from the biological to the psychical, from what Freud saw as a raw quantitative force to the more qualitative affects affiliated with thoughts that we call feelings. And because affects move, because they are unconsciously repressed, suppressed, and split off, they are always playing hide and seek with the ego. We could say that a theory of affects has been repressed in Freud's thinking. This means that although we have been happy to discuss the latent and manifest contents of dreams, and the unconscious representations that tell the story of our personal self and history, when it comes to a question of affects in Freud's legacy everyone forgets or disqualifies the importance of the question. Freud is seen to have already dismissed it along with his thinking on seduction, hysteria and the failed techniques of hypnosis and abreaction. In Freud's early work on hysteria, affects were seen as a frustration, denied by the mind, which was then expressed through the body. In *Project For a Scientific Psychology and The Interpretation of Dreams*, affects are the clues to the missing ideas or representations. So, for example pain gives rise, not to an external perception, but to an inner one that energises the memory system and wakes it up.

Feeling pain, something hysterics wish to avoid, is the key to remembering. What we feel is not so much a register of what is happening to us now, but a reminder of what has gone before. In his Dream book Freud understands affects as suppressed in order to make way for the free reign of wishes; but of course the analysis of dreams shows Freud how inseparable wishes and affects really are. Dreams are evidence of how early memory traces are completely mixed up with affectual responses. We see things in dreams, but we can't really perceive them, as we are asleep. Thus, in dreams we are in touch with an affectual memory where our first perceptual responses are intact. Dream memories are particularly instinctual, and wishes are driven by the affects that drive them. This of course ushered in Freud's momentous discovery of child sexuality and the notion of sexual drives, showing how if quantitative bio-energy is the root, then fantasy and wishes are the branches of the affectual structure we call the unconscious.

In his historic paper on the unconscious, Freud suggests that the true aim of repression is to stop affect from developing; when affects are suppressed they are unconscious. So, "strictly speaking" Freud says there are no unconscious affects, in the way there are unconscious ideas. But, he says "there may very well be in the system Ucs. affective structures which, like others, become conscious". Freud goes on, stipulating that the difference,

> arises from the fact that ideas are cathexes—basically of memory traces—whilst affects and emotions correspond to processes of discharge, the final manifestations of which are perceived as feelings. (Freud, 1915: p. 178)

What Freud means here, is that in order for affects to have some kind of form in the unconscious they have to be attached to ideational material and memory. Raw affects, the beginnings of unconscious life, are a structure-less and quantitative energy, flowing and discharging, moving through the drives; to become bound and cathected into a network of representations, which discharge affects as feelings, but only after they have been allowed to proliferate. As a tree of life this unconscious affectual structure contains a trunk full of sap corresponding to the force or flow of quantitative energy, whilst the branches and the unfurling leaves are linked to the more qualitative affects and feelings that are inseparable from ideas. This metaphor of a tree becomes more usable when we take Freud's later structural model into account of *The Ego and the Id*. Because in this later picture the unconscious is something that envelops both ego and id. It is only the upper parts of the tree that equate with the conscious ego, but the structure of affects runs through from roots to leaves moving through a network of multiplying forms and associations.

Although Freud famously pictured the unconscious as a repressed container, it is probably more accurate to see the mind as clothes that drape and envelop the more naked affectual body. To think of the unconscious as an affectual tree, means we have to see it in all its quantitative sameness and force, and in all of its qualitative, representative difference. Affects don't simply structure the drives as Otto Kernberg believes, or exist as some kind of replacement of the drive in original ego states; for affects move in search of form and ideation. As Freud realised when writing *The Ego and the Id*, the unconscious is affectual and perceptual in ways that bypass the repressive hypothesis. Or, to put it more simply there are things we actively repress and banish into the unconscious and then there is a more communicative non-repressed unconscious, which is receptive and perceptive. And yet I don't see what Bollas calls the generative unconscious as distinct from the repressed. If a receptive "maternal" unconscious allows for the empathic and telepathic communication between analyst and patient, elaborating forms for our feelings, then the repressed unconscious is also the force and energy behind our drives. Without this force, the mysterious and ultimately unknowable kernel of our desire, there would be no passion to fuel our creativity, to seek out and find the evocative objects with which we fashion a self. There is no creativity without trauma, no harmony in Freud's picture of psychic life; if there was, our minds would simply cease to move. And this brings me to consider how the affectual tree which structures unconscious life is one in which temporality is embedded.

This temporality, as André Green reminds us is heterogeneous (Green, 2002). Our affects come to life in relation to the living forms that surround us; the sea or say trees, have a rhythm which is matched by our own internal affectual waves and juices. It is in his paper on pleasure and death that Freud starts to wonder about how temporality alters affects through rhythm and repetition. Binding and non-binding of affects, their repetition and compulsion, become the ways in which we obtain pleasure, and avoid un-pleasure, but these repetitions also lead beyond pleasure to the stillness of death. And yet there is no easy way the life and death drives are opposed in Freud's thinking. We can't just equate the binding of affects in the ego, with pleasure, and their unbinding outside of the ego with deathly hate. Just as there is a binding integral to the ego that is involved in containing the spread of hate, so there is unbound energy turning up in dreams, as wishes. Unbound energy opens us to the more plastic world of sensory perceptions, but also to the affects and forms carried by another.

The question in *Beyond The Pleasure Principle,* is one about rhythm, about how our passions travel. It is through rhythm that our passions move and through rhythm that they become fixated and stuck. Just as it is through rhythm we build the self, so it is within the rhythm of the object or the dream that we lose ourselves again. Rhythm feels good, but when is it bad? Freud saw in the repetition of the transference, a malignant and deathly refusal of difference, a reproduction of the same that refuses all remembering or interpretation. But I am not sure this stuck transference, the refusal to let go, or process new material is simply the unbound rhythms Freud associated with the death-drive. What if these rhythms are the affects that exist unbound, but are prevented from moving onto new forms, by the fixity of the old ones? The malignant death-drive or regression we see in the transference, the inability of the patient to move between primary and secondary processes, or between passion and more qualitative feelings, is not simply because our passions lack necessary form. It is also because they are unbound in relation to an ego that won't bend or style itself to fit them. Affects as Freud saw are always out of step with the ego and they turn up as symptoms, as desire that needs sculpting into different spaces, shapes, and patterns. If the ego and our passions both want their own way as the one way, then we are always left with a cruel division between our violent needs and an equally punishing super-ego.

Rhythm is the introduction of time to the straight and urgent quantitative flow of affects. Life is made of rhythms. We can think of the animal rhythms of our bodies and of the natural world; the rhythm of the waves or the rhythm of growing trees, where the patterns of the bark is reproduced in finer detail in the budding leaves. Our feelings have rhythms translated in various forms; trauma becoming tragic drama, or the very particular beat that accompanies the comic provoking our laughter. Rhythm is how we master pain and regulate our pleasures, creating the ego. But rhythm is also involved in how we elaborate what we want and feel in relation to others. One of the things the child learns is how to wait and tolerate the absence of the maternal object. As Freud showed with his famous Fort Da game, rhythm becomes the way a child learns to master the mother's absence through play. But for rhythm to be pleasurable it has to take its time between one thing and another. Too much haste, or an inability to wait, destroys the creative experience of rhythm. Just think of an infant sucking at the breast, and as any midwife will tell you, the attachment between mum and baby is all about them both being relaxed enough to get into rhythm with each other. Creative rhythm also entails destruction, the build up and binding together of representations in the ego, and their break up, as driven affects burst the ego's boundaries and move beyond them. And so if Freud's pleasure principle is one rhythm that binds together the ego, the death drive as the unbound rhythms of our affects must be double.

As opposed to the affects of pleasure and life, there is the really negative aspect of the death-drive that clinicians know as malign regression; a transference that has no appreciable duration, because it is stuck and repetitive. This rhythm is immediate, no beat of time to separate self and other, and so affects can't move beyond either ego, or object, becoming adhesively fastened to what Julia Kristeva calls the primary thing. Deep depression and a mad "powers of horror" are the outcome of this mad mimicry onto a primal maternal object, where affects can't move or change, or find their own forms. Breaking out of this lock-in are the repeated attempts by the ego to murder this primeval object and move on. And without this killing, there is no creative destruction of the ego's representations and boundaries; no third rhythm or movement of affects beyond the ego to seek recreational new life. The use of the object, as Winnicott tells us is necessary in being able to both find and create a shared reality, to shape emotions into experience. Breaking the early mother up, ruthlessly destroying her, allows our passions a rhythm and then a form, in which we can go travelling unconsciously beyond her. This busting up of the primary maternal object is as André Green describes, the way of putting the object, and the subject, into psychical time and motion. So, in this scenario one kind of death-drive has to abolish another, or to put it more specifically you need a death-drive to explode the force of attachment to the mummified object. It is the killing of this formless mummy that brings life and time into being.

There is a force, of the impersonal id that must be deployed in smashing the object in fantasy. This destruction "plays its part in making reality", but this reality is only achieved, if the mother (or analyst) can survive the attacks of the baby (or the client) and return their passions differently (Winnicott, 1969: p. 714). The mother empathises with the infant's need to devour her body and soul (because she feels it too) but instead of simply matching this passion she translates it back to the child in what Sándor Ferenczi called a language of tenderness. Possessive love is both acknowledged and held and then passed back, in a modified state, and with tolerable delay. Thus, passion gets mixed with affection. Rhythms of laughter, and voice or an impulse to be playful, merge with the projectile missile of the child's primitive affects, changing their temperament. In the clinical situation too, the patient's love is reciprocated, but time and the analyst intervenes, holding and interpreting its raw materials. The analyst waits, holds off from interpretations that might pre-empt this attempt to move from a deadly repetition with the maternal objects that exists outside of unconscious time, to a more rhythmic form within it. Our passionate energies are vital ingredients, building into quick flowing drives. Growing and developing, if things go well enough, into the ever more qualitative branches of affects and ideas, these drives enter into more and more complicated networks that give our unconscious worlds their circuitous routes and chains of associative meaning. If rhythm is what moves this tree and brings it to life, then it is within the many branches of what Freud calls the Oedipal complex that these rhythms are both creative and repetitiously fixated. But when are the repetitions of our Oedipal complex simply more of the same and when can they become something new? To put it another way, how do we leave the tree, or move the tree (this is Lily's dilemma) which has been the house of our first passions?

Within the branches of this unconscious tree of affect, our objects, quite arbitrarily it seems, come to rest. Mrs. Ramsay watches the old rook in the trees, father John, squabbling with Mary his wife and she laughs merrily, "Look! she said laughing. They were actually fighting. Mary and Joseph were fighting" (Woolf, 1992: p. 88). And yet Mrs. Ramsay can't see them clearly enough, unable to recognise the ambivalence of love, she keeps turning these Oedipal birds into winged and holy ideals. So, when her son Jasper (an embodiment of the pleasure principle) starts shooting them down, breaking their wings, she can't really rebuke him:

> Don't you think they mind', she said to Jasper, having their wings broken?' Why did he want to shoot poor old Joseph and Mary? He shuffled a little on the stairs and felt rebuked, but not seriously, for she did not understand the fun of shooting birds; that they did not feel; and being his mother, she lived away in another division of

the world, but he rather liked her stories about Mary and Joseph. She made him laugh. But how did she know those were Mary and Joseph? Did she think the same birds came to the same trees every night? he asked. (Woolf, 1992: p. 89)

Jasper manages easily what Lily finds so hard. Being able to shoot your fantasy parents out of the tree, break and replace their ideals is the necessary psychodrama of our Oedipal stage. Mr. Ramsay is tolerant of his son's delight in maiming live creatures, it's "all natural in being a boy" he says sagely (Woolf, 1992: p. 73). Freud, of course agrees, and sees smashing Oedipal objects more the boy's province than the girl's. But is Freud saying this is more natural for the boy, or just easier? Being feminine arguably makes the Oedipal complex, more complex, because smashing up your mother will also feel self-destructive, like destroying a version of you. How you get angry with your mother, as a daughter, from a psychoanalytic point of view is interesting, because this daughterly rage has to find a form or a fiction, to make that destructive smashing of wings, into a good use of the object. And in order to be used, the mother has to supply enough of her idiom, to keep the daughter going as it were, while primary passions can be transcribed within more qualitative feelings and forms.

A third rhythm

These aesthetics of the ego are, I suggest, how our repressed desire gets carried and transported through rhythms and enabling us to bear and shape what we feel. In the beginning our affects exist in a realm of the senses without a subject, and our first forms which carry these affects are the rhythms from non-personal and external physical objects. Interrupted in cutting out magazine shapes for James, by the sounds that surround her, Mrs. Ramsay hears, the tap of "balls upon bats" and the "fall of the waves on the beach, which for the most part beat a measured and soothing tattoo to her thoughts". Like a "cradle song murmured from nature", these rhythms repeat over and over again binding pleasure and life within the ego. But then, as she moves her attention, Mrs. Ramsay becomes aware of a less kind meaning to the movement in her mind: "a ghostly roll of drums remorselessly beat the measure of life, made one think of the destruction of the island and its engulfment in the sea" (Woolf, 1992: p. 20). Beyond reading to the child, beyond the pleasure principle, beyond what can be bound in relation to the object, are the thunderous sounds and waves of our affect like id, terrifyingly ready to swamp us. As both id and idiom, Mrs. Ramsay is a maternal metaphor who embodies different kinds of rhythm and transference, the one that offers creative pleasure and form to the ego, through reading stories to James. And beyond that, the more frightening id, fundamentally driven, immediate in its supplies and demands, that is forever attached to a dead maternal object. And yet there is another death-drive, in the novel, that is not a stuck repetition to the maternal thing. This stroke, in tune and in time with the light house beam, as "the last of the three" is a rhythm that lies beyond the familiar self in relation to a virtual other; a transference onto the non-personal and evocative object that is transformative (Woolf, 1992: p. 70).

This third creative death rhythm of Mrs. Ramsay is, "the losing of personality" beyond the fret, the hurry, "the stir" of the ego. In the freedom, the peace and dark, after her children are sleeping, she sinks down, a dissemination of herself into "inanimate things; trees, streams, flowers". And it is in this sinking down of life that she is able to unconsciously receive, and become, the objects around her, so that they feel like they "expressed one..became one...knew one..in a sense were one" (Woolf, 1992: p. 70). In this losing and loosening of the ego, objects are not just found they are created, an entering and merging into non-personal forms, which enables the new rising of the ego.

> There rose, and she looked and looked with her needles suspended,
> there curled up off the floor in her mind, rose from the lake of one's
> being, a mist, a bride to meet her lover. (Woolf, 1992: p. 71)

Now we can see this uncanny and romantic haunting, as a Jungian archetype, Mrs. Ramsay as some female anima, but I want to argue the definition of the forms at stake, are different. Freud never saw the unconscious representations that haunt the ego, as transcendental myths in the way that Jung did. Instead he saw them like dreams, always a negotiation between the affectual drives of the id and the structures of the object. The ego is born and re-born through this marriage, although such change in character is arguably too difficult for the ego, unless it can untie the knots that bind it together. Losing your ego, after all, is much harder than losing the object; if they were both at a party, the ego would always be the last person to go. Losing your personality is, in a sense, integral to its elaboration, like finding another dance that is less familiar. Only when the ego can let itself go in this transference, between the passionate id and the aesthetics of that affect (given by the virtual other), only then can the ego find its style. Finding your idiosyncratic style as every adolescent needs to know, is all about getting the right mix between the non-personal and the familiar. It is as if this losing of personality and finding of style is paradoxically the pathway through which the ego can realise his true self.

So, rather than seeing Mr. and Mrs. Ramsay as rather tired versions of gendered archetypes, we can see them and their marriage as a relationship between passions and the ego, affects entwined with living forms. Mr. Ramsay is the ego that rigidly won't bend, that is bound tight in knots, loving his wife. He wants to devour her, is frightened of being devoured by her, above all he wants, no, he demands sympathy. Like his friendship with William Bankes, Mr. Ramsey's ego has lost its pulp and become a repetition that "has taken the place of newness" (Woolf, 1992: p. 26). It is Lily and not his wife who refuses to enter Mr. Ramsey's egoic knots: his double binds of give me sympathy and leave me barren. Refusing his drama of grief, holding her skirts away from his puddles of self pity, means Mr. Ramsay has to stop making demands and notice his needs. And he notices that his shoelaces are undone. Lily refuses to sympathise and instead praises his boots,

> What beautiful boots!" she exclaimed, She was ashamed of herself. To praise his boots when he had asked her to solace his soul.
> (Woolf, 1992: p. 167)

But Mr. Ramsay smiles, "his pall, his draperies his infirmities fell from him". He shows Lily how to knot and unknot her shoes, "Three times he knotted her shoe; three times he unknotted it". As we learn Mr. Ramsay's knots are his own invention and Lily can eventually feel compassion for him when this is acknowledged. Lily also has to unwind the knots in her mind. She has to confront the difficulty in her painting of connecting "this mass on the right hand with that on the left"; how to connect, in other words, her internal "house full of unrelated passions" to the hedge, the step, the wall (Woolf, 1992: p. 60). For it is Mr. Ramsay, in spite of his knots and melodramas, who has known all along how to fashion objects, with his exquisite boots and his beautiful face that has taken on the "unornamented beauty which so deeply impressed her", of the bare and austere kitchen table (Woolf, 1992: p. 170).

Despite his love for his wife, it is not Mrs. Ramsay's immediate and unmediated passion that gives the necessary lived form to Mr. Ramsay's feelings, but the kitchen table of his work and his books. For this table has moved, no longer simply metaphysics lying on top of vegetable life, it is an embodied, living experience:

> He must of had his doubts about the table, she supposed; whether
> the table was a real table; whether it was worth the time he gave it;
> whether he was able after all to find it. He had had doubts, she felt,
> or he would of asked less of people. (Woolf, 1992: p. 170)

In his paper *The Dynamics of the Transference*, Freud discusses how there are at least two transferences in the clinical situation, one positive and one negative. Both go back to erotic sources, as "originally we knew only sexual objects" (Freud: 1912: p. 105). When negative transference becomes too strong (Freud gives the examples of paranoics), then analysis is impossible. But the positive transference, too, has its roots in ambivalence. And it is the erotic source, at the heart of the transference, which produces repetition of the symptom. Breaking up this resistance in analysis entails breaking up the transference, being able to move from one rhythm to another. This working-through, Freud reminds us in his famous companion piece on remembering and repeating can be theoretically likened to "the 'abreacting' of the quotas of affect strangulated by repression" (Freud, 1914: p. 156). But of course such discharge of affects through feelings, as Freud realised all too well, was not enough to bring about change in the analysis. What distinguishes psychoanalysis from hypnotic treatments or body therapy goes back to Freud's realisation that the discharge, or abreaction of affect, is not enough. The same feelings come back, and if they have been lifted hypnotically, more strongly than before. Such is the power of repression. It is the ability, through the transference to change the nature and structure of what we feel, to move and modify our passionate love, that makes psychoanalysis a necessarily less economic and more drawn out affair, than say going to a prostitute, or having our anxieties washed away through hypnotherapy.

So the question remains, how do affects move, what rhythms move them and where to? Freud highlights two clinical transferences or rhythms onto the figure of the analyst. Of course in life and in the analytic session there are many more, the rhythms of symptoms, internal objects, and past and present loves. These rhythms are collected into particular streams or branches that become attached to the therapist. A rhythm moves backwards and forwards, like a branch in the breeze, or a wave in the sea. Back to the past and forward to the future, our affects are moved in particular time, in relation to their objects. The pleasure principle or the love that binds the ego is always moving backwards, to old times and familiar haunts, before it can move forward; such uncanny staging of the old with the new, means confronting what a beyond the pleasure principle might mean. Because we all have to face a before, an after, and the disappointment of what living beyond the pleasure principle entails. We can do this, Freud tells us, more or less creatively. And the creative way of the death-drive, in *To the Lighthouse*, is the third rhythm, the third stroke from the lighthouse, the third tying and untying of shoes or egos that allows Mr. and Mrs. Ramsay to move from one transference to another, one rhythm of affect to another. We have a positive and negative transference on to the analyst, but there is a third one which comes, in time, with the ability to paint.

Rhythms of reading and sexuality

If Mr. Ramsay encounters the reality principle at the end of this novel of rhymes, shapes, and rhythms, it is because he can allow a transformative relationship within his ego, in relation to the object. Only when his ego can become undone like his bootlaces, can the demanding passion for his wife, be returned through the more lasting and austere beauty of the table. I don't think Woolf is insinuating that real passions and life can be substituted for, through books and academic study, quite the reverse. But in *To the Lighthouse*, Mrs. Ramsay is not real to anyone, even herself, And getting beyond her imaginary order, to what Lacan would call the Symbolic, is the ability for the ego to create its own living forms: to beautifully boot, tie, and untie its affects. Through reading with our mother we combine passion with the beginnings of finding new rhythms and forms. It is as if through reading this novel, and through the unconscious reading in it, love can last. Not because reading is a substitute for love, but because it is a real continuation of its form, it's what sustains us, in the presence and through the absence of the object. It allows us to translate our desires, to have them heard and returned differently. Reading in a clinical session is how the analyst and patient unconsciously listen and translate bits of each other, telling and hearing the symptoms and making them up together, into different stories and genres. And it is through unconscious reading that we can move from the repetition of our drives to the rhythm of our affects. We can move through the tree of our affects, to their finer constellation in the branches.

It is through reading that Mr. and Mrs. Ramsay finally hit their stroke together, finding a third rhythm. He can realise that the whole world does not revolve around going to bed with a woman, he can return "to Scott and Balzac, to the English novel and the French novel". And as Mrs. Ramsay reads in a light trance she manages to move through the mass or trunk of her passion, to a crystallisation of its affects, informed by the object: the shape of her feelings in a sonnet, sitting in the branches:

> She was climbing up those branches, this way and that, laying hands on one slower and then another.
>
> Nor praise the deep vermilion in the rose,
>
> she read, and so reading she was ascending, she felt onto the top, the summit. How satisfying! How restful! All the odds and ends of the day stuck to this magnet; her mind felt swept, felt clean. And then, there it was, suddenly entire shaped in her hands, beautiful and reasonable, clear and complete, the essence sucked out of life and held rounded there—the sonnet. (Woolf, 1992: p. 131)

For if Woolf acknowledges in her androgynous modernist book, that there can never be a third sex, there can, perhaps by a third rhythm. Love, without the ego's aesthetics of form, without an idiom to give it a third rhythm, simply falls back into the divide between the ego and its passions, the mind and the body. We have repression or an impossible desire. In this scenario, sexual difference becomes a sadomasochistic stand off, in life and in literary theory. But just as we can put the ego and its passions into a time, a rhythm that can show them some new moves, so can we understand how the quantity and the quality of our love is something we have to be able to mould into different shapes and temporalities.

Reading, I suggest, is not simply desire, but about the forming and informing of our internal worlds. We have to begin reading with someone, but then we can read on our own. How is this similar or different from having sex? You can have sex on your own, either before or after having it with someone else, but in order to make sex a relational exchange, you have to enter into an unconscious reading of the other, with all the foreplay, emotional response that this entails. We can read without desire and we can desire without enough reading or care. But reading arguably adds something to sex; it creates a delay and different pathways, a kind of free association on the way to the primary wish or need. And yet it is this free association, the dissemination of ideas and feelings, integral to our imaginative life, which breaks up the wish into other shapes and constellations of thoughts and affects, keeping us unconsciously travelling. In his essay *On The Universal Tendency to Debasement in the Sphere of Love*, Freud tells us that when it comes to love, affection and sensuality are at odds (Freud, 1912b). Affection is older than erotic love and is part of the self-preservative drive, the early ego's devotion and attachment to the parents. Libidinal desire comes later and attaches itself to the same objects, which are of course incestuously forbidden. Happy love in adult live depends on being able to combine affection and desire, but because our affectionate ties are all too often familial in nature, they take us back to the early fixations where tenderness and desire are incompatible. As Freud says this means for people, the commonly acknowledged dilemma "Where they love they do not desire and where they desire they cannot love" (Freud: 1912b: p. 183). The way and the way out for our desire, is then to find those people who can remind us of our parents, without actually becoming them.

Something, in other words, must be added to desire to make it work and that is the translation of our ego's affections into forms and figures that resemble our first Oedipal loves and also replace them. Unconscious reading and translating between the ego and its objects, paints, and re-paints the pictures of our ego's internal gallery. And yet reading or painting, devoid of the force of desire becomes an inhibited return to forbidden incestuous objects, like the frigid woman who is too ready to care, but unable to fuck. But maybe the reading between mother and child, between Mrs. Ramsay and James, between the ego and its internal objects, can pave the way and create the step whereby desire can enter into a rhythm and time; where its repressed self can find expression. But because this desire, has by its very nature, to be delayed and translated in order to gain its rhythm, the self or ego will have to accept the death of Mrs. Ramsay. It will have to lose, and fail, and finally find a workable shadow or shape for Mrs. Ramsay's immediate, straight as an arrow, passion.

The reading and painting of our desires, in life and in *To the Lighthouse*, is a journey through the tree of our affects, to their finer distillation in the branches. Of course, not all affects are transformable or bearable, and it in the Oedipal branches of our desire that we learn to repress, and delay, our more incestuous wanting. Mrs. Ramsay reads and paints a fairy world for her youngest children to hold their desires and fears, to give them time and rhythm, so they can fly from their trees, or make the final sailing expedition to the lighthouse. And so maybe there is more to repression that just the banishing of unwanted material; that in addition to repression, or its release, there is the potential in the ego for this desire to be recreated. Maybe for every repression there is a corresponding, potential time and rhythm of our feelings that can be unconsciously read and communicated. If reading and painting are the forms given by another that allow our ego its idiomatic shapes, then our passionate desires are on the other side of this endeavour, because they are the force which break up these figures and allow others to emerge. Desire, then is an essential part of creating the ego's rhythms; a transference, which might capture the object, shoot or wing it. So that for every banished or punished desire, there is also a scattering; a dissemination of that desire into a myriad of internal objects that can fly and be creatively set free.

When Lily contemplates the pear tree and examines all the contradictory things fissured and humped forever into its woody bark, she sees the different currents of her affection and desire: her own repressed ego in the figure of Mr. Ramsay. She sees him in all his spoilt tyranny and need. But then she sees him, again, as a father who is simple and true, loving his dogs and children. These contradictions dance up and down in Lily's mind, "like a company of gnats, each separate, but all marvellously controlled within an invisible elastic net" and as they dance up and down she becomes aware of Mr. Ramsay's aesthetic form, the scrubbed table, still etched in the branches. Along with this impression comes,

> her thought which had spun quicker and quicker, exploded of its own intensity; she felt released; a shot went off close at hand, and there came, flying from its fragments, frightened effusive, tumultuous, a flock of starlings. (Woolf, 1992: p. 30)

Lily is the flower symbol of rebirth in this novel, but she is also a stereotype of the frigid and dry "old maid". And it is perhaps in this figure of an ageing daughter, that has been so widely acknowledged to be autobiographical, that we can see Virginia Woolf, staging and restaging Freud's famous question, "What does the woman want"? In the novel this question is voiced by the flounder in the fairytale of *The Fisherman and His Wife*, "Well, what does she want then? Said the flounder" (Woolf, 1992: p. 63). And of course in the tale the wife can't stop wanting, because everything she wants, and gets, ends up not being satisfying. This is then the dilemma of desire, because we can't, in a Freudian sense, ever completely have what we want. Sensual, and affectionate love, are forever estranged. Although Freud has been rightly criticised for his sexist views on women, this has also been confused with some very interesting things he has to say about female desire. That because women are given the role of caring, because they mother and are mothered, then their relation to the affectionate currents in their psychic life and to their incestuous objects is very powerful, as is the consequent division between their affectionate and sensual love.

Lily's dilemma is how to find her desire, how to connect her affections with her passions and translate her love for Mrs. Ramsay with her picture. This painting is a re-painting; a reading, translating and in-forming of affects that takes place between the ego and its objects. Killing the Victorian Angel in the House, along with Charles Tansley's patriarchal assumption that "women can't paint and women can't write" is arguably Freud's project where it is in tune with feminism (Woolf, 1992: p. 94). Because the translation of the woman and mother into living art forms for the ego, is what psychoanalytic therapy is all about. Translating her feelings into more painterly forms is how Lily manages to end Tansley's disembodied talk and move her affectual tree so it can mediate passions with the ego, between the feminine and the masculine.

> She remembered that next morning she would have to move the tree more into the middle, and her spirits rose so high at the thought of painting tomorrow that she laughed out loud at what Mr. Tansley was saying. Let him talk all night if he liked it. (Woolf, 1992: p. 101)

The third rhythm that Lily eventually finds is one (like the reading between the Ramsay's), where her painting can give a form to physical love, to the unrelated passions of the house. Like Mr. Ramsay and his beautiful scrubbed table of a mind, this rhythm is one that has learnt to tie and untie boots in styling the affects of the ego. This rhythm is beyond the pleasure principle, a telepathic transference onto the object, that has learnt how to wait and to lose; to bear the death of what we once desired, and desired to be, and yet could never fully have. It is "with a curious physical sensation" that Lily enters into this "dancing rhythmical movement" and although her juices, the passions of her paints are spontaneously squirted, the movement of her brush "was now heavier and went slower, as if it had fallen into some rhythm dictated to her" (Woolf, 1992: p. 173). Managing to make her rhythm work, Lily can finally give a shape and dress sense to the passionate Mrs. Ramsay. And as readers we can follow her desire, giving time to our unconscious tree of affects: its meandering branches and patterned leaves. Fast, and then slow, as it blows through our minds.

CHAPTER EIGHT

Dreaming lilies

W hat would it mean to think of the psychoanalytic unconscious as an immanent entity; something that exists outside as a virtual, suggestive and impersonal world, until it is brought inside us and elaborated within the internal topographies sketched for us by Freud? In this reading the unconscious would exist as a virtual phenomena; something by definition we cannot know, until it becomes elaborated within the personal self or ego. Outside as the unconscious virtual world we select from, and inside as both a receptive potential of being (the unthought known) and the repressed and unknowable constituent of our being, the Freudian unconscious is both dynamically repressed and also receptively and perceptively communicative in relation to another. If we acknowledge the hidden role of unconscious perception in Freud's writings then we have to accept that our unconscious being extends to a virtual and phenomenological world beyond the ego. As Jean Laplanche notes, *A Note Upon "The Mystic Writing Pad"* is Freud's most succinct theory of the operation of durational, perceptual time which moves beyond the subject. The world is an excess in this description, from which we selectively retrench, or cut out from, thus establishing a time and subjectivity for ourselves. This time is not restricted to human beings, but encompasses any living being. In rhythm we move backwards and forwards, becoming excited and interrupted by the virtual world and then retreating, as "a periodical shutting down that opposes the continuous action of the 'not me'" (Laplanche 1999: p. 241).

Laplanche's principal objection to Freud's theory of time is that it belongs "outside psychoanalysis"; placing Freud alongside thinkers such as Merleau-Ponty and Bergson who happily extend their phenomenological analysis from humans to animals. In Laplanche's view, none of the basic tenets of psychoanalysis such as sexuality, repression or transference, can be found in this perceptual psychology. Furthermore, it makes narcissism the basis of human existence with the unconscious as the centre. So, "far from being an alien inside me, the unconscious would be my foundation, my starting-point" (Laplanche, 1999: p. 241). Laplanche thinks that Freud's theory of time is anti-psychoanalytic, whereas I suggest it connects psychoanalysis to a social albeit virtual world, rather than leaving it as an explanation of our elaborate protections against it. If "The Mystic Writing Pad" is Freud's theory of psychological rhythm and time then it is through his understanding of unconscious perception and telepathy, that this model can be integrated with his theory of the rhythms inherent to the repressive personal self. I have argued in this book for a hidden account of telepathy and unconscious perception in Freud's work and that without this more receptive unconscious a theory of unconscious repression or indeed the psychoanalytic transference could not exist.

Freud's dandelions

Freud's early thinking on unconscious perception is contained within his description of screen memories. Strachey notes how curious it is that the type of screen memory considered in Freud's early paper where "an early memory is used as a screen for a later event—almost disappears from the later literature" (Strachey, 1950: p. 302). Strachey is referring to Freud's subsequent understanding, formulated only two years after in *The Psychopathology of Everyday Life*, which places screen memories as later memories covering over earlier, autoerotic fantasies of childhood. However, in Freud's first thoughts on *Screen Memories*, it is the unconscious perceptions and fantasies of the present that are projected back into a childhood memory and so veiled. The case that illustrates these ideas is presented by Freud as being that of a university educated man of thirty-eight, but as we learn shortly afterwards in Freud's letter to Fliess this case history is autobiographical. In the story Freud is a young man who remembers an incident from childhood in an unaccountably intense way. He is with his two cousins, a girl and a boy, and they are all aged between two and three years old. The scene is of a lush green, sloping meadow and at one end is a cottage with a farmer's wife and a nursemaid in conversation. The children are playing and picking dandelions:

> The little girl has the best bunch; and, as though by mutual agree-
> ment, we—the two boys—fall on her and snatch away her flowers.
> She runs up the meadow in tears and as a consolation the peasant-
> woman gives her a big piece of black bread. Hardly have we seen
> this than we throw the flowers away, hurry to the cottage and ask
> to be given some bread too. And we are in fact given some; the
> peasant-woman cuts the loaf with a long knife. In my memory the
> bread tastes quite delicious—and at that point the scene breaks off.
> (Freud, 1899: p. 311)

Freud is puzzled by the vividness of the yellow flowers and the deli-cious flavour of the bread. The way they seem to make the memories really present. He then remembers how he first came upon the memory, during a visit to the same cousins when he was seventeen, and on this occasion he fell madly in love with the girl as a young woman. Unfortu-nately he encounters her for only a few days before she departs to board-ing school. She is wearing a yellow dress and Freud links the flower memory from childhood with the girl he has fallen so hopelessly for. He has the memory again a few years later on the occasion of another visit, but this time Freud is "a slave" to his studies and is uninterested in his past love. Instead, his father and uncle get to work plotting his future marriage to the girl; in part because they think marriage will lead to a more sensible bread and butter occupation than his fanciful stud-ies. Taking the role of an analyst with himself Freud proceeds to draw associations to the two memories noting that the sweet tasting bread denotes fantasies of a happy marriage to the young woman. The yel-low of the flowers stands in for the repressed memories; yellow being the colour of the childhood dandelions, the dress and the dark yellow flowers that Freud discovers walking in the Alps (the only pleasures he allows himself when being such a work slave). The snatching of the flowers in the childhood memory are the symbolic code for wishing to deflower his dream woman and Freud acknowledges that it is precisely the "coarsely sensory element in the phantasy" that prevents it from developing consciously (Freud, 1899: p. 317).

What are we to make of this early understanding of the screen memory, where early impressions are created and "worked over" at a later date? "It looks", Freud remarks,

> as though a memory trace from childhood had here been translated back into a visual and plastic form at a later date—the date of the memory's arousal. But no reproduction of the event had ever entered the subject's consciousness. (Freud, 1899: p. 321)

This is Freud's idea of deferred memory in action, and yet the explanation of this story only makes sense if we understand that there are unconscious perceptions in the present that are hidden through the cover and creation of a more innocent childhood memory. This understanding of unconscious perception does not cancel out Freud's later emphasis on screen memories as innocent screens of more sexual impulses situated in the past, but it gives them a new twist, because if unconscious perception is always at work in the creation of vivid memories, then how do we know what is memory and what is unconscious perception? Unconscious perception and memory work backwards and forward, but distinguishing them becomes more and more difficult. If as Freud says the "raw material" of our memories are unknowable in their first forms, then this fact must dissolve the distinction between screen memories and all other memories. So much so, that it remains a question, according to Freud, "whether we have any memories at all *from* our childhood: memories *relating* to our childhood maybe all we possess" (Freud, 1899: p. 322).

It is significant I think that the relationship between unconscious perception and memory in the above story is linked to an association with flowers. As I have argued in chapter two, flowers are lived forms associated with a maternal holding and telepathy which read memory and perception (past and present) in relation to each other; inhabiting borderlands between the real and the imaginary. But Freud's unconscious reading of the dandelion memory also makes us think about fantasy in a different way because fantasy here is not just some false imaginary we have to escape from in order to reach the symbolic or reality. Fantasy as unconscious perception is our view point onto reality; it is the means by which we correspond to the present and the past. Dreaming in other words, by day, and in relation to the other, is how we create our relations not just with the world that surrounds us, but with our history. We dream up our relationship to our past through our unconscious reading of current reality, and we read our current dreams through our relationships with a past which can only exist through our ability to unconsciously read and imagine it.

Leo Bersani in his recent essay "Psychoanalysis and the Aesthetic Subject" argues that, "the unconscious never is" it is always a virtual world waiting in the wings for realisation within our being. So we are in a way simply a continuation of that wider world. "It is as if", Bersani suggests, "the world stimulated the activity of desiring fantasy, not by lacking objects of desire, but by their very proliferation" (Bersani, 2010: p. 148). Fantasy is, for Bersani, a correspondence between the world and the self which becomes more elaborated as we find more forms to stimulate and fit our desires. Fantasy is not therefore an inability to have an exchange with reality. "On the contrary", says Bersani,

> it is the sign of an extremely attentive, highly individuated response to external reality. It is not the result of pressure from pre-existent, dominant unconscious impulses; the only sense in which it is revealing about psychic depths is that an intrinsically undifferentiated unconscious provides the material for psychic composition. Fantasy is thus on the threshold between an invisible (and necessarily hypothetical) inner world and the world present to our senses. (Bersani, 2010: p. 148)

Through unconscious perception and reading we elaborate and transport our repressive fantasies, so connecting them with the world. In Freud's dandelion memory the vivid sensory perception of the yellow flowers and the sweet bread amounting to "almost a hallucination", contain more than one, conflicting fantasies from the present. They signify Freud's wish to marry and settle down with the girl in the yellow dress and they also point to an opposite ideal, more in line with his super-ego, of how he should obey his father's plans, give up his "impractical ideas" and take on a "bread and butter occupation". Talking to himself, Freud says, "You projected two phantasies into one and made a childhood memory of them" (Freud, 1899: p. 315). The yellow Alpine flowers that give Freud such pleasure are the "stamp of manufacture", as it were, of their origin in the present rather than the past; they are the fantasies that spell out this young man's attentive "individuated response" to external reality. However, as Freud continues to argue with himself, he realises that things are not straightforward and that the early childhood scene seems genuine too, concluding that the childhood memory is innocent enough to be a screen for the later wishful fantasies.

Follow the wild flowers

Thus the dandelion memory becomes a screen for Freud's current desires and fantasies of reality, and it is also a cover for earlier infantile wishes. As a scene of deferred memory the dandelions signify Freud's infantile desires, blossoming into his adult wishes to snatch away these flowers from the girl in the yellow dress. How do we work out, in this fascinating vignette, where repression stops and unconscious perception starts, or vice versa? And yet without Freud's fantasies of the world around him, none of these desires would be set into motion; without his unconscious reading of the girl in her yellow dress, or the matching colour of the mountain flowers, the dandelions are just repressed or forgotten. Freud travels to his childhood home, meets his dream girl, only to lose her; he then goes to University to study, taking pleasure and solace in his Alpine walks. Fantasies of the yellow flowers, and the memory traces they carry from childhood, are inseparable from the unconscious perception of them, as resonating forms in the world. And yet without these flowers no movement or re-translation between past and present would have occurred. Freud's dandelions are arguably the artistic and maternal forms of his ego that move beyond his personal self to inscribe an unconscious that resides in the virtual world. They are a telepathic and unconscious reading of his repressed incestuous desires, as well as a telepathic perception of the non-personal forms and flowers that lie in waiting, beyond any knowable identity. In short, these dandelions are how Freud travels with his desires between the inside and the outside perhaps constructing what Lacan (in another language) would call topological forms.

As topologies and translations of an unconscious beyond the self these flowers create new possibilities of who Freud can become; and it is notable that the Alpine flowers, signifying his study and future career as a psychoanalyst, are the sublimations that begin to take precedence over his more carnal desires for the cousin in the yellow dress. In fact, the dress, the dandelions, and the mountain flowers are all connected through colour, smell, and shape to what we might call the changing and flexible contours of Freud's body ego. Past, present and future patterns of the ego are at stake here, those that have been repressed, but also the forms of being the ego can still become if it follows its wild flowers and does not just forsake them as common garden plants. Dandelions are simply troublesome weeds in the domestic backyard of the personal ego; the neurotic fantasies that have to be repressed or uprooted. And yet it is only beyond the familiar boundaries of the ego; outside the haven of our home, that we can find the truly wild or unknowable side of these flowers and of ourselves.

The ego, we could say, is enabled to dream and therefore to travel, through its screen memories (its unconscious perceptions); and it is through these dreaming screens that we construct our psychic reality in relation to a virtual and material world in which we live. Telepathy and the unconscious communication with non-psychological objects (beginning with the early mother), is a translation of our secret and repressed memories, through which our psychological memories and experiences are born, or come to exist. Psychic reality is the interweaving of the world and our passions, an inseparable mixing of material and psychic space. And it is the yellow flowers or lived maternal forms of Freud's autobiographical self or ego, which show how memories are always raw experiences that have been worked and worked over through an unconscious filming of the virtual world that lies beyond that personal self. If Freud's flowers are the lived maternal forms that rework past memories and desires to bring new experiences into being, then they also shape those early impressions or memories of the ego, through unconscious readings of the non-human material spaces of our everyday life. There is no access for Freud to his first impressions, until they have been unconsciously read and translated into their flowery forms. For it is these forms, we could call them typologies, that give moving shape to the body ego, stretching and twisting everyday and psychic spaces into new shapes and new places we can inhabit. We exchange eating our mothers for smelling them and sensing them, appreciating their colours and patterns, turning them into imaginary and real forms or flowers that shape the ego. In so doing we move our passions into a new place from the one in which they initially arose.

These passions or early memories are not "complete inventions" says Freud, "they are false in the sense they have shifted an event to a place where it did not occur" (Freud, 1899: p. 322). Follow these wild flowers, says Freud, and we can unconsciously read our way, back to the past and forward to our futures, through the virtual landscapes that exist beyond personal experience. Flower forms are, in Freud's unconscious perception and memory, the maternal lived shapes of an ego, carved out from the landscapes around him; elements of sublimated being, carrying him towards his future.

These yellow flowers are fantasies and typologies that don't simply elaborate Freud's personal self (the repressed ego); they open up the topographies of the unconscious (Freud's topographical and structural model) to changing geographies of a more impersonal material world. Freud's dandelions, in other words, are the forms through which he travels from inside and outside, and between present and past. But it is in their wilder design and habitat that they actually illuminate the world and his desires together. We can't, in other words, find or pick the wild flowers of our desires through just turning up to our privatised therapy sessions, falling in love with our analyst or free-associating on the couch. We need do all these things, reading and re-describing the neurotic dandelions of the transference through the unconscious communication of the clinical session. And yet arguably, to really follow the flowers, we have to also walk through the garden door to territories beyond our familiar experience. Transference onto the analyst, like the screen memory, has to be read as a desire whose form is always shifting shape and location. The therapist is our earliest primal tie (and dandelion), an imaginary lover (the cousin in the yellow dress), and the virtual mountain forms that signal the becoming of who we can be. It is only through turning his back on his longing for his cousin and the tasty black bread, that Freud eventually re-finds them, stretched and changed through time and place, on his mountain climbs towards his future. If the dandelions and the cousin in the yellow dress, are reminiscent of our incestuous, symptom ridden Oedipal forms, then it is their unconscious translation into the wilder more unknowable forms of the ego, that will open up the landscapes in which we live. Follow the wild flowers Freud seems to say, in all of their uncanny colours and semblances, if you want to elaborate your deepest and most intimate wishes.

Unconscious reading of the transference

Christopher Bollas observes how unconscious perception and reception take place in the free association between the unconscious of two people: the analyst and the analysand. Calling this the analytic work of the Freudian Pair, Bollas, reminds us that free association was Freud's original meaning of transference: the transfer of unconscious material onto consciousness. Distinguishing free association from "Transference" as it is generally understood within mainstream British analysis (the projection of past unconscious wishes and libidinal ties onto the therapist), Bollas stoutly declares that; "Modern psychoanalysis should return to Freud's earlier view to recover its wisdom" (Bollas, 2007: p. 85). Whereas, interpretation of the erotic transference, in the here and now, has been the mainstay of particularly Kleinian analysis, the original Freudian emphasis on the patient free associating in relation to everyday life within the session has been more ignored because according to Bollas it can't be shored up with the more knowing authority of the analyst.

If an omniscient belief in "here and now" interpretations obscures the intuition and play of the free associating Freudian pair, then it is the telepathic reading and replication of forms that accompanies such free association that mitigates the ferocity of our transference passions. One of the reasons that the analysis of the transference from Dora onwards, has been such a central concern in psychoanalysis is because it is irresolvable, and by that I don't mean that therapy can't help, because I think it helps enormously. But no amount of interpretation of the passionate transference actually modifies it, quite the reverse. Dora's analysis with Freud failed because she could not bear his literal interpretations of her desire. This does make Freud's observations wrong, if anything they were sexually too near the mark. But Freud missed, as he later acknowledged, Dora's maternal transference onto Frau K. This transference as I have argued includes the crucial significance of Dora's rapt daydreaming in front of the painting of the Sistine Madonna, which is one of Dora's associations (a screen perception/memory), she makes with her second dream. Thus, I suggest that we can see the screen perception of the Madonna painting much like Freud's yellow flowers, in that the painting figures as an unconscious perception working backwards to the "real" of an early passionate tie with the maternal body. As a typology or lived maternal form that can carry and aesthetically sublimate Dora's passions, the painting of the Madonna was the free association and screen memory with which Freud could have worked with. In creating maternal forms to carry Dora's passions, this free associative transference would have served to modify and unconsciously read her imaginary Oedipal relations; translating those familiar bonds into the virtual forms of what she could become, beyond her familiar ego, in relation to her future.

Lacanian analysts have realised for quite a while that simply interpreting the transference as an imaginary object relation, just shores up the ego's fantasmatic relationships. I want to suggest that unconscious perception and reading between analyst and patient, the telepathy between them, is a way of elaborating new lived forms for the ego that read the past; thereby returning to the repressed history of our personal selves. However, this unconscious reading and free association passing between analyst and client also moves beyond the self in relation to the non-psychological forms and resemblances of our everyday world. As Bollas insists the unconscious is not to be found in some deep and secret place, it is happened upon, like Freud's dandelions and the yellow Alpine flowers, or in Dora's visit to an art gallery, in the most ordinary, cultural objects and places. Most importantly, the unconscious is not to be found shut up within the self or within some private retreat from the world. The therapy's couch should be a viewpoint onto the world, because it is only through our fantasies, our unconscious perceptions onto the virtual landscapes that surround us that we can move towards a reception of the anything new.

Unconscious perception, as Freud realised in relation to his personal and wild flowers, is a screen memory; something that coats and covers our past memories and desires, carrying them to and fro, in rhythm with the virtual world in which we live. And narcissism in a relational sense is the glue that allows us to identify and fantasise with that world beyond the self, because we have to dream the world in order to socially inhabit it. "We might speak of sociability" suggests Leo Bersani, as an ascetic conduct'; one that is prepared to lose or bypass the sadomasochistic pain of the repressive ego. And,

> once stripped of these interests, we discover a new type of being, as well as a new type of pleasure. The pleasure does not serve an interest or fulfil a desire. It is an intransitive pleasure intrinsic to a certain mode of existence, to self-subtracted being. A willingness to be

less—a certain kind of ascetic disposition—introduces us (perhaps reintroduces us) to the pleasure of rhythmed being. (Bersani, 2010: p. 48)

So it is in our unconscious rhythms, beyond the pleasure ego, where we encounter the everyday objects and people as the dream screens and forms with which we go travelling. Back to the past and our repressed and familiar self, but also forward to what is our unknowable future. Without our unconscious reading of the everyday life around us, neither are night dreams, nor our preferred stories of ourselves and our pasts could possibly exist. We have to unconsciously read the rhythms of the spaces that surround us in our daily existence in order to make and re-make the ones that build our so-called internal, psychic reality. And yet we also need the pleasures of our narcissism, not incarcerated or repressed within the self but as open feelers, ready to illuminate and respond to the virtual forms, which come our way. Mediation of the erotic transference can only be achieved through the unconscious reading of lived forms that begin beyond the ego's walls; situated within the objects and people that we relate to. Unconscious reading of each other within the clinical session is a form of ascetic conversation because it is an intimacy where actual sex is bypassed, or sublimated through the art of elaborating a more virtual world. Freud's interpretation of Dora's erotic transference was only ever going to lead to more extreme first forms of love or hate, and this was played out in the way that she left him. And yet as I have suggested, if Freud had understood Dora's transference onto the painting of the Madonna, as her need to unconsciously read him as a more impersonal object, then maybe he would of refrained from some of his more explicit sexual interpretations, that merely put her back inside the repressive ego and incestuous family she was trying to leave. In other words Dora needed her love shaping into a lived maternal form that could be a shared ideal form of becoming. Not a substitution for the object that Dora had lost; more a wilder, self-subtracted version of it.

Wild flower forms

Freud's dandelions are the screen memories that come to him through his unconscious fantasies and perceptions of the young woman he falls for in his adolescent passion. They also read and bring to life the earlier more personal drama of his childhood. Freud is certain the memory is constructed as a response and a cover for his passionate transference onto his beautiful cousin. The hallucinatory and sensual parts of the screen memory, the brightness of the yellow flowers, the sweet bread are reminiscent, Freud reminds himself, of the two principal childhood drives of love and hunger associated with the mother. Figuring as the different currents of affection and sensuality, the bread and dandelions become more sexually explicit with the associations Freud then makes with paintings of ladies bustles and a recent burlesque he has visited. Like Woolf's first memories, Freud's dandelion memories are a mixture of unconscious perception and memory; they are both real and imaginary. They are, I suggest, the lived maternal forms which both elaborate and mediate his early passions. More importantly they carry and communicate those unconscious desires, thus transferring his current daydreams of the girl in the yellow dress back to the past where they can read and translate more buried memories. Arguably it is the role of such cover memories to read the past familiar forms of the self in relation to new fantasies that propel us into the world. Screen memories carry us back to the past, but they are also the aesthetic covers that carry our desires onwards in our travels with current reality. For the girl in the yellow dress is both familiar and new, she is scene of Freud's early Oedipal love and hate, as well as being a current unfinished form; a pleasurable "foretaste" of what is to come.

As in Woolf's memory, it is the lived form of the yellow flowers and dresses which unconsciously read and cover Freud's more sensual passions; moving them unconsciously and imaginatively. Interestingly the imaginative daydreams of the girl in the yellow dress arise in the young Freud as he walks in the lovely woods, the same woods that he used to escape from his father before he could barely walk. And yet, after going to University, Freud soon forgets his cousin. She is too associated with his father's plans for a safe "bread and butter career", and as such she is ultimately an inhibition: desire strapped too tight with super-egoic injunctions. So the woods in which Freud wanders seems a way out of filial guilt, a way beyond the ego of his knowable self and family to something much more unchartered. The escape to the woods of Freud's young narcissism becomes an escape to mountain climbs with their wild yellow flowers, whose lived form carries the exact colour and pleasures of the girl Freud has loved. These wild flowers are not anything immediately knowable, and so they brook no immediate satisfactions. As such, they are virtual and formal; an aesthetic pattern of what has come before and a promise of some as yet non-definable future.

Freud finds the freer associations and sublimations of his passions that release him to his future, away from his father. Being wedded to his books rather than his cousin gives him the route out to his future life carrying him away from his more familial self. If life as a scholar in the city is a struggle: "hard pressed by the exigencies of life and when I had to wait so long for a post", then it is through the only pleasures Freud allows, the climbing trips and mountain flowers, that he arrives at a continuation of his passions in exchange with reality (Freud, 1899: p. 314). The wild flowers are a continuation of the dandelions and the yellow dress beyond his personal ego; lived forms that aesthetically provide for the ego, the kind of intransitive or aimless pleasure Bersani describes—a pleasure in being.

Indeed in an essay on *Creative Writers and Day-dreaming* written just a few years later, Freud spells out this form of unconscious reading in relation to the creative art of writing and literature. "The essential ars poetica" of the writer, says Freud,

> lies in the technique of overcoming the feeling of repulsion in us which is undoubtedly connected with the barriers that rise between each single ego and the others. (Freud, 1908: p. 153)

The technique of the writer, Freud continues is twofold, he

> softens the character of his egoistic daydreams by altering or disguising it, and he bribes us by the purely formal—that is, aesthetic-yield of pleasure which he offers us in the presentation of his phantasies. (Freud, 1908: p. 153)

Freud also calls this aesthetic pleasure an "incentive bonus" or "fore-pleasure" because it allows us to anticipate and wait, thus enabling us to create the rhythm of time and space intrinsic to the ego's being. The fore-pleasure that creative writing offers us as readers is the unconscious pleasure of reading and elaborating our fantasies through aesthetic forms. And it is this fore-pleasure that is at stake in the unconscious screen memories, the living forms and wild flowers that both disguise and elaborate our passions; liberating them into our future life beyond the familial ego.

If this is so, how can we follow these wild flowers in thinking about the clinical session? Of course psychoanalysis began in the wild, there was nothing familiar or tame about psychoanalysis in the beginning either theoretically or in terms of practice. It was one big experiment. Psychoanalysis today appears to have lost this adventuring spirit. In his paper on "'Wild' Psychoanalysis", Freud criticises a young doctor for his literal advice to a hysterical, middle-aged woman who subsequently approaches Freud for a consultation. The woman who is divorced is suffering acute anxiety. The physician tells her she is ill because of a lack of sexual relations and gives her the alternatives of going back to her husband, finding a lover or of satisfying herself through masturbation. This advice is useless, Freud scathingly informs us, because it reduces sexuality to its literal popular meaning.

With psychoanalysis, Freud argues,

> we prefer to speak of psychosexuality, thus laying stress on the point that the mental factor in sexual life should not be overlooked or underestimated. We use the word sexuality in the same comprehensive sense as that in which the German language uses the word lieben ['to love']. We have long known, too, that mental absence of satisfaction with all its consequences can exist where there is no lack of normal sexual intercourse; and as therapists we always bear in mind that the unsatisfied sexual trends (whose substitutive satisfactions in the form of nervous symptoms we combat) can often find only very inadequate outlet in coitus or other sexual acts. (Freud, 1910b: pp. 222–223)

Psychically we are not just beings who are full with desires, we also repress those wants, and so the young doctor's practical advice to the hysterical woman is beside the point, says Freud. She knows perfectly well the avenues open to her, such as taking a lover. Her anxiety stems from the strength of her inner resistances. Even if she manages to have sex, this woman will not so easily resolve the repressions and the neurotic conflicts estranging her from love. And yet by the end of the paper Freud concludes that the wild analyst at least points the patient in the right direction and is preferable by far to a "highly rated specialist who would have told her she was suffering from a 'vasomotor neurosis'" (Freud, 1910b: p. 227).

So it seems that what Freud is actually criticising in wild analysis is a lack of imagination on the part of the analyst: the wild analyst is not wild enough. It is not just that this woman won't allow herself sexual pleasure; she both wants, and refuses her own desires. There is no right or most rigorous practise that will solve this pernicious dilemma. All analysis must be wildly imaginative if it is to move the patient's symptoms into the scene of unconscious reading that advances the reader (be it patient or analyst) into producing more creative forms for her fantasies. For without these transferential forms the patient is stuck; there is nothing to dress her passions or to carry them forward into her future life. We don't just go to analysis to return to dreams about our parents and our past. If working with and reading the psychoanalytic unconscious means anything, it is a way to follow the unconscious through its sequence and rhythm of lived forms. Free association is one route to doing this, and the shapes that evolve between analyst and patient are dream-like in that they do not separate or obey any law of the senses. Just as a dream selects the residues of the day and uses these perceptions unconsciously to read and bring to life our most secret wishes; so the analytic session is a place where we begin to dream the virtual world, its objects and settings, using them to carry and communicate our desires.

In Freud's "wild" analysis with himself, the free associations and lived forms of the dandelion memory create shapes of flowers, colours, and tastes. This synaesthesia as sensory perception akin to the dream, elaborates Freud's sexuality aesthetically. It is precisely the promiscuity of these senses, their refusal to be separated, which allows his desire, movement, expression, and synthesis; thus bridging barriers between past and present, and between perception and memory. All the barriers erected in other words by the repressive, personal ego. We can think similarly of the synaesthesia produced within the unconscious communication in the analytic session. However, this mixing of the senses is not as a regression to a place where they are blurred to the point of being undistinguishable, rather the senses are in rhythm and unconscious conversation with each other.

Corresponding forms and senses

The senses of the analytic session can be likened to Baudelaire's famous poem "Correspondances" where one sense is taken up and received in a different modality.

Correspondances

The colonnades of Nature's temple live
And babble on in tongues half-understood
Man wanders lost in symbols while the wood
With knowing eyes, keeps watch on every move.
Like echoes from infinity drawn out
Into a dappled unison of light
Beyond the dawn of day or dead of night,
All scenes, all sounds and colours correlate.
Some fragrances resemble infant skin,
Sweeter than woodwinds, green as meadow grass—
Others expand to fill the space they are in.
Endlessly rich, corrupt, imperious,
Amber and musk, incense and benjamin
In sense and spirit raptures sing as one. (Baudelaire,
1997: p. 19)

In this poem, nature is a temple, where man "wanders lost in symbols". Half understood this watchful wood is a non-personal form which does not metaphorically transcend the bodily senses, so much as read, care, and carry them within a different imaginary register. Scents, colours and the pulses of our senses, omnipotent and perverse, or cool to touch like a baby's skin, are not so much substituted as moved somewhere else in their response. Leo Bersani argues that in this poem,

> we move from vertical transcendence to horizontal "unity". . . . stimuli ordinarily associated with one of our senses can produce sensations "belonging" to another sense. (Bersani, 1977: p. 32)

These communicating senses are unconscious, they talk telepathically; and as Bersani observes they don't actually "remind us of anything else"; rather they "expand" and "transport," they become the echoes that infinity draws out (Bersani, 1977: p. 33). Senses become spiritual, the last lines of the poem tell us, emerging as a singing passion of the soul; a form that does not substitute for feelings, but shapes and changes them.

This enlargement of the senses, their expansion into infinite echoes and things can also be seen as the changing shape and space-time of the ego, as it literally develops its lived forms beginning at the mother's breast. Indeed, in Baudelaire's poem of the Giantess, the girl giant is a monstrous shape changing landscape, sheltering the poet "under the shadow of her breast—a sleepy hamlet under the mountain's foot" (Baudelaire, 1997: p. 53). The Giantess is an impersonal force and form of nature, symbolically moving the poem's senses into a self that is carved out of, and in-between, the shadow of those mountainous breasts. The ego, here, is a geography; a topography and space that shifts and changes according to the correspondence and telepathy of the senses within the analytic session. Baudelaire's sensual correspondences, his poems, are like dreams. When we are within them and their surreal landscapes, our senses are exchanged and perceived in ways that allow them to move and change.

We see things in dreams but we don't really see; perception and memory seem mixed up; we see what cannot be actually seen, our dreams talk but physically we hear nothing. As in dreams, in the analytic session, senses become exchanged as analogies of each other and as they become exchanged they become returned differently by the free associating freudian pair. It is perhaps no accident that it has been in child analysis that the "painting" and elaborating of the senses has been explored more than in other therapies. Paradoxically, it is through these non-verbal techniques of play and transitional phenomena that we can understand the proper function of language within adult psychoanalysis. Language is a medium in analysis to put synaesthesia into play. In other words the importance of language in analysis is not so much its role as a linguistic entity, but its role as a form through which the affects and senses, between analyst and patient, are transported and put into conversation. When language becomes stripped of this illusory capacity, whether that is through badly placed or cut off analytical interpretations, or with a patient who uses languages in an overly intellectual way, then the illusory space of the session is jettisoned.

In his paper "The Role of Illusion in the Analytic Space and Process", Masud Khan describes two case histories. In the first, the patient destroys the illusory space of the analysis by a language substituting for the maternal body, as an "addictive mental state" usurping more sensual functions of sight and touch. Language, here, has became a perversion of the more sensual aspects of the ego. This girl, says Khan, is unable to experience what Winnicott called a natural hesitation; a hesitation that ushers in transitional phenomena and illusory experience for the young infant. As a result this patient could not allow, her body to have its natural physical say in the matter. Miss X was held by her language and mentation, and to this nothing external could ever find access or entrance. (Khan, 1973: p. 244)

However, the second female patient that Khan describes manages to elaborate the necessary symbolic and illusory space within the session, precisely because language is not used prematurely. Symptoms for this patient are less articulate or precocious and yet Khan's ability to hold and unconsciously read the girl's needs enables her to touch and see the objects and outlines of his consulting room, before as it were she can speak within its walls. Khan shows how he intuitively understands this girls' need to create and build the aesthetics of being and relating which will furnish her ego. He writes:

Through staying silent and thus unknowable, and by touching the walls with her hands and the whole of her body, and looking and exploring the space with her sight, she would gradually create that trust in relating and being related to which allowed for her privacy and yet crystallized very slowly that dimension of illusion. (Khan, 1973: p. 244)

A young woman I saw was similar and yet different from either of Khan's patients in that language for her was an intellectual means of defending herself against the world and mastering reality. She was like Khan's first patient exceptionally articulate and used her intellectual powers to ward off her more passionate feelings and dependency needs in relation to me. And yet silence was also an issue, because unlike the second girl that Khan talks about she could not use the silence in the sessions either, and would simply experience them as persecutory, as I became the parts of her mother that had been unavailable and depressed, or indeed the father who had adored and then abandoned her through neurotic disappointments in his own career. This woman had loved and been loved by both her parents and there were many internal resources to facilitate creative work and yet this woman's refusal to let her dream and real life experiences coalesce meant that she had a tendency to retreat to living out her desiring life in fantasy; as she would like it to be in her mind, rather than in actuality. The reality of the men my client had relationships with were either far less exciting, or far more cruel than her preferred father had been. Subsequently, men that could be both attractive and dependable were always for some reason unavailable.

Winnicott describes in his brilliant essay, "Dreaming, Fantasying and Living", the fate of a female patient who is so stuck in being unable to bring her fantasy and real worlds together, that real life and fantasy become represented in the dead end games of patience and the immovable daydreams of pink clouds in which she experiences this dissociation. Winnicott makes a distinction in this paper between the creative or poetic value of dreaming, and the sterile activity of daydreams. Whereas, this woman's daydreams of pink clouds keep her estranged from creative living, they are just fixated thoughts that had become split off from bodily feeling. Her dreams are the poetic way through because they contain "layer upon layer of meaning related to past, present and future, and to inner and outer" (Winnicott, 1974: p. 42). Dreams get to an arena of what Winnicott calls formlessness and without this formlessness no new forms can be created. His patient experienced her life as constructed by other people and she describes this as being patterned and cut out like a dress pattern according to someone else's sense and style. "Her childhood environment", says Winnicott,

> seemed unable to allow her to be formless but must, as she felt it, pattern her and cut her out into shapes conceived by other people. (Winnicott, 1974: p. 40)

I understand what Winnicott means by formlessness to be a loss of the ego's circumscribed boundaries and a more fusional state with the other, reminiscent of the early bond between child and mother, where forms and their accompanying affects are shared and passed backwards and forwards through rhythm. And yet I have a problem with Winnicott's categorical separation of daydreaming and dreaming in this paper. In Freud's essay, *Creative Writers and Day-dreaming*, daydreams are neither rigid nor disembodied but come laden with affects that are too extreme for the ego's ideals and injunctions. Here, it is the aesthetic practice of writing that moves and mediates the passionate daydream into differing forms that will be accepted by the ego. But I also wonder if Winnicott is trying to distinguish between fantasying that is a result of defensive and intellectual dissociation and the more embodied idea of repression. Repression is more embodied for the simple reason that it is much more unstable and produces fantasies attached to bodily symptoms.

Like Freud I think fantasy can be creative if it can move like a dream between past and present and between inside and outside. And yet as Winnicott makes clear, fantasies can also become intellectually fixated, masking the equally entrenched but split off passions of the id. So, what if fantasies and all our psychic representations are simply the re-presentations of what lies beyond the ego? The parts of the id that were initially the world before it became inscribed as the unknowable "non-me" that uncannily haunts the personal self. Then the question becomes not what is the status of fantasy, but what moves it? And where to? Fantasies are the forms through which we make and break the ego, through and against a non-personal world that both surrounds us and lives inside us.

Fantasies that live their life as intellectual ideas can exist, like the woman in the pink clouds, as both independent and uninterrupted. Symptoms on the other hand, have an urgency that calls for a response from the other. We could say that symptoms are looking for a correspondence with the ego that can only be found in identification with the analyst or other. Like Baudelaire's correspondences the symptoms and the sexual transference in the analytic session become put into a rhythm and identification with the analyst as a representation, not simply of the personal past but of memories that are less recognisable. These more contingent memories are inseparable from a telepathic sensory perception through which the analyst becomes unconsciously read as a virtual being. The telepathic reading between analyst and patient is formless in Winnicott's sense, in that it moves like a dream between the outside and the inside, and between the past and what is current.

It is the movement of affects and senses beyond the ego in search of corresponding forms which arrive from another, that enables the clinical scene to be more than a repetition of the patient's personal history. When we unconsciously and telepathically correspond with our clients in therapy we are doing more than empathising: feeling their feelings or thinking their thoughts. We are, when the therapy is alive, involved in a recreation of forms that in their mobility change shape and perspective. Leo Bersani argues that Baudelaire's poetry can be seen as a series of horizontal correspondences where forms open out from the "I" to the "non-I", so preventing individuation or completion. Baudelaire enacts a "generic mutation", argues Bersani, through "the novelizing of poetry, a displacement of the aesthetic from an act of representation to the deployment of a perspective" (Bersani, 1977: p. 33). Like the poet lying under the mountainous mounds of the Giantess, identification between analyst and patient is unconsciously communicated in an ongoing way. It is regularly interrupted through the rhythms, the coming and going of the analyst and patient, the breaks and the miscommunications. There is always difference at stake within this familiarity, the greatest "non-identical replication" being the analyst himself.

Like Baudelaire's poet who dreams the world into being from the house of his ego, sheltering under the body of the Giantess, so the analyst and patient have to dream each other into being through the analytic sessions. The woman fantasying about pink clouds, has sterile daydreams or fixed thoughts, rather than a poetic experience, because Winnicott is unable to join her in dreaming them. Necessary "formlessness" which would allow her to move inside and outside her dreams, backwards and forwards in time, only arrives when both analyst and patient can start dreaming and elaborating on fantasies and dream material together.

Dreaming lilies

The young woman in analysis with me would lie on the couch and free associate to her daily life and her dreams and yet I was never allowed to really join in. If I made interpretations of her self-critical inner world, she would respond as though these were certainties of some inner persecutory truth. And yet when I made free associations to the parts of her that I perceived as really kind and thoughtful, they were ignored as being woolly, or simply went unheard. Dreams were not remembered, or when they were, they turned up in the sessions in a similar fashion to the day's dreams of the woman fantasying pink clouds. Her dreams were her affair and whatever free associations I made she could not use them to go travelling in relation to her own unconscious perceptions and memories. We could not dream together; either the dreams that she brought, or the past experiences that had made her suffer. Her associations seemed to be constantly stamped on by the severity of her super-ego. And whatever interpretation or association I would try and make, she remained intellectually aloof. My patient could often be very intense, but the meaning of her dreams and the recounting of her everyday life was often conveyed in language which was stripped of its sensual and illusory capacity.

My response to this woman was to interpret her evasions but I also refused to give up my dreaming within the session. I would free associate to the material she brought, mindful of the creativity at stake in her anger, and how being able to feel some of this destruction would have prevented it from becoming more of the self-mutilating guilt she was so used to. Dreaming the patient's experience into being has been described by Winnicott, Khan, and more recently by Christopher Bollas and Thomas Ogden. Ogden suggests that the analyst participates, "in dreaming the patient's 'undreamt' and 'interrupted dreams'"(Ogden, 2005: p. 23). Like Bion's transformation of beta elements or Winnicott's ability to unconsciously hold and help shape his patient's poetic dreams into shared experience, dreaming in analysis is a process by which analyst and patient can metabolise experience which is unbearable or just too unknowable. And yet we can't, it seems to me think about any of this as simply a process of projective identification. Unconscious communication and perception, as telepathy, are at the heart of how we read and listen to the material of the clinical session, jointly translating past passions and traumas, into new forms that will in turn create new experience.

My patient taught literature in secondary school, a career inherited from her mother, but what she really wanted to be was an artist. But when her mother had died she had dropped out of art school and embarked on teacher training. The mother's death had severed the family; the brother drifted off into a fairly staid career with a possessive wife and the father remained disappointed and melancholic. The material and the work of this analysis unfolded gradually. Getting to know someone unconsciously takes time, and this is no different when the person you are getting to know is another side to yourself. In order to have a view to the different parts of being that exist inside and outside the preferred self, the ego has to have what Virginia Woolf would call a reading room. A room furnished aesthetically with requisite new forms which are constructed through rhythms that move, not just in time with the sessions, but with the life lived beyond them. The pleasure in being a therapist is not goal directed, however much the symptoms and the accompanying transference might at times make us think otherwise. This young woman was intelligent and loving, but her self-punishment and guilt, her need to be the nursemaid to both her parent's sadness and loss, kept her chaste and unfulfilled. And being a bit of a Nun meant she ran no chance of waking up to the need and competition with her mother, or replacing the adored father of her earlier years.

Then one day she brought a dream. Not just any old dream, but one which became the dreaming experience of the analysis. This woman was in love with one of her older male colleagues at the school she worked in, who flirted with her and befriended her, and yet remained happily married. In the dream this man, James, was playing the guitar and paying no attention to her, or any of the other students who were sitting listening to him with rapt attention. And then, as she watched he started visibly changing into a young curly-haired, green eyed boy. At this point in the dream the sexual longing was palpable and so was the need and loss she felt. "It was like he came right off the page" she said, and was so real she could have touched him. But the dream continued and the man changed again. This time he was middle-aged, as he was in real life, except she was a little girl holding his hand, the adoring version of her father in a tweedy jacket and corduroy trousers, and they were in a shop buying flowers together for his wife. My patient chose and pointed to some flowers in a dusty corner of the room, which were a milky-white colour and they were also encased inside a glass dome or bell jar. Then the dream changed again and the curly haired boy was back, whispering in her ear, teasing her and laughing at her sexual longing for him. He seemed to be flying through the air around her. She looked into his face and he brushed her gently with a flame coloured scarf. As she looked down at him and then herself, she realised he was laughing because they were children with bodies that were more similar than different. The next moment he was flying away, through the trees, pulling her with him, and she realised with pleasure that she hadn't lost him and could still love him because he was not her lover but her childhood playmate or twin.

"Who is the changeling man/boy in the dream?" I asked and she replied, "He reminds me of the first boy I fell in love with in the sixth form. He was called Mark and had brown curly hair and these amazing sea coloured eyes". These sea-green eyes in turn reminded her of playing with her brother as a child by the seaside and in the woods. The man she was in love with in the present was an older version of this boy and in the dream he was also the loving father she remembered as a child. When I asked her about the flowers she told me that they were lilies and that maybe they were buying them for the man's wife, because she had died, and of course they also symbolised the death of her real mother. Musing more about the lilies she said that they were like her depressed mother, but they were also her own feelings trapped under a bell jar. Lilies were noticeable, however white, because they exuded such heady perfumes. I said, "Perhaps the jar is a way of shutting the smells out?". She went very quiet. "Smell is the first thing you notice about someone, when you become intimate with them" she said, "And it's the last trace you have of them when they leave." But of course smells wake us up to what we feel; our longings, our greed, and the pain associated with being hungry or empty, "Flowers only smell nice when they are alive", remarked my patient, "but when they die they really start to stink". And in the face of this incontrovertible fact, and the dead and depressed mother in the transferential bell jar of the session, we wondered about how frightening it was when her feelings smelt bad and hateful. Conversely, we also thought about the reassurance of someone's smell and how when they have gone a person's smell is their last wild form, a way of keeping them present with us. Dreams of course are also the forgotten forms of the other we carry around with us.

The lily's hesitation

Winnicott argues that it is reality that makes our fantasies more bearable, enriching them so we can start to experience them in a lived way. This means putting our perceptual senses into correspondence with a dream other; the night dream and the daydream and the dream we experience with our analyst. If I am honest, there is no way I can give you an account of the clinical session in narrative form, because clinical sessions are like dreams, they are more like poetry than straight prose and the conversation is neither fully conscious nor necessarily within a language of words. Indeed, the unconscious conversations that make up the clinical session mean that all case studies are fictions, or screen memories. Like dreams they are impossible to catch, there is always a disjunction and a translation between these unconscious communications and their arrival, into prose, or onto the page. The white lilies that appeared in the unconscious correspondence between me and my patient were a hesitation in Winnicott's sense, in that they ushered in illusory experience for both of us. "I have frequently made the experiment of trying to get the spatula to the infant's mouth during the stage of hesitation", observes Winnicott,

> Whether the hesitation corresponds to my normal or differs from it in degree or quality. I find that it is impossible during this stage to get the spatula to the child's mouth apart from the exercise of brutal strength. (Winnicott, 1941: p. 54)

When Winnicott tries to insist in overcoming this pause and still expectation of the child, the baby responds by screams, even intestinal colic. But what kind of hesitation were the lilies in the bell jar? If they are part of a poem, can a poem be a hesitation ushering in the kind of transitional experience, the overlapping circles of illusion between mother and child that Winnicott describes?

Giorgio Agamben's understanding of the hesitation of poetry is informed by the repetition and stoppage of the image that is at stake in cinema, specifically the films of Guy Debord. The two transcendental conditions for Debord's cinema, repetition and stoppage return us, in Agamben's view, to Walter Benjamin's messianic sense of history. "Repetition restores the possibility of what was" writes Agamben:

> And renders it possible anew; it's almost a paradox. To repeat something is to make it possible anew. Here lies the proximity of repetition and memory. Memory cannot give us back what was, as such: that would be hell. Instead, memory restores possibility to the past. This is the meaning of the theological experience that Benjamin saw in memory, when he said that memory makes the unfulfilled into the fulfilled, and the fulfilled into the unfulfilled. Memory is, so to speak, the organ of reality's modalization; it is that which can transform the real into the possible and the possible into the real. If you think about it, that's also the definition of cinema. Doesn't cinema always do just that, transform the real into the possible and the possible into the real? (Agamben, 2008: p. 330)

The second transcendental is stoppage, cinematic interruption. It is this interruption or stoppage of the image that makes cinema, in Agamben's view, closer to poetry rather than prose. Through the caesura and enjambment, the poet creates a "non-coincidence, a disjunction between sound and meaning" (Agamben, 2009: p. 331). I want to suggest that the hesitation inherent to poetry, and to Winnicott's baby with the spatula, is also a disjunction of the senses as forms and shapes that don't coincide with familiar meanings.[1] Just as the sound to a poem stops and starts, plays a familiar melody only to pause and arrest us, so it juxtaposes both sense and meaning with what is surprising and non-coincidental: our senses become disordered and confused. Rhythm in analysis is its unconscious composition, a poetic interruption, which we must read and yet allow for its unconscious and unknowable elements, the montage if you like, that is inherent to the dream.

Cinema and poetry are forms that bring repetition and interruption of the image or scene and in doing so they confront us with the presence of what is alien and new, something we unconsciously perceive and feel. And yet it is in the power of rhythm to try and bind this alien stuff to what is more familiar. In the face of the inviolable we are either paralysed or we improvise, and with the latter we find the corresponding forms within our memory to shape whatever is coming our way. And so it is in therapy we bring along the rhythm and repetition of our preferred stories and pasts, the narrative pleasures of our ego, if you like. But rhythm is never just a return of the same, there is always the unknowable break or hesitation in the face of what is strange, that we respond to by making it uncanny, both familiar and new. Indeed any repetition of the ego that does not acknowledge this temporal disjunction or interruption is in fact a fantasy, like Lacan's imaginary, the ideal of self-completion.

And it is for this reason, the presence of an unknowable otherness that makes up the poem, and sits besides ourselves, that pulls me away from Agamben's historical sense of the poem as being situated within Walter Benjamin's messianic order or disorder of history. Because what does it mean to redeem our traumatic and therefore missing or forgotten past? Isn't the theological experience Benjamin speaks of an ideal history, one where our wishes to save and restore what we have lost are paramount? But, if repair of some kind of magical before-land to our traumas is arguably what we can never achieve, then what use are our histories, and the psychoanalytic deconstruction of our personal lives to us? To be fair to Benjamin he does say we salvage ourselves through the wreckage and debris of history, but I don't believe that we can actually repair trauma, or for that matter salvage anything from the broken dreams of our past. Agamben's reading of poetry as restoring possibility to the past is arguably different from Benjamin's restoration of some past authentic aura or ideal. We can't repair trauma in therapy, or make up for the lost experiences that have been foreclosed or abolished. But we can use the past as a virtual landscape, as something that exists in memory and in our unconscious perceptions of the world that surrounds us, as a potential of what we can wish for and imagine in our futures.

History, then, as a series of clues to be followed, and yet where they lead is always a mystery, because for wishes to work they have to remain unfinished as works in progress. Oedipal identifications are our psychic melodramas that are constantly seeking different genres. Endings, after all, whether they occur in analysis, novels, and life don't mean their completion, and the satisfaction they bring is arguably simply an inability to imagine a different kind of a future. Within the clinic, the correspondence of memory and unconscious perceptions between analyst and patient can restore possibility to the past, by translating what we didn't have into something we might still encounter. Loss and wishing, the ego and libido, have to discover their potential as playmates, not as independent substitutes.

What we learn from psychoanalysis is how we are always excluded, from a past that is full of pain, not least because our experience and awakening to it is always delayed. We arrive in our traditions and families, in our cultural milieus that have carried on before us. We can join in, or opt out, but we can never catch up, and even first born children always come second to their parent's lives that preceded them. There are no firsts in psychoanalysis, one good reason perhaps why therapy will never become a university of life, because what we discover is not how to win, but how submitting to the inevitable second class experience of being in a family or a culture, has costs and benefits. And if this submission is ever going to be more than a sadomasochist solution to the reality of the non-exceptional place of the ego, then it is through our ideals and identifications that we must move. Not as some fixed and nostalgic recuperation of our losses, but as a re-sexualising of our ideals into forms that correspond with us. This exchange replicates desire into ever changing shapes that refuse the inner alienation of the ego and its unobtainable ideal.

Redemption of the past is a fixed ideal, but sublimation of what we feel through the living forms we passionately identify with, makes our ideals more plastic and flexible. Perhaps we can learn from psychoanalysis the ability to acknowledge and indeed recapture what we might call, following Bersani, a non-redemptive being; the capacity to be more receptive and ready to tune into the rhythms and cultural shapes that surround us. Because what we find is not the unrealisable ideal, but our own potential in those secondary forms and their ability to take us somewhere new. And this does not mean compliance. Being alive to our second class forms means that we can be led by our ideals but not be fooled by them, in that they will never be complete, they are always capable of being re-read and yet like the best essays they are always being rewritten by a plurality of selves that we pick from the pleasure, in moving from one form to another.

The repetition and interruption of rhythms within analysis don't restore what we have missed out on in the past, but they open us to, and light up our world, by inscribing the secondary forms of that world within us. Thus rhythm goes hand in hand with mimesis; the identifications with others that unconsciously flow and become interrupted. In Bersani's account of non-redemptive being, sublimation is not a secondary substitute for our autoerotic desires, or a decoy that leads us away from them, but a return to primary narcissism. As forms of expansive narcissism and self-love, the sublimations of our work and play "have to be defined in terms of turning away from the objects we love and back to the objectless jouissance in which, as Freud suggests, we were perhaps born into sexuality"(Bersani, 1990: p. 43).

The lily as being and desire

Marion Milner says something similar in her paper, "the role of illusion in symbol formation". Following Ernest Jones, Milner argues that there is an early form of symbolic equivalences, where the symbol is not the result of repression, but of the forward identification with reality.[2] Primary symbol formation is a regression involving artistic ecstasy which allows for the necessary identification and adaption to reality. In this scenario the world is not a substitute, wrought through repression, of our first libidinal loves, but is made up, and made through our primary narcissistic fantasies. Fusion with the object or other, in order to re-find loved parts of the self, is an illusion of oneness with the environment, which Milner argues is an essential part of artistic work and analysis. She describes a young patient, a boy, who has to either make her up as part of his own creation, or abject her as some alien and devil other:

it seemed as if it was only by being able, again and again, to experience the illusion that I was part of himself, fused with the goodness that he could conceive of internally, that he became able to tolerate a goodness that was not his own creation and to allow me goodness independently. (Milner, 1987: p. 103)

The symbolic illusion of our world, Milner seems to be saying, is the only way we can feel alive in it. And the illusion and fusion she describes, particularly in the boy's play with his toy soldiers is as much a shattering of the boundaries of the self. The boy's play therapy consists in making fires and furnaces, melting his toy soldiers down. "The sacrifice of the toy soldier by melting it down", says Milner,

expressed the wish to get rid of the bad object, particularly the cramping and cruel aspect of his superego, and also his sense of the need to absorb his inner objects into his ego and so modify them. But in addition to this I think it represented his feeling of the need to be able, at times, to transcend the common-sense ego; for common sense was very strong for him, his conscious attitude was one of feet firmly planted on the ground. (Milner, 1987: p. 96–97)

I think we can see symbolic illusion, the imaginative making of our objects and surroundings, as an expansive primary narcissism, where the object is burnt, lost, or turned away from. And yet, this illusion as a living symbolic form, is a passionate destruction of "the common sense ego" and the re-finding of the self within a more virtual landscape. Milner gets rather tired of being utilised as the boys bodily materials, "of being continually treated by the boy as his gas, his breath, his faeces" until she understands that this non-personal usage, is not a substitute or a retreat from reality, but a generative regression that moves towards apprehending it. Once Milner realises the creative nature of the boy's repetitive and narcissistic shaping of her, the analysis changes and the boy allows her to exist as a more real and external object in the world.

My client's associations to the white lilies under the glass bell jar in her dream, lead her to the writing and poetry of Sylvia Plath. We talk in one session about the poem *Lady Lazarus* and how it reflects the tight control of her anger and her familiar inner self-torture. The very real fear she feels about letting her devouring passions escape through the seal of her ego. Shared associations to her dream are also caught up, and interrupted, with my perception of her lying on the couch with its blue-green cover and of a picture hanging above of Leighton's *Flaming June*. The young woman lying in front of me had dark hair with these auburn lights that reflected the gauzy orange material of the sleeping woman above her in the picture. I don't comment on this, but find myself saying:

"The Lilies also remind me of Emily Dickinson. Except the Lily she preferred was the Cow or day Lily which was orange like the flame coloured scarf in your dream. The white lilies are your passions that are somehow trapped but the orange ones are like the boy with the scarf and make me think of your desires and where they might lead."

She thought about this and replied:

"The desire in the dream I feel for the young man is really painful, because he is unavailable like James. The longing for him makes feel empty. But as my father he feels right, when we are in the flower-shop, I am back home with my father as he loved me when I was a child. Also the green eyed boy is wicked, he is mocking my need of him. It's like he is saying we don't have to have sex silly, we can just fly away together. Lost boys stuff." She continues, "you know at the end of the dream I feel really happy because we are together, he is not my unavailable lover but an intimate part of me".

We talked about the loss of her father and how staying out of real sexual experiments with men kept him eternally with her, like the Peter Pan figure in her dream. But I also felt intuitively that the elusive impish boy was something more creative, her incomplete Oedipal desires seeking future replications. Eventually my client said;

"The milky lilies remind me of my rage at my mother's unavailability and maybe signals my jealousy of James' wife, but they are also my guilty feelings getting trapped in being the good teacher. In the dream, James is playing a guitar and all his student's are listening to him, but actually he is listening to himself...but not in a bad way, because if you can't listen to yourself then you can't play music. If I don't listen to what I really feel then I won't ever break out and do what I really want with my life".

Of course this girl's father and mother had stopped listening and conversing with her emotionally at crucial times when she was a child. And James was too plugged into his own family life to ever become a part of hers. And yet the dream of the changeling and the lilies was a way in which we both started to unconsciously listen and correspond to each other within the therapy. My own fantasies of this girl in relation to Emily Dickinson, with her flame coloured passion hidden under a white bell jar of her nun-like behaviour in real life, was also matched by my interest of what lilies meant in Dickinson's poetry. Emily's poetry and her love of flowers were inseparable: words and gardens were living forms to be shaped and cultivated. Like her mother before her, Emily lived a secluded life. The self-enclosure of this life; the self, becoming a soul, captured in its own virginal dream world is symbolically illustrated in a poem about the white Calla lily.

> Through the Dark Sod—as Education-
> The lily passes sure-
> Feels her white foot—no trepidation-
> Her faith-no fear-
> Afterward—in the Meadow-
> Swinging her Beryl Bell-
> The Mold life all forgotten—now-
> In Extasy—and Dell—(Dickinson, 1975: p. 187).

The mouldy bulb form that emerges to swing as a single white Beryl Bell, doubles as another kind of form, that of the ego reaching towards an ecstatic and mystical existence. This then is a kind of narcissism and self reverie that involves no-one else. However, it was not the Calla lily but the day lily or the Cow lily that Emily associated herself with. Offering two of these flaming flowers to Thomas Wentworth Higginson as signal of their friendship, Dickinson envisages the day lily as symbolic of herself and her love. The poem of the day lily still symbolises a narcissistic relation to a flower self, but it is one which promises intimacy and belonging. For the day lily the inner distances between the ego and its ideal have been crossed, and the latter is returned as a living presence and meeting of the self and its desires, not spiritual transcendence.

> Where I am not afraid to go
> I may confide my Flower
> Who was not enemy of Me
> Will gentle be, to Her-
> Nor separate, Herself and Me
> By Distances become-
> A single Bloom we constitute

Departed, or at Home—(Dickinson, 1975: p. 698).

This poem seems to be offering a communion of passion and sexuality with a female other, which is also the self. It is the Cow lily as both sexuality and form; we could call it a living maternal form, which Emily Dickinson sees as symbolically representing a loving correspondence with herself and her friend Higginson. If the poem about the Calla lily expresses a kind of pre-Raphaelite depiction of virginal femininity that is often associated with Emily Dickinson's secretive existence, then the Cow lily poem is all about the giving of those secrets to another who is in a different place, but is fundamentally the same as herself. The lily poems represent changing shapes and forms of not just flowers but also of the psyche and soul. And of course these associations to flowers are not exactly my client's but nevertheless are my response to her, and both interrupt and colour my sense of her dreams and passions.

For me the curly haired boy was synonymous with the "formlessness" that Winnicott talked to with his patient, in that the flying boy represented a poetic correspondence between my patient's dreams and her real life, and between her present and her past. But the boy was also like the flaming lily: an ego infused with unrepressed desire: a changing shape of what and who she could become. Dream experiences in analysis are constructed and moved by telepathy; they are co-created as the après coup of the original traumatic experience, just as Freud tried to create a dream experience for the Wolfman, so they could metabolise together, his primal scene. And it is the mutual unconscious reading of our passions and senses that creates the forms in which they can travelling, like the flight of the changeling boy through the trees. Khan's second patient creates a sense of self, a reading room and architecture for her ego. It is as though she is aesthetically shaping the actual room that surrounds her into one that she can live in within herself. And Khan's telepathic holding of her, his ability to unconsciously read her sensual forms and return them in a meaningful way is how she begins to symbolise her being within language. When language works in therapy it carries our senses, affects, and fantasies as forms which can enable our dream worlds an exchange with reality. But to do this, language has to communicate the kind of sensual and poetic correspondences that Baudelaire describes.

"Shouting Flowers" and new shapes of the ego

I suggest that the maternal lived form that is unconsciously communicating our senses and feelings in analysis can be carried by language and poetry, but that if language is devoid of this emotional and sensual underpinning, then it becomes linguistic mentation. The kind of intellectual warfare practised by Khan's first patient against him, whilst with my client it became the critical lacerations, "Lady Lazarus style" that she visited upon herself. So what we may ask are Freud's screen memories? Are they not also the unconscious perceptions and readings of fantasies and dreams, the past, present, and future forms of the ego that we initially find outside in the world, before we carry them and re-create them within ourselves? Fantasising, for Freud, holds the same poetic value as dreaming does for Winnicott. For fantasies, in Freud's mind, are not fixed so much as having an ability to move in time and place and change shape according to new impressions. Where fantasy was, new shapes of the ego can be, we could say. The subject's mental activity he writes,

> is linked to some current impression, some provoking occasion in the present which has been able to arouse one of the subject's major wishes. From there it harks back to a memory of an earlier experience (usually an infantile one) in which this wish was fulfilled; and it now creates a situation relating to the future which represents a fulfilment of the wish. What it thus creates is a day-dream or phantasy, which carries about it traces of the origin from the occasion which provoked it and from the memory. Thus past, present and future are strung together, as it were, on the thread of a wish that runs through them. (Freud, 1908: pp. 174–148)

Wishes can work for us, if we allow then to travel back to the past and forward to our futures, but in order to travel they need forms to carry them. Daydreams and fantasies are like screen memories in that they have to be opened up and translated as they move inside and outside the ego, backwards and forwards in time. And just as Freud blurs the distinction between fantasy and dreaming so dreams are also akin to memory. Famously, with the Wolfman it is the dreaming experience entered into with Freud and his patient that resurrects and reworks earlier trauma; the Wolfman cannot actually reproduce a memory of his own. Of this therapy writes Freud,

> It seems to me absolutely equivalent to a recollection , if the memories are replaced (as in the present case) by dreams the analysis of which invariably leads back to the same scene and which reproduce every portion of its content in an inexhaustible variety of new shapes. Indeed dreaming is another kind of remembering, though one that is subject to the conditions that rule at night and to the laws of dream-formation. (Freud, 1918: p. 51)

Dreams, like fantasies, don't just rework the past as a constant après coup of earlier traumas; they are the unconscious communications, which make new shapes and experiences for the ego. But this reworking and re-shaping, this movement from representation to a new perspective can only take place through an unconscious dreaming between what lies beyond the ego and what exists within it. Fantasies that are fixed, whether they are figured through dissociated pink clouds or more actively perverse sexual wishes need more curiosity, enabling them to search for the forms and patterns that can elaborate them. Without this artistic elaboration, our fantasies runaway home; shrinking back from current life, taking the libido with them. In Freud's autobiographical essay he sets his own dreaming and analytic couple up, by talking and free associating to himself, and it is through this conversation that his screen memories move from the present to the past and then forward again to the future. The flowers that become unconsciously read or dreamt between two, in Freud's personal story, are not lilies but dandelions and yet they change colour and shape just like the lilies in my patient's dream.

Thus the dandelions, which Freud snatches away from his little cousin, become the older wallflower yellow of her dress as she becomes the young woman he falls in love with. These screen memories are sensory and they move aesthetically in their crafting of new forms. The tasty black bread sliced and given to Freud at the end of the first screen memory by the farm woman is followed by sexual association of painted ladies in bustles and the fantasy of sexually deflowering the cousin, first in a temper and secondly through passionate love.

The wild yellow flowers that Freud follows on his mountain walks, towards his future, combine the deep sensuality of Freud's passion for the girl, with an escape from his father's ideals, and one reading of Freud's mountain flowers is that they figure as the first blossoming forms of what will become psychoanalysis. Free association in analysis is not just a way of detecting our mysterious and unknowable early passions; it is a matter of translating them into new spaces and worlds that exist beyond the personal ego or self. As such, free association is not just in relation to our so called internal worlds, it is a means of inscribing the world, carving from it the fantasies that can carry us both back to the past and forwards to new experiences. The dandelion in Emily Dickinson's poems holds none of her more reclusive qualities but is a "shouting flower" whose tubular stem "astonishes the grass":

> The Dandelion's pallid tube
> Astonishes the grass
> And Winter instantly becomes
> An infinite Atlas—
> The tube uplifts a single Bud
> And then a shouting Flower—
> The proclamations of the Suns
> That sepulture is o'er. (Dickinson, 1975: p. 636)

Freud's dandelions in this poetic reading, are thus the suns and screen memories that noisily proclaim the ego's openness to the virtual landscapes that surround it. Follow these wild flowers and you can exchange a wintry burial crypt of the repressive self, for the ego as an atlas: the virtual, yet to be explored ground of our future existence. The yellow flowers, of Freud's autobiography and the lilies of the analysis I have described are memories and fantasies that become unconsciously dreamt between self and other, but they are also unconscious perceptions that telepathically translate those secret memories and move them into a correspondence between the ego and its ideal other.

So the white stopped-up lilies in my client's dream and the too loud shout of Freud's dandelions, find a responding flaming passion or less incestuous form, with the unconscious conversations that take place in the requisite clinical space or autobiography. And perhaps it is important in analysis, not to worry too much about what bits are unconsciously perceived or made up. After all, one leads to the other and just as artists have to remember an inner form or what they imagine in order to perceive and represent a living resemblance, so analysts and clients have to bring and cherish the passions of the transference within their encounters. But such desires will always be too excessive or idealistic and so the work and play is to allow the relational search of these passions and symptoms for new forms of being. The movement of desire is thus to break and remake the ego's boundaries in tune with the new shapes and patterns that exist beyond the self. If crudely naming the transference or indeed dissolving it is often neither a desirable or possible event, then thinking of interpretation as a kind of unconscious translation or telepathy is not so much about finding some lost key of meaning, but the beginning of joining our hopes and dreams to a more facilitating reality. For if the transference is always more excessive than either analyst and client can acknowledge or know, then our interpretations are never right in the sense of being complete, but are always infinite. The point is not to define or master, but to reconfigure this bond in ways that can lead the ego into a more friendly and less inhibited relation to its passionate and ideal other.

Rhythms of analysis—without conclusion

The rhythms of a telepathic maternal form that I have tracked in this book are partial in the sense that they do not substitute for other psychoanalytic accounts or readings of Freud, and they can never make up for the sheer intractability of the repression that exists between our characters and our history. Indeed, telepathy in its Freudian, uncanny sense, will never be the magical clairvoyance it seems to assume in more supernatural explanations, because of its nearness to the repressed. In abolishing distance between the ego and its ideal, telepathy sublimates our passions but only ever incompletely. Passions are by their very nature the incestuous, enigmatic currents that dog our lives. Telepathically sublimating and illuminating these intensities means understanding that the transference and analysis can never be completed. And this is a good thing, especially if we also acknowledge that analysis reads and runs alongside our daily symptoms and existence; it is not some prerequisite for full knowledge or "cure".

One reason, perhaps, that we have such a meagre repertoire to describe the unconscious conversations that take place during analysis is that we can't talk about them with any certainty; the danger is that language becomes mystical or romantic, and idealism becomes fixed rather than deconstructed and moved into a less terrifying testimony of our desires. Still, we can't know the unconscious, it is by definition unknowable at a conscious level and so all we are left with are our skills to receive, perceive, and describe this unknowable and mysterious force. Perhaps the answer is not to try and know the unconscious or the transference, but to move it, make it together into something less sado-masochistic, less unobtainable, and less buried. Like Dickinson's flaming lilies and Freud's shouting sunflowers, the passion infused forms that break and remake the ego are its passport to a more creative life.

Theodor Reik talks of the music, the "haunting melody", that puts us in touch with the unknowable unconscious beyond the ego and I think it is not just music but all the lived expressive forms such as dance and aesthetic expression that allows us this access. The original meaning of the word empathy is embedded in the aesthetic appreciation of corresponding non-human forms, which of course return us to the early rapport with the mother and the unconscious perception and reception of her gestures. The transference is the backdrop, the canvas if you like, of all analytic work, a constant presence in the space of the session, whether we pay explicit attention to it or not. The repressed passions and symptoms that constitute this bond are never completed or mastered, but they can be translated within the responding forms, repetitions, and interruptions that make up the rhythms of the analytic session. It is this poetry, an unconscious maternal telepathy which gives a dress sense to our passions and provides perspective and new shapes for the ego, thus allowing access to a lived experience that has hitherto been alien.

Notes

1. I am indebted to Josh Cohen's analysis of Winnicott, hesitation and poetry made in a talk given to the *Psychoanalysis, Literature and Practise Seminar* at Senate House, London, in December 2011.
2. See Marion Milner's fascinating discussion of primary symbolism which she traces back through Herbert Read, Ernest Jones, Otto Rank and Hanns Sachs. Milner argues that not only is the primary symbol a poetic equivalence and primitive adaptation to reality, but it can be seen as a primary form of expression. Regression to this archaic symbolism in analysis engenders ecstasy and fusion which constitutes the creative illusion of the transference. The poetic, telepathic maternal forms that I have argued for in this book would be of apiece with the primary symbolism that Milner describes. See Milner, M. (1987) (1952). "The role of illusion in symbol formation" in: *The Suppressed Madness of Sane Men*, pp. 84–86.

REFERENCES

Agamben, G. (2008). Difference and repetition: on Guy Debord's film. In: T. Leighton (Ed.), *Art and the Moving Image: A Critical Reader* (pp. 328–333). Tate Publishing: London.

Almodóvar, P. (1999). *All About My Mother*.

Anzieu, D. (1989). *The Skin Ego*. New Haven, CT: Yale University Press.

Austen, J. (1969). *Sense and Sensibility*. London: Penguin Books.

Ballaster, R. (1995). Introduction. In: J. Austen, *Sense and Sensibility* (pp. xi–xxxv). London: Penguin Books.

Baudelaire, C. (1997). Complete Poems. W. Martin (trans.) Manchester: Carcanet Press.

Benjamin, W. (1978). On the mimetic faculty. In: P. Demetz (Ed.), *Reflections* (pp. 333–336). New York: Schocken Books.

Benjamin, W. (1978). Surrealism. In: P. Demetz (Ed.), *Reflections* (pp. 177–193). New York: Schocken Books.

Benjamin, W. (1933). Doctrine of the similar. *New German Critique, 17*: 65–69.

Berlant, L. (2005). Introduction: Compassion (and Withholding.) In: L. Berlant (Ed.), *Compassion: The Culture and Politics of an Emotion* (pp. 1–27). New York: Routledge.

Berlant, L. (2008). *The Female Complaint: The Unfinished Business of Sentimentality in American Culture*. Durham: Duke University Press.

Bergson, H. (1908). Memory of the present and false recognition. In: K. A. Pearson & J. Mullarkey (Eds.), *Henri Bergson: Key Writings* (pp. 141–157). New York: Continuum (2002).

Bersani, L. (1977). *Baudelaire and Freud*. Berkeley: University of California Press.

Bersani, L. (1986). *The Freudian Body: Psychoanalysis and Art*. New York: Columbia University Press.

Bersani, L. (1990). *The Culture of Redemption*. Cambridge, MA: Harvard University press.

Bersani, L. (2010). Psychoanalysis and the Aesthetic subject. In: *Is The Rectum a Grave? and Other Essays* (pp. 139–154). Chicago: University of Chicago Press.

Bersani, L. & Phillips, A. (2008). *Intimacies*. Chicago: University of Chicago Press.

Bion, W. R. (1962). *Learning From Experience*. London: Basic Books.

Bollas, C. (1987). *The Shadow of the Object: Psychoanalysis of the Unthought Known*. London: Routledge.

Bollas, C. (1993). *Being in Character*. London: Karnac.

Bollas, C. (1995). *Cracking Up*. London: Routledge.

Bollas, C. (2000). *Hysteria*. London: Routledge.

Bollas, C. (2007). *The Freudian Moment*. London: Karnac.

Booth, M. R. (1965). *English Melodrama*. London: Jenkins.

Boothby, R. (2005). *Sex on the Couch*. London: Routledge.

Borch-Jacobsen, M. (1992). *The Emotional Tie: Psychoanalysis, Mimesis and Affect*. D. Brick & C. Porter (trans.), Stanford, California: Stanford University Press.

Brooks, P. (1976). *The Melodramatic Imagination, Balzac, Henry James, Melodrama, and the Mode of Excess*. New Haven, CT: Yale University Press.

Butler, J. (1997). *The Psychic Life of Power: Theories in Subjection*. Stanford, California: Stanford University Press.

Campbell, J. (2006). *Psychoanalysis and the Time of Life; Durations of the Unconscious Self*. London: Routledge.

Campbell, J. (2009). Rhythms of the suggestive unconscious. *Subjectivity*, 6.4: 29–51.

Campbell, J. & Pile, S. (2010). Telepathy and its vicissitudes: Freud, thought transference and the hidden lives of the (repressed and non-repressed) unconscious. *Subjectivity*, 3.4: 403–425.

Campbell, J. & Pile, S. (2011). Space travels of the Wolfman: phobia and its worlds. *Psychoanalysis and History*, 13.1: 69–89.

Conner, S. (2004). *The Book of Skin*. Ithaca, New York: Cornell University Press.

Dean, T. (2000). *Beyond Sexuality*. Chicago: University of Chicago Press.

Derrida, J. (1980). On narrative. *Critical Inquiry*, 7.1: 55–81.

Dickinson, E. (1975). *The Complete Poems (1830–1886)*. In: T. H. Johnson (Ed.), London: Faber & Faber.

During, S. (1988). The strange case of monomania: Patriarchy in literature, murder in Middlemarch, drowning in Daniel Deronda. *Representations* 23: 88–104.

Eigen, M. (1999). *Toxic Nourishment*. London: Karnac.

Eigen, M. (2004a). Abstinence and the schizoid ego. In: A. Phillips (Ed.), *The Electrified Tightrope* (pp. 1–8). London: Karnac.

Eigen, M. (2004b). A little psyche-music. In: *The Sensitive Self* (pp. 74–85). Middletown, CT 0649: Wesleyan University Press.

Eliot, G. (1963). Silly novels by lady novelists. In: T. Pinney (Ed.), *Essays by George Eliot* (pp. 300–324). London: Routledge and Kegan Paul.

Eliot, G. (1999). *Daniel Deronda*. New York, London, Toronto: Everyman's Library.

Eliot, T. S. (1997). Hamlet and his problems. In: *The Sacred Wood: Essays on Poetry and Criticism* (pp. 81–87). London: Faber & Faber.

Elsaesser, T. (1987). Tales of sound and fury: observations on the family melodrama. In: C. Gledhill (Ed.), *Home is Where The Heart Is: Studies in Melodrama and Women's Film* (pp. 43–69). London: B.F.I.

Federn, P. (1952). *Ego Psychology and the Psychoses*. New York: Basic Books.

Ferenczi, S. (1951). The Dream of the Clever Baby. In *Further Contributions to the Technique and Theory of Psychoanalysis*. Compiled by J. Rickman, (trans.), J. T. Suttie. London: Hogarth Press.

Ferenczi, S. (1955). Confusion of Tongues between Adults and the Child. In: M. Balint (Ed.), *Final Contributions to the Problems and Methods of Psychoanalysis* (pp. 156–157). London: Hogarth Press.

Ferenczi, S. (1995). *The Clinical Diary of Sándor Ferenczi*, J. Dupont (Ed.), M. Balint & N. Zarday (trans.). Cambridge, MA: Harvard University Press.

Freud, S. (1953–1974). *The Standard Edition of the Complete Psychological Works of Sigmund Freud*, (trans.), J. Strachey. London: Hogarth.

Freud, S. (1893–1895) (with J. Breuer). *Studies on Hysteria. S.E., 2.* London: Hogarth.

Freud, S. (1899). *Screen Memories. S.E., 3.* London: Hogarth.

Freud, S. (1900). *The Interpretation of Dreams. S.E., 4–5.* London: Hogarth.

Freud, S. (1905). *Fragment of an Analysis of A Case of Hysteria. S.E., 7.* London: Hogarth.

Freud, S. (1905). *Three Essays on Sexuality and Other Works. S.E., 7.* London: Hogarth.

Freud, S. (1908). *Creative Writers and Day-Dreaming, S.E., 9.* London: Hogarth.

Freud, S. (1908). *Hysterical Phantasies and their Relation to Bisexuality. S.E., 9.* London: Hogarth.

Freud, S. (1909a). *Some General Remarks on Hysterical Attacks. S.E., 9.* London: Hogarth.

Freud, S. (1909b). *Family Romances. S.E., 9*. London: Hogarth.

Freud, S. (1910). *Five Lectures on Psycho-Analysis. S.E., 11*. London: Hogarth.

Freud, S. (1910b). *'Wild' Psychoanalysis. S.E., 11*. London: Hogarth.

Freud, S. (1912). *On The Universal Tendency to Debasement in the Sphere of Love. S.E., 11*. London: Hogarth.

Freud, S. (1912a). *The Dynamics of the Transference. S.E., 12*. London: Hogarth.

Freud, S. (1913). *The Disposition of Obsessional Neurosis: A Contribution to The Problem of Choice of Neurosis. S.E., 12*. London: Hogarth.

Freud, S. (1914). *Remembering, Repeating and Working-Through. S.E., 12*. London: Hogarth.

Freud, S. (1914a). *On Narcissism. S.E., 14*. London: Hogarth.

Freud, S. (1915). *Instincts and their Viccisitudes. S.E., 14*. London: Hogarth.

Freud, S. (1915). *The Unconscious. S.E., 14*. London: Hogarth.

Freud, S. (1916). *Some Character-Types Met With in Psycho-Analytic Work. S.E., 14*. London: Hogarth.

Freud, S. (1916a). *On Transience. S.E., 14*. London: Hogarth.

Freud, S. (1917). *Mourning and Melancholia. S.E., 14*. London: Hogarth.

Freud, S. (1917a). Lecture VII The Sense of Symptoms. In: *Introductory Lectures on Psychoanalysis. S.E., 16*. London: Hogarth.

Freud, S. (1917b). Lecture XXVII Transference. In: *Introductory Lectures on Psychoanalysis. S.E., 16*. London: Hogarth.

Freud, S. (1917c). Lecture XXIII The Paths to the Formation of Symptoms. In: *Introductory Lectures on Psychoanalysis. S.E., 16*. London: Hogarth.

Freud, S. (1918). *From The History of an Infantile Neurosis. S.E., 17*. London: Hogarth.

Freud, S. (1919). *The Uncanny. S.E., 17*. London: Hogarth.

Freud, S. (1920a). *Beyond the Pleasure Principle. S.E., 18*. London: Hogarth.

Freud, S. (1920b). *Civilisation and its Discontents. S.E., 21*. London: Hogarth.

Freud, S. (1922). *Dreams and Telepathy. S.E., 18*. London: Hogarth.

Freud, S. (1923). *The Ego and the Id. S.E., 19*. London: Hogarth.

Freud, S. (1925). *Negation. S.E., 19*. London: Hogarth.

Freud, S. (1925). *A Note Upon 'The Mystic Writing Pad' S.E., 19*. London: Hogarth.

Freud, S. (1926). *Inhibitions, Symptoms and Anxiety. S.E., 20*. London: Hogarth.

Freud, S. (1938). *Findings, Ideas, Problems. S.E., 23*. London: Hogarth.

Freud, S. (2006). *Concerning the Most Universal Debasement in Erotic Life* (1912). In *The Psychology of Love*. S. Whiteside (trans.), The New Penguin Freud, General Editor Adam Phillips, (pp. 250–261). London: Penguin Books.

Frow, J. (2006). Genre and interpretation. In: *Genre* (pp. 100–104). London: Routledge.

Gledhill, C. (2000). *Rethinking Genre, in Reinventing Film Studies*, (Eds.), C. Gledhill & L. Williams. (pp. 221–244). Berkeley: University of California Press.

Green, A. (1997). *On Private Madness*. London: Karnac.

Green, A. (2002). *Time in Psychoanalysis*. A. Weller (trans.), London: Free Association Books.

Hertz, N. (2005). Poor Hetty. In: L. Berlant (Ed.), *Compassion: The Culture and Politics of an Emotion* (pp. 87–104). New York: Routledge.

Irigaray, L. (1991). The bodily encounter with the mother. In: M. Whitford (Ed.), *The Irigaray Reader* (pp. 34–46). Oxford: Basil Blackwell.

Irigaray, L. (1993). Flesh colours. In: C. G. Gill (trans.), *Female Genealogies* (pp. 153–165). New York: Columbia University Press.

Jacobus, M. (1999). *Psychoanalysis and the Scene of Reading*. Oxford: Oxford University Press.

Khan, M. M. (1973). The role of illusion in the analytic space and process. In: *The Annual of Psychoanalysis, Vol. 1*: 231–246.

Khan, M. M. (1983). Beyond the dreaming experience. In: *Hidden Selves, Between Theory and Practice in Psychoanalysis* (pp. 42–50). London: Hogarth.

Kris, E. (1936). The psychology of caricature. *International Journal of Psychoanalysis, 17*: 285–303.

Kristeva, J. (1987). *Black Sun: Depression and Melancholia*. L. Roudiez (trans.), New York: Columbia University Press.

Kristeva, J. (1981). Women's Time. *Signs*, Vol. 7, No. 1, 13–35. A. Jardine & H. Blake (trans.), Chicago: University of Chicago Press.

Lacan, J. (1992). *The Seminar of Jacques Lacan, Book V11, The Ethics of Psychoanalysis*, (Ed.), J. Miller, (Trans.), D. Porter. London: Routledge.

Langer, S. (1953). *Feeling and Form: A Theory of Art*. New York: Scribner's.

Laplanche, J. (1985). Why the death drive? In: *Life and Death in Psychoanalysis* (pp. 102–126). J. Mehlman (trans.), Baltimore: John Hopkins University Press.

Leavis, F. R. (1962). George Eliot. In: *The Great Tradition* (pp. 79–125). London: Chatto and Windus.

Lee, H. (1992). Introduction. In: *To the Lighthouse* (pp. ix–xliii). London, Penguin Books.

Lewes, G. H. (1898). The principle of vision. In: *The Principles of Success in Literature* (pp. 22–46). London: Walter Scott Publishing.

Lingis, A. (1996). We mortals. In: *Sensation: Intelligibility in Sensibility* (pp. 1–13). New York: Humanity Books.

Matus, J. (2008). Historicising trauma: The genealogy of psychic shock in *Daniel Deronda*. *Victorian Literature and Culture, 36*: 59–78.

Miller, C. R. (1984). Genre as social action. *Quarterly Journal of Speech 70*: 151–167.

Milner, M. (1987). The role of illusion in symbol formation. In: *The Suppressed Madness of Sane Men* (pp. 83–113). New Library Psychoanalysis, London: Routledge.

Mulvey, L. (1994). It will be a magnificent obsession—the melodrama's role in the development of contemporary film theory. In: J. S., Bratton, J. Cook & C. Gledhill (Eds.), *Melodrama: Stage, Picture, Screen* (pp. 121–134). London: B.F.I.

Ogden, T. H. (2005). *This Art of Psychoanalysis*. New Library of Psychoanalysis, London: Routledge.

Oliver, K. (1998). *Subjectivity Without Subjects: From Abject Fathers to Desiring Mothers*. Lanham, MD: Littlefield Publishers.

Penner, L. (2002). Unmapped country: Uncovering hidden wounds in *Daniel Deronda*. *Victorian Literature and Culture, 30*: 77–97.

Phillips, A. (2006). *Side Effects*. London: Hamish Hamilton, Penguin Books.

Phillips, A. (2006a). Talking nonsense and knowing when to stop. In: *Side Effects* (pp. 21–42). London: Hamish Hamilton.

Phillips, A. (2006b). Two lectures on expectations. In: *Side Effects* (pp. 218–263). London: Hamish Hamilton.

Rak, J. (2012). *Boom! Manufacturing Memoir for the American Public*. Wilfred Laurier University Press, Waterloo, ON: Canada.

Reik, T. (1972). *Listening With The Third Ear: The Inner Experience of a Psychoanalyst*. New York: Arena Press.

Royle, N. (1991). On second sight: George Eliot. In: *Telepathy and Literature; Essays on the Reading Mind* (pp. 84–110). Oxford: Basil Blackwell.

Rycroft, C. (1985). Psychoanalysis the literary imagination. In: *Psychoanalysis and Beyond* (pp. 261–277). London: Hogarth.

Scarry, E. (2001). *Dreaming by the Book*. Princeton: Princeton University Press.

Sharpe, E. (1950). Sublimation and delusion. In: M. Brierley (Ed.), *Collected Papers on Psychoanalysis* (pp. 125–136). London: Hogarth.

Sharpe, E. (1950b). An examination of metaphor. In: M. Brierley (Ed.), *Collected Papers on Psychoanalysis* (pp. 155–169). London: Hogarth.

Shepherdson, C. (2000). *Vital Signs: Nature, Culture, Psychoanalysis*. London: Routledge.

Stern, D. (1985). *The Interpersonal World of the Infant*. New York: Basic Books.

Stone, C. (1993). George Eliot's *Daniel Deronda*: The case of Gwendolen H. *Nineteenth Century Studies 7*: 57–67.

Stonebridge, L. (1998). *The Destructive Element, British Psychoanalysis and Modernism*. Basingstoke: Houndmills.

Tanner, T. (1969). Introduction. In: *Sense and Sensibility* (pp. 7–34). London: Penguin Books.

Toise, D. (2010). Sexuality's uncertain history: or 'narrative disjunction' in *Daniel Deronda*. *Victorian Literature and Culture 38*: 127–150.

Tromp, M. (2000). Gwendolen's madness. *Victorian Literature and Culture 28*: 451–467.

Trotter, D. (2004). The invention of agraphobia. *Victorian Literature and Culture 32*: 463–474.

Vrettos, A. (1995). *Somatic Fictions: Imagining Illness in Victorian Culture*. Stanford: Stanford University Press.

Williams C. (2005). Moving pictures. In: L. Berlant (Ed.), *Compassion: The Culture and Politics of an Emotion* (pp. 105–144). New York: Routledge.

Williams, L. (1998). Melodrama revisited. In: N. Browne (Ed.), *Refiguring American Film Genres: History and Theory* (pp. 42–88). Berkeley: University of California Press.

Williams, L. (2001). The american melodramatic mode. In: *Playing The Race Card, Melodramas of Black and White from Uncle Tom to O. J. Simpson* (pp. 10–44). Princeton: Princeton University Press.

Winnicott, D. W. (1941). The observation of infants in a set situation. In: *Through Paediatrics to Psychoanalysis* (pp. 52–70). London: Karnac.

Winnicott, D. W. (1969). The use of an object. *International Journal of Psychoanalysis, 50*: 711–716.

Winnicott, D. W. (1974). Dreaming, fantasying and living. In: *Playing and Reality* (pp. 31–43). London: Penguin Books.

Winnicott, D. W. (1982). Communicating and not communicating leading to a study of certain opposites. In: *The Maturational processes and the Facilitating Environment* (pp. 179–192). London: Hogarth.

Winnicott, D. W. (1984). Primitive emotional development. In: *Through Paediatrics to Psychoanalysis* (pp. 145–157). London: Karnac.

Wollstonecraft, M. (1985). *A Vindication of the Rights of Woman*. London: Penguin Books.

Woolf, V. (1977). *The Letters of Virginia Woolf, Vol. 3, A Change of Perspective*, (1923–1928) (Eds.), N. Nicolson & J. Trautmann. London: Hogarth.

Woolf, V. (1988). Reading (1919). In: *The Essays of Virginia Woolf, 1919–1924*, vol. 3, (pp. 141–161). London: Houghton Mifflin Harcourt.

Woolf, V. (1990). *A Sketch of the Past*. In: *Moments of Being* (pp. 69–174). London: Grafton Books.

Woolf, V. (1992). *To the Lighthouse*, London, Penguin Books. [1927].

Wright, K. (2009). *Mirroring and Attunement: Self Realisation in Psychoanalysis and Art*. London: Routledge.

INDEX